Why Jane and John Couldn't Read— And How They Learned

A NEW LOOK AT STRIVING READERS

ROSALIE FINK

Lesley University
Cambridge, Massachusetts, USA

INTERNATIONAL
Reading Association
800 BARKSDALE ROAD, PO BOX 8139
NEWARK, DE 19714-8139, USA
www.reading.org

The International Reading Association attempts, through its publications, to provide a forum for a wide spectrum of opinions on reading. This policy permits divergent viewpoints without implying the endorsement of the Association.

Director of Publications Dan Mangan
Editorial Director, Books and Special Projects Teresa Curto
Managing Editor, Books Shannon T. Fortner
Acquisitions and Developmental Editor Corinne M. Mooney
Associate Editor Charlene M. Nichols
Associate Editor Elizabeth C. Hunt
Production Editor Amy Messick
Books and Inventory Assistant Rebecca A. Zell
Permissions Editor Janet S. Parrack
Assistant Permissions Editor Tyanna L. Collins
Production Department Manager Iona Muscella
Supervisor, Electronic Publishing Anette Schütz
Senior Electronic Publishing Specialist R. Lynn Harrison
Electronic Publishing Specialist Lisa M. Kochel
Proofreader Stacey Lynn Sharp

Project Editors Shannon T. Fortner and Charlene M. Nichols

Art Cover Design, Linda Steere; Cover and Interior Photography, Rosalie Fink

Library of Congress Cataloging-in-Publication Data

Fink, Rosalie, 1942-
  Why Jane and John couldn't read and how they learned : a new look at striving readers / Rosalie Fink.
     p. cm.
  Includes bibliographical references and index.
  ISBN 0-87207-592-3
  1. Reading--Remedial teaching. 2. Children--Books and reading. 3. Reading interests. I. Title.
  LB1050.5.F545 2006
  372.43--dc22

                                                          2005035295

To
Gerry,
Hal and Adina,
Julia and Uri,
Jennifer and Sarah,
Maya,
Alisa,
and Ben

CONTENTS

Promoting Success With an Interest-Based Model of Reading

Bilingual Readers: Marvelous Mentors and Cultural Pride

LIST OF FIGURES, TABLES,
AND ADDITIONAL RESOURCES

PREFACE

How do striving readers learn to read well and succeed in challenging professions like medicine, law, art, and science—professions that require lots of reading? This question intrigued me and led me to write this book—a book about my study of 66 men and women who overcame their reading problems. In conducting the study, I listened intently to each individual's story. To my surprise, I discovered common themes—themes that point to specific strategies for helping other striving readers. The themes form a consistent approach that I have found works successfully in my own classroom.

My interest in the problems of striving readers was sparked by an observation I made while teaching public school students who had difficulty reading. Despite their obvious difficulties, many of them were very bright. This paradox—bright students unable to read well—piqued my curiosity. At the time, I didn't know much about how to help them become skilled readers. My desire to learn more led me to the doctoral program in reading and language at the Harvard Graduate School of Education, where I was trained in various methods of reading research. The result of that training, and support from The Spencer Foundation and the National Academy of Education, led to this book.

Why Jane and John Couldn't Read—And How They Learned: A New Look at Striving Readers is a comprehensive study of a group of bright striving readers not unlike those I encountered in my public school teaching experience. Of course, this group "made it," and this book is my attempt to tell how it happened. The book comes at a time when there is broad agreement among experts about the essential elements of good reading instruction: systematic teaching of phonemic awareness, phonics, vocabulary development, oral reading fluency, and reading comprehension strategies (Farstrup, 2005; Flippo, 2001; National Institute of Child Health and Human Development [NICHD], 2000). Despite this consensus, many students continue to struggle, never learn to read well, and eventually drop out of school after years of frustration and humiliation. However, the study described in this book had a different result with a happier ending: All of the striving readers in this book ultimately became skilled readers and successful professionals. My goal here is to capture what I learned from them and share how they overcame their reading difficulties.

This book explains how a group of striving readers succeeded in achieving high-level reading ability. The book presents an interest-driven, or interest-based, model of reading. Initially, I did not set out to focus on the role of students' interests. In fact, none of my initial questions were about interest. Yet my study concluded with interest as its main focus because individual interest emerged from the data as a powerful component that could not be ignored. The Interest-Based Model of Reading described in this book has important implications for helping readers of all abilities and ages, K–adult. It is applicable to all developing readers, not only those who struggle. The model emphasizes transactions among reader, text, and teacher and features the following components:

1. A passionate, personal interest that spurs sustained reading.
2. Avid, topic-specific reading.
3. Deep schema knowledge.
4. Contextual reading strategies.
5. Mentoring support.

Why Jane and John Couldn't Read—And How They Learned conceptualizes striving readers in a new way that moves away from a deficit model to an **interest-driven model based on students' strengths and abilities**. Throughout the book, I use the terms *striving readers* and *struggling readers* interchangeably, but I prefer the term *striving readers*, which is gaining increasing acceptance because it connotes the positive qualities of motivation and effort—qualities often overlooked in students who struggle (Farstrup, 2005).

In the book, I explain how the developmental theories of Vygotsky, Piaget, Gardner, and others inform our understanding of uneven development in different individuals' pathways to reading. By *uneven development* I mean great disparities within a student between the student's high-level skills in one area (such as mathematics) and low-level skills in another area (such as reading).

This book highlights new theories and research, new teaching materials, and innovative ways to use traditional materials to maximize learning and joy as students develop as readers. Each chapter describes teaching materials, strategies, and activities, and each chapter features case studies of highly successful men and women who struggled. *Why Jane and John Couldn't Read—And How They Learned* replaces old myths about struggling readers with new, research-based realities about individuals who overcame their reading difficulties and succeeded. After 30 years as a reading teacher, reading researcher, speaker, and writer, I want to give others the benefit of my experience, my insights, and my unique database. The database includes information that I collected from extensive interviews and reading tests that were individually administered to a group of highly successful individuals who struggled with reading yet ended up at the top of their professions. Included in the database are a variety of teaching materials, strategies, and activities that can be used in various settings: homes, classrooms, clinics, and community centers.

Who Should Read This Book?

This book is for teachers, families, reading specialists, and reading coaches and tutors involved with students of all ages and abilities. In addition, administrators, researchers, and policymakers likely will be interested in the interest-driven model that unfolds. The results of the study, the teaching materials and strategies, and the discussions in this book are applicable for teaching all types of readers, not only those who struggle. I hope that readers are inspired, as I was, by the captivating stories and impressive achievements of the men and women in this book. And, I hope that the concrete suggestions of materials, activities, and strategies in each chapter are useful to a wide variety of professionals and families involved with students at all levels, K–adult.

How Is the Book Organized?

Why Jane and John Couldn't Read—And How They Learned balances individual case studies with practical teaching suggestions. The case studies illustrate different aspects of the Interest-Based Model of Reading. The cases present examples of how different individuals learned to read through a variety of genres based on their passionate, personal interests—genres that included biographies, manuals, romance novels, and so forth. Each case study exemplifies a different pattern or theme common to all 66 cases (e.g., marvelous mentors, "hands-on" activities).

Each chapter contains a section titled "What Teachers and Families Can Do," which systematically discusses instructional strategies and materials intended for teachers, reading specialists, students, and families. Readers can use the strategies and materials to develop lessons and activities for striving readers in their own classrooms, clinics, or homes. Additional resource lists at the end of chapters 1–4 are organized by topic to help families and teachers use each student's interests to motivate reading. The resource lists are organized by grade level to make it easy to locate appropriate materials for each student.

Chapter 1, "Promoting Success With an Interest-Based Model of Reading," presents an overview of the study and its major results. (Readers interested in a more detailed description of the background, goals, and methods of the study should consult the Appendix.) Chapter 1 presents the following topics: the Interest-Based Model of Reading, the timing and mechanisms involved in striving readers' fluency development, the evidence for these striving readers' high level of reading achievement, and the evidence for three distinct subgroups of striving readers.

Chapter 2, "Bilingual Readers: Marvelous Mentors and Cultural Pride," presents case studies of two Latino Americans who struggled with reading: a Nobel Prize–winning immunologist and an early childhood educator. Two key elements highlighted in this chapter are (1) pride in diverse languages and cultures and (2) marvelous mentors at home, school, and work. The chapter describes activities, materials, and strategies to help students develop deep cultural knowledge and pride in their heritage. Also emphasized is the role of mentoring by families, teachers, specialists, and peers. This chapter contains activities and annotated additional resource lists that are especially useful for teaching bilingual students.

Chapter 3, "Learning to Read Through Multiple Intelligences," presents the case study of a renowned scientist whose abilities in science compared with his abilities in English, history, and French showed enormous disparities; that is, there were huge gulfs between his extremely high and extremely low skill levels. Topics in this chapter include multiple intelligences, disparate abilities, sociocultural support, content area reading, "hands-on" learning experiences, and the mechanisms underlying content area variations in reading fluency. The chapter features engaging science texts and activities that can be used in homes, classrooms, clinics, and field trip sites.

Chapter 4, "Debunking Some Myths About Gender and Reading," explores similarities and differences between the reading skills, attitudes, and experiences of boys and girls, men and women. Highlighted here are case studies of a filmmaker, a lawyer, a gynecologist, and others. The chapter focuses on boys' and girls' preferences for certain types of texts, boys' and girls' different reading experiences, and strategies that help students explore alternative concepts of gender and the world. The chapter emphasizes reading lessons that incorporate creative and critical questioning, discussion, drama, writing, and art.

Chapter 5, "Identifying Striving Readers," deals with assessment issues at all developmental levels. The chapter provides an overview of several types of assessment tools—their strengths, caveats, and limitations—and the use of ongoing assessment to inform instruction. The importance of early intervention is stressed, as well as the need to consult a reading specialist when in doubt about a student's progress. Also noted is the need for continuing assessment and systematic reading instruction through high school and beyond.

Chapter 6, "Conclusions and Implications," addresses the results of this study for policy, practice, and research. In addition to addressing issues for teachers, reading specialists, administrators, and policymakers, the chapter connects findings from the study to programs and legislation related to reading instruction today.

What Are My Hopes for Readers?

I hope that readers of this book are inspired, as I was, by the stories of these fascinating individuals, who overcame their difficulties and succeeded at high levels, both in literacy and in life. They opened their souls to me, telling their poignant stories in moving detail with the hope of inspiring others who struggle. I hope that this book will motivate the use of innovative educational approaches that enable struggling readers not only to learn to read, but to learn to read well.

Acknowledgments

I am deeply indebted to each individual who participated in the study—the striving readers who succeeded as well as members of the comparison group. They opened their hearts, sharing personal stories, taking challenging tests, and responding to my questions. I appreciate their courage, trust, and candor. Without them, I could never have conducted the study or written this book.

I am grateful also to my friends and colleagues at the Harvard Graduate School of Education: Kurt Fischer, Howard Gardner, David Rose, Judith Singer, Catherine Snow, John Strucker, and Terry Tivnan. A special thanks to Kurt Fischer and Catherine Snow for inviting me to be a Visiting Scholar in Education at the Harvard Graduate School of Education. This opportunity enabled me to expand the size of the original study and investigate new questions.

Thanks also to The Spencer Foundation and the National Academy of Education for supporting my research by honoring me with a Spencer Postdoctoral Research Fellowship. This support enabled me to travel throughout the United States to conduct the study.

I also wish to acknowledge the researchers, teachers, friends, and colleagues who helped to enhance the book through their publications, presentations, and conversations: Dick Allington, Hester Brooks, Collette Daiute, Bridget Dalton, Nell Duke, Alan Farstrup, Esther Feldman, Rebecca Felton, Rona Flippo, Barbara Foorman, Paul Gerber, Carol Gilligan, Cathy Gronwold, Minnie Gross, Jane Holmes-Bernstein, Vicky Jacobs, Linda Kerr, Joan Knight, Lindsay Moffatt, Victoria Purcell-Gates, Jeff Gilger, Diane Lefley, Lynn Meltzer, Lynn Miller, Bruce Pennington, K. Ann Renninger, S. Jay Samuels, Bennett and Sally Shaywitz, Larry Silver, Jim Slattery, Margaret Snowling, Joe Torgesen, Susan Vogel, Ellen Winner, Amy Weinberg, Evie Weinstein-Parks, Susan Whitehead, Mary Ann Wolf, and Julie Wood.

I especially appreciate the support and encouragement of my Program Director at Lesley University, Christine Evans. Thanks also to other Lesley colleagues for their ongoing interest in my work: Karen Allan, Marcia Bromfield, Terry Bromfield, Donna Cole, Mary Beth Curtis, Mary Dockray-Miller, Paul Fideler, Irene Fountas, Barbara Govendo, Lori Grace, Catherine Holmes, Solange Lira, Mary McMackin, Susan Merrifield, Margery Staman Miller, David Morimoto, Frances Osten, Anne Pluto, Maureen Riley, Arlyn Roffman, Prilly Sanville, Robin Schwarz, Stephanie Spadorcia, William Stokes, Robert Wauhkonen, Marjorie Wechsler, and Frances Yuan.

In addition, thanks to the children and teachers at the William H. Lincoln School in Brookline, Massachusetts. I am grateful to Jan Preheim for inviting me to visit her school and to Principal Barbara Shea for the opportunity to observe and photograph children during their reading lessons. I wish to thank the children and teachers, all of whom accommodated me most graciously: Linda Cohn, Liz Dennis, Jessica Gelb, Liz Gelotte, Mrs. Howard, Marti Katz, Erin Kelley, Kathy Tower, Pam Redlener, Joe Reilly, Paula Reilly, and Mrs. Thorn. Thanks as well to everyone at Dryden Central School in Dryden, New York.

I also want to acknowledge my editors at the International Reading Association, who worked tirelessly on drafts of the book and whose professional insights improved the final product: Dan Mangan, Teresa Curto, Shannon Fortner, Charlene Nichols, and Corinne Mooney. While I am grateful to all who encouraged me to conduct the study and helped to make this book a reality, I alone bear full and sole responsibility for any errors or oversights.

Finally and most important, thanks to my loving family. First, thanks to my beloved parents, Hal and Adina Lewis; to them I owe my excitement about reading, which began many years ago when they read to me each day.

I am also grateful to my wonderful children—my daughter Julia Feldman and her husband, Uri, and my daughter Jennifer Fink and her partner, Sarah. A special thanks to Julia for her invaluable help and superb expertise with legal issues and her enduring pride and interest in my work. A special thanks to Jennifer for her endless supply of encouragement and enthusiasm for my work and her invaluable help and suggestions based on her expertise as an accomplished novelist and English professor.

Thanks also to my three wonderful grandchildren—Maya, Alisa, and Ben—who enable me to revisit the excitement of learning to read all over again and add joy to my life each week.

Finally, thanks to my loving husband, Gerry, for his unique sense of humor, enthusiastic spirit, and lifelong support. No words can express my deep appreciation for his dedication to me and to my work.

CHAPTER 1

Promoting Success With an Interest-Based Model of Reading

One year I noticed five bright, enthusiastic students who stood out in my language arts class. They sparked class discussions with their creative ideas, yet something about them perplexed me. Each one of them had extraordinary difficulties with the basics of reading, writing, and spelling. There seemed to be a deep gulf between their complex ideas

1

about literature on the one hand and their basic lower level reading skills on the other hand. I wondered, What's going on here? At the time, *Scholastic Magazine* had printed an excerpt from Eileen Simpson's *Reversals* (1979), which included intriguing vignettes about Simpson's travails as a girl with dyslexia. Moved by Simpson's story and thinking it might be relevant to my students, I read aloud an excerpt to my class, hamming up the most dramatic sections. I was in for a surprise.

Within a few days, I received letters from several mothers, each one thanking me for reading *Reversals* to the class, each one telling me how much it had helped her child to learn that other smart people—in this case Simpson, a well-known author—had suffered similarly, yet ultimately succeeded. The letters were filled with an outpouring of emotion and gratitude. Hearing Simpson's story was definitely a turning point, both for my students and their parents. The powerful impact of this single story convinced me to embark on a study and write a book about other readers who had struggled, yet ultimately succeeded.

Striving Readers Who Succeeded

My biggest challenge was to find successful men and women who had struggled with severe reading problems as children, yet ultimately succeeded in professions that require extensive reading. I located a group of striving readers who had succeeded in a variety of such fields, including medicine, law, business, theater, art, psychology, education, biology, physics, and so forth. Many of them were outstanding professionals; some were the veritable movers and shakers in their fields. For example, the group included Baruj Benacerraf, a Nobel laureate in medicine and physiology; Lora Brody, a television/radio personality and author of *Cooking With Memories* (1989); George Deem, an internationally known artist; Donald Francis, a doctor and AIDS researcher; Florence Haseltine, a gynecologist and coauthor of *Woman Doctor* (Haseltine & Yaw, 1976); Robert Knapp, a cancer researcher and Chair of the Department of Gynecology at Harvard Medical School; Sylvia Law, a New York University Professor of Law, Medicine, and Psychiatry and author of *The New York Times* Outstanding Book Award–winner *Blue Cross: What Went Wrong?* (1974); Nancy Lelewer, a writer and author of *Something's Not Right: One Family's Struggle With Learning Disabilities* (1994); and Thomas G. West, a writer and author of *In the Mind's Eye* (1991). (Table 1 shows the name, profession, and workplace of each striving reader who participated in the study.)

TABLE 1
Successful Striving Readers

Name	Profession and Workplace
	Men
J. William Adams	Headmaster, The Gow School, South Wales, New York
S. Charles Bean	Neurologist, Clinical Associate Professor, Jefferson Hospital, Philadelphia, Pennsylvania
Baruj Benacerraf	Immunologist, Professor of Immunology and Chair, Dept. of Pathology, Harvard Medical School, Cambridge, Massachusetts
James R. Bensinger	Physicist, Brandeis University, Waltham, Massachusetts
William Brewer	Psychologist, Professor of Psychology, University of Illinois, Champaign, Illinois
Michael L. Commons	Psychometrician, Lecturer/Research Associate, Dept. of Psychiatry, Harvard Medical School, Cambridge, Massachusetts
Heriberto Crespo	Social Worker, Latino Health Institute, Boston, Massachusetts
Roy Daniels*	Biochemist, Director, Stanford DNA Sequencing/Technology Center, and Professor, Stanford University School of Medicine, Stanford, California
George Deem	Graphic Artist, Adjunct Professor of Art, University of Pennsylvania, Philadelphia, Pennsylvania
G. Emerson Dickman	Attorney at Law, Maywood, New Jersey
Charles Drake	Founding Director, The Landmark School, Beverly, Massachusetts
H. Girard Ebert	Interior Designer and Chief Executive Officer, H. Girard Ebert, Inc., Baltimore, Maryland
Donald Francis	Virologist/AIDS Researcher, Genentech, Inc., and Founder and President, VaxGen, Inc., San Francisco, California
Miles Gerety	Attorney at Law, State Public Defender, Bridgeport, Connecticut
Daniel Gillette	Learning Specialist and Coordinator of Advising, Boston Architectural Center, Boston, Massachusetts
Alexander Goldowsky	Program Developer, New England Aquarium, Boston, Massachusetts
David Gordon	Marketing Consultant, Adaptive Computing, Beverly, Massachusetts
Philip Hulbig	Tutor, Walpole, Massachusetts
Robert Knapp	Gynecologist, Professor and Chair, Dept. of Gynecology, Harvard Medical School, Cambridge, Massachusetts
John Moore	Social Worker, Boston, Massachusetts
Jonathan Pazer	Attorney at Law, Law Offices of Pazer & Epstein, New York, New York
Bart Pisha	Computer Specialist, Director of Research, Center for Applied Special Technology (CAST), Peabody, Massachusetts

(continued)

TABLE 1 (continued)
Successful Striving Readers

Name	Profession and Workplace
Cruz Sanabria	Early Childhood Educator, Boston, Massachusetts
Michael Schweitzer	General and Vascular Surgeon, Virginia Surgical Specialists, Richmond, Virginia
David Selib	Sales Manager, Reebok International, Medfield, Massachusetts
Larry B. Silver	Psychiatrist and Writer, Clinical Professor of Psychiatry, Georgetown University School of Medicine, Washington, DC
Hilary Smart	Chief Executive Officer, Industrial Products Company, Boston, Massachusetts
James Soberman	Dentist, Clinical Assistant Professor of Prosthodontics, New York University, New York, New York
Michael Spock	Codirector/Researcher, Chapin Hall Center for Children, University of Chicago, Chicago, Illinois
Michael Van Zandt	Research Scientist, Institute for Diabetes Discovery, Branford, Connecticut
A. McDonald Vaz	Writer, Miami Beach, Florida
Thomas G. West	Writer, Visualization Research Institute, Washington, DC
Glenn Young	Learning Disabilities Program Specialist, Washington State Dept. of Social & Health Services, Seattle, Washington

Women

Name	Profession and Workplace
Hannah Adams	Elementary Teacher, Cambridge, Massachusetts
Tania Baker	Biochemist and Professor, Massachusetts Institute of Technology (MIT), Cambridge, Massachusetts
Barbara Bikofsky	Special Educator, Adjunct Instructor, Lesley University, Cambridge, Massachusetts
Lori Boskin	Director of Alumni Relations, Special Projects & Promotions, University of California Los Angeles School of Law, Los Angeles, California
Lora Brody	Cookbook Author, TV and Radio Personality, Newton, Massachusetts
Terry Bromfield	Special Educator, Adjunct Assistant Professor, Lesley University, Cambridge, Massachusetts
Dale S. Brown	Program Manager, The President's Committee on Employment of People With Disabilities, Washington, DC
Susan E. Brown	Filmmaker, New York, New York
Ann L. Brown (deceased)	Researcher/Educator, Professor of Education, University of California, Berkeley, California
Jane Buchbinder	Fiction Writer, Boston, Massachusetts

(continued)

TABLE 1 (continued)
Successful Striving Readers

Name	Profession and Workplace
Susan Cobin	Administrator/Principal, Talmud Torah Day School, Saint Paul, Minnesota
C. Ellen Corduan	Theater Set Designer/Teacher, The Walnut Hill School, Natick, Massachusetts
Ellen Gorman	Social Worker, New Haven Adult Education, New Haven, Connecticut
Stacey Harris	Attorney at Law, Brookline, Massachusetts
Florence Haseltine	Gynecologist and Director, Center for Population Research, National Institutes of Health, Washington, DC
Marlene Hirschberg	Arts Administrator/Director, Jewish Community Center, Milwaukee, Wisconsin
Melissa Holt	Head Teacher, South Shore Day Care, Quincy, Massachusetts
Annette Jenner	Neurobiologist, Biology Teaching Fellow, Harvard University, Cambridge, Massachusetts
Sylvia Law	Attorney at Law, Professor of Law, Medicine, & Psychiatry, New York University School of Law, New York, New York
Nancy Lelewer	Writer, Research Associate in Neurology, Harvard Medical School, Cambridge, Massachusetts
Joanne Lense	Social Worker, Bronx Lebanon Hospital & Knight Education, New York, New York
Susan Marlett	Artist, Clearway Technologies, Fort Lee, New Jersey
Robin Mello	Storyteller/Actress, Adjunct Instructor, Tufts University & Lesley College, Boston and Cambridge, Massachusetts
Fiona Moore	Social Worker, Human Resource Institute, Brookline, Massachusetts
Tania Phillips	Elementary Teacher, Northampton, Massachusetts
Priscilla Sanville	Arts Educator, Adjunct Assistant Professor, Lesley University, Cambridge, Massachusetts
Maureen Selig*	Social Worker, Easton Hospital, Easton, Pennsylvania
Charlann Simon	Author & Program Developer, Speech/Language and Learning Specialist, Tempe, Arizona
Amy Simons	Attorney at Law, Assistant State Attorney, Dade County State Attorney's Office, Miami, Florida
Jane Smith*	Anthropologist, American University, Washington, DC
Beth Steucek	Manager, Executive Vice President, New England Innkeepers, Portsmouth, New Hampshire
Lezli Whitehouse	Speech/Language Specialist, Boston, Massachusetts
Kathleen Yellin*	Hotel Manager, Boston, Massachusetts

* Indicates a pseudonym.

Overview of the Study

Goals and Questions

Initially my project began as a small pilot study of 12 individuals and was part of my doctoral program at the Harvard Graduate School of Education. After completing my doctorate, I received a Spencer Post-Doctoral Research Fellowship from the National Academy of Education, which enabled me to expand the original study to a larger sample of more than 60 striving readers from all regions of the United States. I included equal numbers of men and women in the study, which had two main goals: (1) to learn whether there were any patterns common to the experiences of all of the striving readers and (2) to discover teaching strategies, materials, and approaches that could be useful to teachers, reading specialists, students, and families. My hunch was that the striving readers in my study might have devised unique strategies for learning that could prove useful for teaching others.

Several questions intrigued me: What had contributed to the resilience of these striving readers? What strategies had they used to overcome their reading difficulties? What level of reading ability did they ultimately achieve? At what ages did they develop basic fluency? Are they fluent readers today? If so, according to what definition of fluency? Were there any gender differences and, if so, what were they? Most important, I wanted to know, What do the experiences of these successful striving readers tell us about teaching others to read? These questions were the driving force behind the study described in this book.

The Sample of Striving Readers

The sample was not a random sample; rather, men and women were selected based on their level of educational and career achievement, field of expertise, gender, age, and socioeconomic level. Individuals were considered "successful" if they (a) demonstrated professional competence recognized by peers in an area of expertise that requires sophisticated reading and demands extensive training, skill, and responsibility and (b) supported themselves financially. Individuals were considered "striving readers" if they (a) showed evidence of a childhood history of severe reading difficulties, (b) met the Responsiveness to Intervention definition of a reader who struggled, and (c) met the International Dyslexia Association's definition of an individual with dyslexia. (See Appendix for details.)

Interviews and Assessments

I individually administered formal and informal reading and psychological tests and assessments, including the Diagnostic Assessments of Reading With Trial Teaching Strategies (Roswell & Chall, 1992); the Nelson-Denny Reading Test of Vocabulary, Reading Comprehension, and Reading Rate (Brown, Fishco, & Hanna, 1993); and the Graded Nonword Reading and Spelling Test (Snowling, Stothard, & McLean, 1996). (See the Appendix for complete list and details.) I also conducted lengthy, face-to-face interviews, three to nine hours each, during which participants were encouraged to tell their own stories in their own ways. (See the Appendix for interview questions and methodology.) All except six individuals took the series of reading tests and psychological assessments. All except one gave me permission to use their real names in the hope that their life stories would inspire others who struggle with reading. In writing this book, I decided to use real names for all except three individuals; due to the sensitive nature of the information, in these cases I used pseudonyms to protect their privacy and the privacy of their families (refer to Table 1 beginning on page 3; an asterisk * after a name indicates a pseudonym).

Becoming Highly Skilled Readers

The results of the interviews and reading tests were full of surprises about learning to read. I expected to discover a variety of bypass strategies that enabled the striving readers in my study to learn without doing much reading. (Presumably, continual frustration with basic skills would have led them to avoid reading.) But to my surprise, instead of avoiding reading, I discovered that they loved books and read a lot. Despite their struggles, all had been avid readers in childhood.

And not only were they avid readers; they also became highly skilled readers. According to results of the reading tests administered to them in adulthood, these men and women understood complex, sophisticated texts and scored high on all upper level skills, including vocabulary knowledge and silent reading comprehension. In fact, their mean reading comprehension score equaled 16.9 GE on the Nelson-Denny Reading Test (a grade equivalent above the fourth year of college). I also discovered that, despite years of reading difficulties, they developed most of the characteristics of Chall's (1996) Stage 5—the highest level of skilled reading. (A Stage 5 skill that some of them still lack is rapid reading speed.)

Chall's Stage 5 entails reading materials that are "highly difficult, specialized, technical, and abstract" and entails reading for one's own personal and professional purposes (Chall, 1983, p. 100). Each of these striving readers demonstrates these skills. Their high performance on the reading assessments that I administered attests to their ability to read, understand, make inferences, and create meaning from text—all Stage 5 skills. Many of these men and women have written major books and articles in their fields of expertise. Their impressive scholarly publications demonstrate their creation of new knowledge—a hallmark of skilled reading at the highest level.

Passionate, Personal Interests

The stories of these striving readers revealed a common theme: Each one had had a burning desire to know more about a favorite topic. Spurred by their passion and curiosity, they read voraciously, engaging in what Chall called "reading to learn" (1983, 1994, 1996). Fascinated by a topic, they read avidly to learn more. And, they did lots of their reading on their own—silently.

I did a lot of reading. I loved reading about physics, so I got lots of physics magazines and books, and I just quietly read about physics on my own.

JAMES BENSINGER (PHYSICIST)

I've always been attracted to books about history, decorative arts, architecture.... So I took reading, which was a problem, and turned it around, because it was the only way that I could explore what I was interested in.

H. GIRARD EBERT (INTERIOR DESIGNER)

I loved history.... I'm a [U.S.] Civil War buff, mainly 'cause I like Lincoln. So through reading about Lincoln, I've learned lots of other things—including how to read!

C. ELLEN CORDUAN (THEATER SET DESIGNER/TEACHER)

By reading about narrow topics (e.g., Lincoln and the U.S. Civil War), each of these striving readers became familiar with the specific vocabulary, themes, and scripts of their favorite types of texts. Based on this genre familiarity, they could use the context effectively to guess at new words and develop their conceptual understanding. They engaged in intense and repeated reading about a single, favorite topic, which enhanced their depth of background knowledge and, simultaneously, enabled them to gain reading practice. The repetition and redundant text material itself provided some of the requisite drill and practice needed to develop their skills. Through avid, highly focused reading, each individual became a virtual "little expert" in a favorite domain of knowledge. In Stanovich's (1986) terms, they got richer (or better at reading) as a result of intensive reading practice. Although topics of interest varied among the individuals, lots of practice within a single genre (or domain of knowledge) fostered fluency and the development of increasingly sophisticated reading skills. (See Table 2 for a summary of their topics and genres of high-interest reading.)

Ages When Avid Reading Began

The ages when these striving readers began to read avidly varied. Overall, those who began their avid, high-interest reading the earliest became the highest achievers. This finding fits with results from early intervention studies that suggest that the earlier a child receives appropriate intervention, the more likely it is that

TABLE 2			
Topic/Genre of High-Interest Reading			
Women *n* = 30		**Men** *n* = 30	
Novels	23	Novels	14
Biographies	2	Biographies	2
Science	2	Science	5
Social Studies	1	Social Studies	6
Cooking	1	Automechanics	1
No Data	1	Sailing	1
		Poetry	1

Gender differences in topics of high-interest reading were statistically significant (chi square = 5.71, *p* = .017).

TABLE 3
Ranges of Interests and Ages When Avid Reading Began

Name	Genre/Interest	Age
B. Benacerraf	Biography	age 7
R. Knapp	History	age 7
R. Daniels	Science	age 8
J. Bensinger	Physics	age 10
A. Simons	Math	age 10
E. Corduan	History	age 11
S. Bean	Poetry	age 12
A. Brown	Novels	age 13
B. Bikofsky	Novels	age 17
G. Deem	Novels	~age 22

the child will eventually close the gap and catch up to normally developing peers (Foorman, Francis, Beeler, Winikates, & Fletcher, 1997; Torgesen, Wagner, & Rashotte, 1997). (Table 3 shows a range of the individuals who participated in the study, their interests, and the ages when they began to read avidly about a topic of passionate, personal interest.)

Late Fluency Development

Fluency development occurred late for all of these readers. In fact, I found a consistent pattern of delay: On average, they developed basic fluency (smoothness and ease in reading and understanding connected text) between ages 10 and 12. This was three to four years later than their "normally developing" peers who developed basic fluency between ages 7 and 8 (Chall, 1983, 1996). When they finally learned to read fluently, it was an important turning point, which they recalled vividly. Many of their most poignant recollections featured memorable mentors—teachers and other important adults who were pivotal in helping them to succeed.

> In fifth grade, I finally learned to read; it was a big change! I
> remember it clearly: Mrs. King helped me.
> JAMES BENSINGER (PHYSICIST)

Fascination and Flow

As I listened to the stories of these striving readers, I discovered that fascination with a favorite topic was an overriding theme; moreover, they were not only fascinated, but they were transformed by their favorite texts. They became so deeply engrossed while reading that they lost awareness of everything else around them, often even failing to "hear" their parents calling, "Time for dinner"–even when the parents were standing right in the same room. Csikszentmihalyi (1991) calls this type of total immersion and enjoyment a "flow experience"–the feeling of being carried away by a current, which often results in an exhilarating loss of self-consciousness. For these striving readers, who became anxious in many reading situations, this feeling of flow while reading about a topic of interest was liberating.

Ongoing Problems

But it wasn't smooth sailing. Many of these striving readers continued to grapple with ongoing problems with word recognition and sound analysis–lower level skills that, for some, remain weak in adulthood. This finding suggests that a subset of the group may have followed a different developmental pathway from that of most skilled readers. (See chapter 3 for discussion.) Many of them continue as adults to have difficulty with basic, lower level word recognition and phonological skills. Despite years of instruction and practice in phonics, some who have learned the sound–symbol relationships of English still have trouble applying this knowledge due to ongoing problems with blending and sequencing. So they use phonics, but not very effectively.

> *I can look at a letter and tell you what the sound is, but I can't put it together into a word.*
> MARLENE HIRSCHBERG (ARTS ADMINISTRATOR)

> *Phonics doesn't always work for me. Even though I'll read phonetically, I can't break it down and make sense, because my phonetic sounds don't always fit with everybody else's. Yet it's not important to me; it's the idea that's important.*
> S. CHARLES BEAN (NEUROLOGIST)

Deep Schema Knowledge and Contextual Reading Strategies

The striving readers in this study seemed aware of the ultimate goal of reading: making meaning from print. But how were they able to think about ideas, make sense from print, and develop basic fluency when their lower level decoding skills remained weak? I was especially curious about how they had constructed meaning (a higher level skill) despite their continuing problems with lower level skills such as letter identification, word recognition, and phonics. What I found was that they relied on context.

> *Even today, when I can't figure out a word, I guess from the context.*
> *Yes, I guess what makes sense.*
> BARUJ BENACERRAF (IMMUNOLOGIST)

> *I use the context and get the gist...and I have it pretty much right!*
> C. ELLEN CORDUAN (THEATER SET DESIGNER/TEACHER)

These striving readers use the context to enhance their understanding, and they know when they have it "pretty much right." This suggests that they use metacognitive checking strategies to monitor their word recognition and comprehension accuracy. That is, they regularly check their own word recognition and comprehension and, in their own estimation, are usually correct. This finding fits with results of research by Lefly and Pennington (1991), who found that compensating adults with dyslexia read unfamiliar words nearly as accurately as other skilled readers.

But how had the striving readers in my study *become* accurate in guessing words? I wondered how they had managed to guess words correctly from context clues. What I discovered was that, by reading avidly about a single engaging topic, they developed deep background knowledge and schema familiarity. Schema familiarity allowed them to "fill in the blanks" correctly, because context clues were more reliable in a familiar schema.

According to schema theory, context-reliant reading is effective and accurate when the reader possesses sufficient background knowledge and has a schema for the material (Samuels, 2002). A reader's prior knowledge creates a powerful advantage that facilitates accuracy and comprehension (Recht & Leslie, 1988; Rumelhart, 1980; Samuels, 2002). For example, a reader's familiarity with narrative schema enables the reader to read new narratives with increasing comprehension and fluency. The reason? Familiarity with narrative components (such as character, setting, plot, problem, resolution) enables prediction and fulfillment of expectations. Consequently, the more narratives an individual reads, the more capable the individual becomes of reading and understanding future narratives. Similarly, a person immersed in reading about science develops familiarity with the highly specialized vocabulary, technical concepts, and experimental designs of science. The result? That person is able to read and understand future scientific texts with greater ease and accuracy.

Three Groups of Striving Readers

Based on the reading tests that I administered, three distinct groups of striving readers emerged from this study (see Figure 1). One group of **compensated readers** revealed few, if any, ongoing weaknesses in adulthood, scoring high in every category of reading. However, **partially compensated readers** showed ongoing

FIGURE 1
Profiles of Compensated and Partially Compensated Individuals With Dyslexia

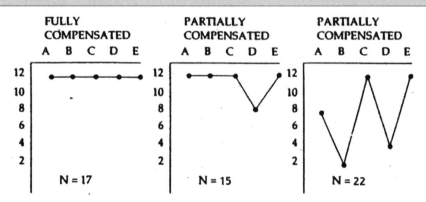

The numbers on the vertical axis represent the grade equivalent score. Maximum performance on this test (DARTT) is 12th-grade level.
A = word recognition, B = oral reading, C = silent reading comprehension, D = spelling, E = knowledge of word meanings. Six individuals did not fit into these types.

Adapted from Fink, R.P. (1998a). Literacy development in successful men and women with dyslexia (p. 329). *Annals of Dyslexia*, *48*, 311–346. Used with permission of the International Dyslexia Association.

jagged, uneven profiles of reading strengths and weaknesses. For example, the two groups of partially compensated readers scored high in upper level, meaning-making skills (such as vocabulary knowledge and silent reading comprehension) on the Diagnostic Assessments of Reading With Trial Teaching Strategies. However, they lagged behind in lower level skills, such as word recognition, oral reading accuracy, and spelling.

One group of partially compensated readers showed weaknesses in spelling (15 individuals); the other group showed weaknesses in word recognition and oral reading, as well as spelling (22 individuals). Six remaining individuals with partially compensated reading difficulties showed similar jagged profiles of strengths and weaknesses. However, their strengths did not quite reach ceiling, and their weaknesses dipped slightly lower than those of other partially compensated readers. Test data for 6 individuals were unavailable.

The striving readers' test results were compared with those of a comparison group. Results showed that, despite the striving readers' high scores on vocabulary and reading comprehension tests, they performed poorly compared to the comparison group on all assessments of phonological decoding. This result indicates that, even though the striving readers caught up to other skilled readers in vocabulary and reading comprehension, they never fully mastered phonological decoding skills.

Table 4 summarizes the reading test results and reveals three main findings: (1) the comparison group outperformed all of the striving readers on every measure of reading; (2) the fully compensated group of striving readers consistently outperformed both partially compensated groups; and (3) for individuals with partially compensated reading difficulties, ongoing jagged profiles of reading strengths and weaknesses persisted in adulthood.

Reading Speed

I wondered whether slow reading speed distinguished the compensated readers from the partially compensated groups. The results of the reading tests showed that slow reading rate was indeed a distinguishing characteristic. On the Nelson-Denny Reading Test, 58% of the total individuals who had struggled were slow readers who used extended time to complete the test (refer to Table 4A). Apparently, without the accommodation of extended time, many of these striving readers would have scored lower on the Nelson-Denny Reading Test. They seemed to need the extra time to process text information and answer questions accurately.

TABLE 4
Reading Test Results

A. Performance on Literacy Tests and Adult Reading History Questionnaire*

	Nondyslexic Controls (*n* = 10)	Individuals With Dyslexia			Contrasts**	
		Fully Compensated (*n* = 17)	Partially Compensated (*n* = 43)	Total Dyslexics (*n* = 60)	Controls v. Total Dys.	Full v. Partial
DARTT (% adults obtaining GE < 12th grade)***						
Word Recognition	0	0	30.2	21.7	.103	.010
Oral Rdg. Accuracy	0	0	55.8	40.0	.014	.001
Silent Comp'n	10	0	6.9	5.0	.528	.264
Spelling	40	0	79.0	57.0	.327	<.001
Word Meaning	0	0	6.9	5.0	.470	.264
Nelson-Denny						
Vocabulary						
raw score *M* (*SD*)	79(.6)	75.9(4.4)	73.9(5.0)	73.5(6.3)	.008	.155
GE *M*	18.9	17.5	16.9	16.9		
GE range	18.9–18.9	14.6–18.9	11.6–18.9	11.6–18.9		
Comprehension						
raw score *M* (*SD*)	75.2(4.4)	70.5(3.9)	67.7(5.6)	68.7(6.7)	.004	.056
GE *M*	18.9	18.6	17.1	17.1		
GE range	16.4–18.9	13.2–18.9	9.6–18.9	9.6–18.9		
Rate (% with *s.s.* < 180)	0	0	33.0	23.3	.088	.007
% using extended time	0	53	60	58	.001	.594
Adult Reading History Questionnaire						
Total Score *M* (*SD*)	.07(.04)	.57(.09)	.61(.09)	.60(.09)	.0001	.126
range	.01–.15	.38–.75	.38–.82	.38–.82		
Florida Passages						
# seconds *M* (*SD*)	25.3(8.4)	78.5(17.8)	106.7(38.9)	98.7(36.5)	.0001	.0060
range	17–50	51–112	51–225	51–225		
# errors *M* (*SD*)	1.5(1.0)	8.8(3.0)	14.5(6.0)	12.9(5.9)	.0001	.0004
range	0–4	4–13	4–27	4–27		
Pig Latin Test						
# correct *M* (*SD*)	44.2(5.6)	40.4(7.5)	30.0(11.9)	33.0(11.8)	.005	.002
range	30–48	24–48	1–47	1–48		
Graded Nonword Tests						
Reading *M* (*SD*)	19.8(.4)	17.1(1.9)	15.0(3.5)	15.6(3.3)	.0002	.0231
range	19–20	13–20	6–20	6–20		
Spelling *M* (*SD*)	18.8(1.3)	16(2.4)	13.0(4.6)	13.8(4.3)	.0007	.0136
range	16–20	11–20	2–19	2–20		

(continued)

* Full data set available upon request (participants' identities withheld)
** Observed probability levels from the statistical contrasts; the first column of contrasts shows comparisons between the nondyslexic comparison group and the total number of individuals with dyslexia; the second column of contrasts shows comparisons between fully compensated and partially compensated individuals with dyslexia.
*** GE = grade equivalent; maximum performance on the DARTT is 12th-grade level (Roswell & Chall, 1992).

Reprinted from Fink, R.P. (1998a). Literacy development in successful men and women with dyslexia (pp. 320–321). *Annals of Dyslexia, 48*, 311–346. Used with permission of the International Dyslexia Association.

TABLE 4 (continued)
Reading Test Results

B. Adult Self-Reported Reading Habits, Using a Scale of 0 to 4 From the Adult Reading History Questionnaire*

| | Nondyslexic Controls (n = 10) | Individuals With Dyslexia | | | Contrasts** | |
		Fully Compensated (n = 17)	Partially Compensated (n = 43)	Total Dyslexics (n = 60)	Controls v. Total Dys.	Full v. Partial
Work-Related Reading						
(% reporting a great deal)	100%	88%	67%	73%	.063	.101
Mean response (*SD*)	3.7(.5)	3.5(1.0)	3.0(.9)	3.1(.9)	.0683	.0652
Range	3–4	0–4	1–4	0–4		
Pleasure Reading						
(% reporting a great deal)	80%	53%	37%	42%	.025	.265
Mean response (*SD*)	3.4(.8)	2.5(1.1)	2.2(1.3)	2.3(1.2)	.0081	.4049
Range	2–4	0–4	0–4	0–4		
Book Reading						
Mean response (*SD*)	3.7(.6)	2.5(1.2)	2.4(1.4)	2.4(1.3)	.0046	.7966
Range	2–4	0–4	0–4	0–4		
Magazine Reading						
Mean response (*SD*)	3.2(1.2)	2.0(1.3)	2.0(1.4)	2.0(1.4)	.0113	1.0
Range	0–4	0–4	0–4	0–4		
Daily News Reading						
Mean response (*SD*)	3.5(1.0)	2.9(1.4)	2.7(1.4)	2.8(1.4)	.1142	.6199
Range	1–4	0–4	0–4	0–4		
Sunday News Reading						
Mean response (*SD*)	3.8(.4)	2.9(1.0)	2.7(1.0)	2.8(1.0)	.0019	.4879
Range	0–1	1–4	0–4	0–4		

* Full data set available upon request (participants' identities withheld)
** Observed probability levels from the statistical contrasts; the first column of contrasts shows comparisons between the nondyslexic comparison group and the total number of individuals with dyslexia; the second column of contrasts shows comparisons between fully compensated and partially compensated individuals with dyslexia.

Reprinted from Fink, R.P. (1998a). Literacy development in successful men and women with dyslexia (pp. 322–323). *Annals of Dyslexia, 48*, 311–346. Used with permission of the International Dyslexia Association.

Reading Attitudes and Habits

The striving readers in this study developed positive reading habits. Most impor-tant, they became lifelong readers. They currently do a great deal of work-related reading. However, I found significant differences among the groups regarding leisure reading. As Table 4B illustrates, the striving readers choose reading for pleasure, but they choose it less often than readers who did not struggle. The good news is that the striving readers do as much work-related reading in adulthood as the skilled readers in the comparison group.

The Interest-Based Model of Reading

These results led to an interest-driven model with important implications for teaching. The Interest-Based Model of Reading explains how striving readers, who may continue to lack strong integration of basic, phonological decoding skills, nevertheless construct higher order "meaning" skills. Key elements of the model include the following:

- A passionate, personal interest that spurs sustained reading.
- Avid, topic-specific reading.
- Deep schema knowledge.
- Contextual reading strategies.
- Mentoring support.

The Interest-Based Model of Reading can be used to promote resilience and success in all kinds of readers, including others who struggle. Teachers and families can use a key component of the model—passionate, personal interest—as a starting point to reverse reading failure and resistance. By providing students with ample opportunities to read about their interests, we can motivate in each student an intrinsic desire to read.

Students who read about a topic of personal interest are likely to become deeply engaged and read more frequently. The sheer volume of this increased reading can supply the requisite repetition and practice that enhances fluency and comprehension of increasingly sophisticated texts. Consequently, reading about a topic of passionate, personal interest can promote reading at higher and higher levels.

What Teachers and Families Can Do

Based on this model and the study's results, there are several specific things that teachers and families can do to help striving readers, both at school and at home:

1. Use students' interests.

2. Balance the reading program.

3. Use irresistible "entry points" into reading.

4. Teach comprehension systematically.

5. Facilitate fluency.

Use Students' Interests

Based on this study's results, teachers and family members should provide compelling materials about each student's interests. The idea that reading materials be tailored to individual interests has strong research support (Fink, in press; Gardner, 1983; Guthrie, 2004; Guthrie & Alvermann, 1999; Guthrie & Wigfield, 1997; Piaget, 1952; Renninger, 1992; Ritchey, 2004; Snow, Burns, & Griffin, 1998). A reluctant reader who has difficulty with typical school texts is likely to be more enthusiastic about books that explore a favorite topic—regardless whether the topic is science, history, sports, automechanics, or romance. This raises the question, How can busy teachers and family members find out what interests each student?

READING INTEREST INVENTORIES. One way to assess students' interests is by using a reading interest inventory such as the one below (adapted from Burns, Roe, & Ross, 1992). Reading interest inventories are easy to administer and modify to fit each student's age or developmental stage.

- What is the best book that was ever read to you?
- What is the best book that you ever read yourself?
- What are your favorite hobbies?
- What after-school activities do you like best?
- What are some of your favorite movies?
- What television programs do you like the most?
- What are your favorite television specials, videos, DVDs, computer games, and Internet websites?
- What school subjects do you find most interesting?
- What pets, sports, or art activities do you like best?
- If you could take a trip, where would you go?
- What careers interest you?

BIO-POEMS. Bio-poems are another way to discover a student's interests. With bio-poems, students write about and draw pictures of themselves. The following bio-poem template, adapted by Florida middle school teacher Minnie Gross (personal communication, May 2, 2004), is useful for students across ages and grade levels.

Line 1: First name only —-

Line 2: Four traits that describe you —-, —-, —-, —-

Line 3: Siblings of —- (or son/daughter of—-)

Line 4: Loves —-, —-, —- (3 people or things)

Line 5: Who feels —-, —-, —- (3 items)

Line 6: Who needs —-, —-, —- (3 items)

Line 7: Who gives —-, —-, —- (3 items)

Line 8: Who fears —-, —-, —- (3 items)

Line 9: Who would like to see —-, —-, —- (3 items)

Line 10: Resident of (your city), (your street)

Line 11: Your last name (draw a picture of yourself).

OTHER RESOURCES FOR DISCOVERING STUDENTS' INTERESTS. Informal interviews are another way to discover a student's interests. Teachers can interview the student by asking questions in the reading interest inventory and inquiring about favorite hobbies (e.g., sports, art, science, travel), movies, television programs, videos, DVDs, Internet websites, and computer games. Use clues from the student's favorite media subjects to discover passionate—or even dormant—interests, then gather reading materials accordingly.

Several books are available to help match students with books on their interests. For example, *A to Zoo: Subject Access to Children's Picture Books* (Lima & Lima, 1993) is a good resource for titles that reflect the interests of young children. This concise book lists preschool and elementary books alphabetically by topic. If, for example, a child is fascinated by dinosaurs, just look under "D" to find good books about dinosaurs. Another good resource is *100 Best Books for Children* (Silvey, 2004), which includes a plot summary and age range for each title. In addition, the Choices booklists provide superb lists of new books selected each year by children, teachers, parents, and librarians through a project of the International Reading Association (IRA; see Additional Resources, pages 30–33).

Leveled books are another good source of interesting titles. To find titles for young children, I suggest *Matching Books to Readers: Using Leveled Books in Guided*

Reading, K–3 (Fountas & Pinnell, 1999). For titles for intermediate and middle school children, I suggest two books: *Leveled Books for Readers, Grades 3–6: A Companion Volume to Guiding Readers and Writers* (Fountas & Pinnell, 2001) and *Guided Comprehension: A Teaching Model for Grades 3–8* (McLaughlin & Allen, 2002). In addition, the Degrees of Reading Power (DRP) system also lists interesting books by readability level. It is available as a CD-ROM and DRP-Booklink online under "Readability of Literature and Popular Titles" (see www.tasaliteracy.com).

In addition to books, student magazines and newspapers provide another way to lure reluctant readers, who usually find the shorter articles less overwhelming than full-length books (see Additional Resources, pages 33–35, for an annotated list of children's periodicals organized by topic and genre; the list also indicates appropriate age or grade levels).

Internet searches are another great way to locate a variety of interesting materials. Students usually benefit from direct instruction on databases, websites, keyword search strategies, and criteria for evaluating Web information. *The Mysteries of Internet Research* (Cohen, 2003) is a good book for grades 4–12. It uses a mystery format to teach students how to check facts on the Internet; it also teaches the research process using print sources. In addition, Story-Huffman's *Caldecott on the NET* (2002a) for grades K–5 and *Newbery on the NET* (2002b) for grades 4–8 have helpful suggestions for integrating award-winning literature with Internet activities and websites.

After helping students locate materials on their interests, teachers and families should plan time for regularly scheduled free reading. Free reading is *not* a frill; rather, it is essential for developing fluency and positive reading attitudes. And free reading is easy to integrate into any reading program. Teachers can incorporate a widely used traditional approach, such as Sustained Silent Reading (SSR), in which each student selects and reads a book silently at a regular time each day. While students read, the teacher also reads silently, modeling good reading behavior. No work is assigned with SSR.

A new approach, Voluntary Reading as Social Practice, includes an added conversational component in which students discuss their books with a peer, tutor, family member, or teacher. The added conversational component increases students' enthusiasm and spurs them to borrow more library books (Parr & Maguiness, 2005).

Both approaches, SSR and the discussion model, fulfill the National Research Council's recommendation that "time, materials, and resources be provided daily for independent reading of texts of interest to each student" (Snow et al., 1998, p. 324). (Figure 2 shows children engaged in independent reading and book discussions at the William H. Lincoln School in Brookline, Massachusetts.)

Balance the Reading Program

In this study, one third of the striving readers never fully mastered decoding, as shown by their reading test results; yet, all of them became skilled, lifelong readers. They received explicit instruction in basic skills, such as phonemic awareness and phonics, and simultaneously read many "real-life" books and magazines. This result underscores the need to balance decoding instruction with authentic text-based approaches. Creating balance is the key to an excellent reading program.

SYLLABICATION FOR DECODING STRATEGY (SDS). We know that phonological decoding should be taught in the early grades until children demonstrate mastery. But how can we teach decoding to older students? And how can we do it without holding them back? SDS, a new strategy that I recently developed, can be helpful. SDS helps students decode multisyllabic words in challenging texts and enables weak decoders to keep up with the content that their peers are learning. The strategy uses sound and rhythm to help students tap, hear, feel, and write the beats in syllables as a way into decoding long words. I created SDS for my own middle school students and have used it successfully with high school and college students as well. It is a lively, fun way to approach syllabication for the purpose

TABLE 5
Syllabication for Decoding Strategy (SDS)

Step 1. As if beating a drum, the teacher taps her desk according to the syllables in her name and each student's name. Students do the same and guess the number of taps (or syllables) they hear. For example: Ros/a/lie Fink (4); Ma/ry Ken/ne/dy (5); John Smith (2).

Step 2. The teacher selects and writes on the board or chart paper words from the student's most challenging reading assignments (i.e., social studies, science, etc.). Words should be underlined by the teacher and written in a phrase or sentence in order to place them in a meaningful context.

Step 3. The student attempts syllabication of each word for decoding purposes by drawing a line between letters to show each new beat (or syllable). The syllable divisions do not necessarily have to follow dictionary rules of syllabication. Syllable divisions are accepted as correct for decoding purposes if they help enable students to pronounce the word. For example, if words from a social studies book include *civilization*, the teacher would accept the following divisions: ci/vi/li/za/tion or civ/i/liz/a/tion or civ/il/iz/a/tion.

Step 4. The student writes the number of beats or syllables heard in each name or word in parentheses after each word. For example: ci/vi/li/za/tion (5); A/mer/i/can (4); pho/to/syn/the/sis (5); gene (1); ba/cil/li (3).

Step 5. After pronouncing a word, the student guesses its meaning from the context or looks up the meaning in the dictionary. The teacher should explain that SDS is primarily for decoding purposes, because traditional rules of syllabication have more constraints.

Adapted from Fink, R.P. (in press). What successful adults with dyslexia teach us about children. In K.W. Fischer, J.H. Bernstein, & M.H. Immordino-Yang (Eds.), *Mind, brain, and education in reading disorders*. Cambridge, England: Cambridge University Press.

of decoding. (See Table 5 for the sequential steps of this strategy. Each teacher can modify the steps to meet each student's individual needs.)

SEMANTIC IMPRESSIONS VOCABULARY METHOD. Teachers should discuss word meanings in context and include a variety of rich vocabulary activities. One excellent approach is the semantic impressions vocabulary method, which develops deep understanding of new word meanings (Richek, 2005). Semantic impressions is a good way to facilitate text comprehension before students begin reading, because it deepens vocabulary understanding and builds schematic background. Students work in groups using new vocabulary words before they read. Instead of the traditional method of writing words in isolated sentences, students work in groups and use all the new words in a coherent story of their own creation.

VOCABULARY CARD GAMES. Research shows that repeated encounters with words are necessary before students internalize word meanings and make new words their own (McKeown & Curtis, 1987; K.D. Stahl, 2005; S.A. Stahl, 1999). To provide repeated word encounters, it helps to have students play a variety of vocabulary games. Many games are available commercially, or they can be easily made. In one teacher-made card game, each student (a) locates the card containing a word that the teacher (or a student) says out loud, (b) gives a correct definition, and (c) creates a sentence using the word orally. Games of this sort not only provide drill and practice but also enliven lessons and make vocabulary learning fun.

Use Irresistible "Entry Points" Into Reading

The striving readers in this study found their own entry points into reading through topics of passionate, personal interest. Sometimes their topics differed from topics in the school's reading curriculum. For example, AIDS researcher Donald Francis loved reading automechanics manuals; until he was 13, he read almost exclusively about automechanics. He told me that he appreciated not being pressured by his parents to read the "right" books. For him, automechanics manuals were effective, irresistible entry points into reading. Eventually, he became a highly skilled reader and a medical doctor.

ALTERNATIVE TEXTS. How can teachers encourage other reluctant readers to find their own entry points to reading? One way is by using alternative texts. This means including any materials that excite the student: automechanics manuals, catalogs, comic books, picture books, easy-to-read books, high-interest/low-vocabulary books, videos, and universal design computer software. Many alternative texts are humorous and are purposely designed to avoid insulting older striving readers.

To integrate alternative texts into the reading curriculum, have students listen to tape recordings of favorite texts while they simultaneously read print versions. Then, gradually help "wean" students from audio support to independent reading by following these steps offered by Florida middle school teacher Minnie Gross (personal communication, May 1, 2004):

1. First, organize materials by readability levels; then show PowerPoint displays of enticing book covers at each level.

2. Next, give short book talks to introduce a variety of books to spark students' curiosity.

3. After each student selects a book, offer both print and audiotaped book options.

Because silent reading is usually faster than listening to tapes, most students are eager to read without the tapes as soon as possible. According to Gross, students usually "wean themselves" of audio support as soon as they feel successful and start to enjoy reading.

Other sources of alternative texts include an annotated list of entry point picture books (see Additional Resources, pages 35–36) and lists of high-interest books with wide appeal at each developmental level, elementary school through adulthood (see Additional Resources, pages 36–39).

Teach Comprehension Systematically

During childhood, the striving readers in this study chose personally fascinating books, sometimes above their instructional levels. How can teachers help other students to comprehend challenging books? By teaching comprehension strategies systematically—before, during, and after reading. Comprehension strategies should be modeled and taught with a gradual relinquishing of responsibility from teacher to student. The goal is for students to learn, practice, and internalize the strategy, ultimately using it independently.

First, help students to select books in what Vygotsky (1934/1978) calls the Zone of Proximal Development (ZPD). This means helping to choose "just right" books in which the student can independently read most of the words, but not all, and independently understand most of the ideas, but not all. Then, teachers should support comprehension throughout the reading process—before, during, and after reading.

BEFORE-READING ACTIVITIES. Begin by teaching vocabulary and questioning activities before reading in order to build background knowledge and enhance comprehension. For example, to prepare students to read current newspaper articles with optimal comprehension, a teacher could capitalize on the students' athletic interests by using articles on football, baseball, or basketball. Before reading, introduce vocabulary, such as *shut out*, *MVP*, *slam dunk*, or any other term likely to be unfamiliar. Write the new word on the board in the context of a phrase; then have students guess, predict, and discuss the word's meaning as it is used in the particular context. In addition, have students work in pairs, creating their own prereading interview questions to ask themselves or one another. The prereading questioning activities that follow enhance comprehension by activating and building schema and background knowledge.

- What do I already know about the topic?
- What do I predict will happen based on previewing the title, subtitles, and pictures?
- What do I want to know and hope to learn from this article?
- How do I feel about the topic, event, people, situation, and so forth? Why?

Several books and websites assist in teaching reading by using newspapers. Two good books with activities to foster newspaper comprehension are *Reading the Newspaper: Middle Level* (Miller & Allan, 1987) for middle school and *Reading the Newspaper: Advanced Level* (Miller & Allan, 1989) for high school. These books use real news stories, editorials, and other types of newspaper articles to teach a wide array of reading skills. Included are articles from actual newspapers on topics likely to engage young people (e.g., sports stories, new immigrants, going to the prom, safe sex, AIDS). To ensure that materials are up to date, teachers can use the engaging activities in these books but substitute more recent news articles. (In addition, consult Newspapers in Education websites that contain current lessons and activities available online through many city newspapers.)

Using newspaper articles to teach reading is a way to address controversial topics that generate deep discussion from multiple perspectives. Students soon discover that there is no single "right answer," but multiple answers to many issues. For example, an article titled "Sex Too Soon" (Miller & Allan, 1989) presents dilemmas faced by many teens and could be a springboard for discussion from various perspectives. Before students read the article, facilitate comprehension by preteaching salient vocabulary concepts (e.g., develop moral values, practice abstinence, practice safe sex). In addition, create stimulating before-reading questions in order to support students' comprehension. Questions might include the following: Do you believe that having sex before marriage is a good idea? Why or why not? What positive and negative consequences are possible when teens have sex? Why? To motivate students further, have them create their own prereading discussion questions in pairs, small groups, or as a class. Then, have them make predictions and discuss possible outcomes. Prereading activities such as these help students to develop the necessary background knowledge and schema that will enhance their comprehension when they actually read the text.

DURING-READING ACTIVITIES. During reading, students also need explicit instruction in comprehension strategies. One useful during-reading approach is the Paragraph-by-Paragraph Comprehension Strategy (Pauk, 2000), which entails reading and thinking about only one paragraph at a time. Tackling single paragraphs, one by one, is extremely effective for students who typically have difficulty understanding and remembering a whole text. To deepen their understanding, encourage students to make connections between information in the paragraph and their own life experiences. The Paragraph-by-Paragraph Comprehension Strategy works well for all kinds of content, but especially informational texts:

1. The teacher models the strategy aloud.

2. Students use the strategy in pairs, taking turns reading and summarizing aloud, one paragraph at a time.

3. Students use the strategy by reading silently and summarizing orally.

4. Students read silently and write short summaries (alone or in pairs).

5. Finally, students share written summaries and give one another constructive feedback on their writing. Some guiding questions for peer feedback:

> What was the main idea or big point of the whole paragraph?
>
> Did you include essential supporting details?
>
> Did you exclude less important details?

Involving students in activities such as these provides them with strategies that they eventually internalize, empowering them to comprehend increasingly challenging texts.

AFTER-READING ACTIVITIES. After reading, students benefit from enriching follow-up activities that reinforce and build on new concepts. For instance, after reading about a historical period, students can work in groups to re-create an event in history by writing it up as a news article. First they might write an attention-grabbing headline that captures the main idea; next they could draw or paint an illustration; then they could write letters to the editor in the voices of historical figures or witnesses to the event (e.g., the events of September 11, 2001; the 1963 Civil Rights march on Washington, DC). Next, each group could display its article on a bulletin board or in a school newspaper. After-reading activities, such as these, deepen students' text comprehension. In addition, they make reading experiences memorable and fun.

Facilitate Fluency

The striving readers in this study developed fluency through avid, even voracious reading about a topic of passionate, personal interest. The repeated vocabulary and syntax of their favorite genres provided the scaffolding that supported their increasing fluency. Teachers can facilitate fluency in other reluctant readers with the Simplified Repeated Reading Method (Samuels, 2002), which has been used with great success and was recently modified. Repeated reading is based on the notion that practice makes perfect. (Table 6 shows a step-by-step approach to

---

TABLE 6
Simplified Repeated Reading Method

Step 1. The teacher begins by asking a motivating question such as, Who are the most highly trained people in our society? Students frequently respond, "Athletes, musicians, dancers." Next, the teacher asks, How did they develop their skills? Students will likely answer, "Practice, practice, and more practice." Now, the teacher leads a discussion about the important role of practice in learning any skill (i.e., swimming, biking, etc.).

A physical demonstration of the benefits of practice may follow. For example, a teacher with ballet training might demonstrate the five basic ballet positions, performed awkwardly, as if by a beginner. Then, to emphasize the role of practice, the teacher demonstrates the same positions, but this time executes them gracefully as they would be performed by a dancer with advanced ballet training. Students then discuss the role of practice in learning to dance well. Finally, the teacher leads a discussion about the role of repeated practice in learning to read fluently.

Step 2. The teacher reads a new passage aloud while students follow along, reading the passage silently. By reading aloud, the teacher models accurate word recognition, appropriate intonation, phrasing, speed, and expression—important hallmarks of fluency.

Step 3. The students read books that they are likely to enjoy, preferably in pairs. If possible, a better reader is paired with a poorer reader. One child is "the student," who reads the text aloud, while the other child is the "teacher," who listens and follows along silently.

Step 4. Finally, students switch roles, taking turns being the reader and listener. They read the same text to each other two times each so that each text is read a total of four times. This practice is based on research by O'Shea, Sindelar, and O'Shea (1985), who found that most gains in reading speed, accuracy, and expression are acquired by the fourth reading. After repeated readings, children's oral reading will likely be smoother and sound increasingly like talking. Formal or informal self-assessment or teacher assessment may follow.

Adapted from Samuels, S.J. (2002). Reading fluency: Its development and assessment. In A.E. Farstrup & S.J. Samuels (Eds.), *What research has to say about reading instruction* (3rd ed., pp. 166–183). Newark, DE: International Reading Association.

using the Simplified Repeated Reading Method.) In addition, I recommend a good book about fluency, *The Fluent Reader: Oral Reading Strategies for Building Word Recognition, Fluency, and Comprehension* (Rasinski, 2003).

COMMERCIAL PROGRAMS. Some commercial programs are also useful for enhancing fluency (Hudson, Lane, & Pullen, 2005). Examples include Carbo Recorded Books (grades K–12), Great Leaps Reading (grades K–12 and adults), Jamestown Timed Readings Plus (grades 9–12), and QuickReads (grades 2–4). Some commercial programs use computer software (e.g., Read Naturally and Soliloquy Reading Assistant).

READERS THEATRE. Readers Theatre is another excellent, exciting way to promote fluency. This engaging approach emphasizes vivid oral reading and accurate interpretation of lines. Readers Theatre focuses attention on text meaning, line by line, word by word. Students do not memorize scripts; instead, they read aloud and concentrate on voice interpretation and characterization. This approach provides practice in oral reading and emphasizes communication of meaning through voice intonation, expression, cadence, and speed. Readers perform with the script in hand, while the audience listens, provides feedback, and sometimes even improvises endings. By engaging students in short, dramatic scenes from great literary works, Readers Theatre can inspire students to read the entire literary work later. Readers Theatre is a lively approach for enhancing fluency for students of all ages and levels (see Additional Resources, pages 40–41).

Conclusion:
Promote Achievement Through Personal Interests

Several key experiences were common to the 66 striving readers in this study. First, although it took them longer than their peers, they ultimately developed high-level literacy by reading avidly about a topic of passionate, personal interest. Second, they developed fluency through schema familiarity—familiarity with the vocabulary and syntax of interesting, content-specific texts. Third, the striving readers who began reading avidly at the earliest ages became the highest achievers. Fourth, all of them received instruction in phonological decoding strategies. However, one third of them *never* mastered phonics. Nevertheless, all of these striving readers read many enticing, authentic texts and mastered the ultimate goal of reading: meaning-making. Fifth, they all needed help from observant teachers and mentors.

These results led to an interest-driven model that explains how students who struggle can learn to read well and succeed at high levels. The Interest-Based Model of Reading has important implications for teaching. Family members, teachers, and everyone interested in helping children learn can use the model to help other students learn to read. Like the striving readers in my study, most students who struggle today can also become skilled readers.

Choices Titles and Other Favorites

Refer to Choices Booklists at www.reading.org/resources/tools/choices.html

Grades K–2

Bano, M. (1999). *When Sophie gets angry—Really, really angry*. New York: Blue Sky Press.

Bedford, D. (2003). *The copy crocs*. Atlanta, GA: Peachtree.

Beers, V.G. (1994). *It's not fair!* Wheaton, IL: Victor Books.

Bright, P. (2003). *Quiet!* New York: Orchard.

Carlson, N. (2003). *It's not my fault!* Minneapolis, MN: Carolrhoda Books.

Connor, L. (2004). *Miss Bridie chose a shovel*. Boston: Houghton Mifflin.

Cronin, D. (2003). *Diary of a worm*. New York: HarperCollins.

Davies, N. (2003). *Surprising sharks*. Cambridge, MA: Candlewick.

Desmini, L. (2003). *Policeman Lou and Policewoman Sue*. New York: Blue Sky Press.

Downey, L. (2003). *Most loved monster*. New York: Dial.

Durant, A. (2003). *Dear Tooth Fairy*. Cambridge, MA: Candlewick.

Falconer, I. (2003). *Olivia...and the missing toy*. New York: Atheneum.

Florezak, R. (2003). *Yikes!* New York: Blue Sky Press.

Foreman, M. (2004). *A trip to dinosaur time*. Cambridge, MA: Candlewick.

Freymann, S. (2003). *Baby food*. New York: Arthur A. Levine.

Freymann, S., & Elffers, J. (1999). *How are you peeling?* New York: Arthur A. Levine.

Gray, K. (2003). *Billy's bucket*. Cambridge, MA: Candlewick.

Greene, R.G. (2003). *This is the teacher*. New York: Dutton.

Hartman, B. (2003). *Grumblebunny*. New York: G.P. Putnam's Sons.

Heidbreder, R. (2003). *Drumheller dinosaur dance*. Cambridge, MA: Kids Can Press.

Horn, E. (2003). *Excuse me...Are you a witch?* Watertown, MA: Whispering Coyote.

Katzwinkel, W., & Murray, G. (2003). *Walter the farting dog: Trouble at the yard sale*. New York: Dutton.

Krosoczka, J.J. (2003). *Annie was warned*. New York: Alfred A. Knopf.

Krosoczka, J.J. (2003). *Bubble bath pirates!* New York: Viking.

Kroll, V. (2003). *Busy, busy mouse*. New York: Viking.

Lessem, D. (2002). *Tyrannosaurus Rex*. Cambridge, MA: Candlewick.

Lewin, B. (2003). *Cat count*. New York: Henry Holt.

Lundgren, M.B. (2003). *Seven scary monsters*. New York: Clarion.

Malkin, M. (2003). *Pinky's sweet tooth*. New York: Dutton.

Martin, B. (2003). *Panda bear, panda bear, what do you see?* New York: Henry Holt.

Middleton, C. (2003). *Enrico starts school*. New York: Dial.

Nelson, D. (2003). *Hunting sharks*. Minneapolis, MN: Lerner Publications.

Numeroff, L. (2003). *Beatrice doesn't want to*. Cambridge, MA: Candlewick.

Palatini, M. (2003). *The perfect pet*. New York: HarperCollins.

Palatini, M. (2003). *Stinky smelly feet: A love story*. New York: Dutton.

Reiss, M. (2003). *Late for school*. Atlanta, GA: Peachtree.

Rinehart, S.C. (2004). *Eliza and the dragonfly*. Nevada City, CA: Dawn Publications.

Rubin, C.M. (2003). *Eleanor, Ellatony, Ellencake, and me*. Columbus, OH: Gingham Dog Press.

Salzberg, B. (2003). *Crazy hair day*. Cambridge, MA: Candlewick.

Shore, D. (2003). *Bus-a-saurus bop*. New York: Bloomsbury Children's Books.

Smith, S. (2003). *Goldilocks and the three martians*. New York: Dutton.
Spinelli, E. (2003). *Moe McTooth*. New York: Clarion.
Stewart, S. (2003). *The friend*. New York: Farrar Straus Giroux.
Thompson, L. (2003). *Little quack*. New York: Simon & Schuster.
Vrombaut, A. (2003). *Clarabella's teeth*. New York: Clarion.
Williams, B. (2003). *Albert's impossible toothache*. Cambridge, MA: Candlewick.

Grades 3-4

Arbogast, J.M. (2004). *Buildings in disguise: Architecture that looks like animals, food, and other things*. Honesdale, PA: Boyds Mills Press.
Cameron, A. (1981). *The stories Julian tells*. New York: Pantheon.
Cameron, A. (1995). *The stories Huey tells*. New York: Knopf.
Cristaldi, K. (2003). *Samantha the snob*. New York: Random House.
Cronin, D. (2003). *Duck for president*. New York: Simon & Schuster.
Davies, N. (2004). *Poop: A natural history of the unmentionable*. Cambridge, MA: Candlewick.
Estes, E. (2001). *The hundred dresses*. New York: Voyager/Harcourt.
Estes, E. (2005). *Miranda the great*. Orlando, FL: Harcourt.
Evans, R.P. (2001). *The tower: A story of humility*. New York: Simon & Schuster.
Figley, M.R. (2004). *The schoolchildren's blizzard*. Minneapolis, MN: Carolrhoda
Flood, P.H. (2004). *It's test day, Tiger Turcotte*. Minneapolis, MN: Carolrhoda.
Geras, A. (2003). *The cats of cuckoo square: Callie's kitten*. New York: Yearling.
Jeffrey, L. (2004). *Dogs: How to choose and care for a dog*. Berkeley Heights, NJ: Enslow.
Lowry, L. (1988). *All about Sam*. Boston: Houghton Mifflin.
Lowry, L. (1988). *Anastasia Krupnik*. Santa Barbara, CA: ABC-Clio.
Lowry, L. (1999). *Zooman Sam*. Boston: Houghton Mifflin.
Lowry, L. (2002). *Gooney Bird Greene*. Boston: Houghton Mifflin.
Markle, S. (2003). *Great white sharks*. Minneapolis, MN: Carolrhoda.
Markle, S. (2004). *Polar bears*. Minneapolis, MN: Carolrhoda.
Mason, S. (2002). *The Quigleys*. New York: D. Fickling Books.
McDonald, M. (2004). *Judy Moody, M.D.: The doctor is in!* Cambridge, MA: Candlewick.
Mead, A. (2002). *Junebug in trouble*. New York: Farrar Straus Giroux.
Pilkey, D. (1994). *Dog breath: The horrible trouble with Hally Tosis*. New York: Blue Sky Press.
Pullman, P. (1991). *Spring-heeled Jack*. New York: Knopf.
Shannon, D. (1998). *A bad case of stripes*. New York: Blue Sky Press.
Sharmat, M.W. (2004). *Nate the great*. New York: Dell.
Smith, C.R. (2004). *Hoop kings*. Cambridge, MA: Candlewick.
Tang, G. (2001). *The grapes of math*. New York: Scholastic.
Teague, M. (1994). *Pigsty*. New York: Scholastic.

Grades 5-6

Cowell, C. (2004). *How to train your dragon by Hiccup Horrendous Haddock III*. New York: Little Brown & Company.
Derby, K. (2004). *The top 10 ways to ruin the first day of 5th grade*. New York: Holiday House.
Estes, E. (1990). *Ginger Pye*. New York: Odyssey/Harcourt.

Estes, E. (1990). *The middle Moffat*. New York: Odyssey/Harcourt.

Estes, E. (1990). *The Moffat Museum*. New York: Odyssey/Harcourt.

Estes, E. (1990). *The Moffats*. New York: Odyssey/Harcourt.

Estes, E. (1990). *Pinky Pye*. New York: Odyssey/Harcourt.

Estes, E. (1990). *Rufus M.* New York: Odyssey/Harcourt.

Estes, E. (1990). *The witch family*. New York: Odyssey/Harcourt.

Holzer, H. (2004). *The president is shot! The assassination of Abraham Lincoln*. Honesdale, PA: Boyds Mills Press.

Janeczko, P.B. (2004). *Top secret: A handbook of codes, ciphers, and secret writing*. Cambridge, MA: Candlewick.

Konigsburg, E.L. (1998). *Altogether, one at a time*. New York: Simon & Schuster.

Konigsburg, E.L. (1998). *From the mixed-up files of Mrs. Basil E. Frankweiler*. New York: Simon & Schuster.

Konigsburg, E.L. (1998). *Jennifer, Hecate, Macbeth, William McKinley, and Me, Elizabeth*. New York: Simon & Schuster.

Konigsburg, E.L. (1998). *The second Mrs. Giaconda*. New York: Simon & Schuster.

Konigsburg, E.L. (1998). *Throwing shadows*. New York: Simon & Schuster.

Konigsburg, E.L. (1998). *The view from Saturday*. New York: Simon & Schuster.

Mercado, N.E. (Ed.). (2004). *Tripping over the lunch lady and other school stories*. New York: Dial.

Nevins, C. (2004). *Karate hour*. New York: Marshall Cavendish.

Norton, M. (1990). *The Borrowers*. New York: Odyssey/Harcourt.

Norton, M. (1992). *The Borrowers afield*. New York: Odyssey/Harcourt.

Norton, M. (1992). *The Borrowers afloat*. New York: Odyssey/Harcourt.

O'Keefe, S.H. (2004). *Death by eggplant*. Brookfield, CT: Roaring Brook Press.

Packer, T. (2004). *Tales from Shakespeare*. New York: Scholastic.

Wenzel, G. (2004). *Feathered dinosaurs of China*. Watertown, MA: Charlesbridge.

Wilber, J. (1996). *Totally private and personal: Journaling ideas for girls and young women*. Minneapolis, MN: Free Spirit Publishing.

Williams, M. (2004). *The golden hour*. New York: Harry N. Abrams.

Zinneen, L. (2004). *Holding at third*. New York: Dutton.

Grade 7–Adult

Bowler, T. (2003). *Storm catchers*. New York: Margaret K. McElderry Books.

Bradley, K.B. (2003). *For freedom: The story of a French spy*. New York: Delacorte.

Byng, G. (2003). *Molly Moon's incredible book of hypnotism*. New York: HarperCollins.

Curley, M. (2003). *The dark*. New York: Bloomsbury.

Donnelly, J. (2003). *A northern light*. New York: Harcourt.

Draper, S.M. (2003). *The Battle of Jericho*. New York: Atheneum.

Flake, S.G. (2003). *Begging for change*. New York: Hyperion.

Graham, R. (2003). *My not-so-terrible time at the Hippie Hotel*. New York: Viking.

Hautman, P. (2003). *Sweetblood*. New York: Simon & Schuster.

Holm, J.L. (2003). *The creek*. New York: HarperTrophy.

Johnson, A. (2003). *The first part last*. New York: Simon & Schuster.

Mackler, C. (2003). *The Earth, my butt, and other big round things*. Cambridge, MA: Candlewick.

Naylor, P.R. (2003). *Patiently Alice*. New York: Atheneum.

Paolini, C. (2003). *Eragon*. New York: Knopf.

Pattou, E. (2003). *East*. New York: Harcourt.

Paulsen, G. (2003). *The Glass Café*. New York: Wendy Lamb Books.

Peck, R. (2003). *The river between us*. New York: Dial.

Prose, F. (2003). *After*. New York: HarperTempest.

Rees, C. (2003). *Pirates!* New York: Bloomsbury.

Rees, D. (2003). *Vampire High*. New York: Delacorte.

Rottman, S.L. (2003). *Shadow of a doubt*. Atlanta, GA: Peachtree.

Schreiber, E. (2003). *Vampire kisses*. New York: HarperCollins.

Shusterman, N. (2003). *Full tilt*. New York: Simon & Schuster.

Soto, G. (2003). *The afterlife*. New York: Harcourt.

Spinelli, J. (2003). *Milkweed*. New York: Knopf.

Springer, N. (2003). *Blood trail*. New York: Holiday House.

Steer, D.A. (Ed.). (2003). *Dr. Ernest Drake's Dragonology: The complete book of dragons*. Cambridge, MA: Candlewick.

Tashjian, J. (2003). *Fault line*. New York: Henry Holt.

Theodore, W. (2003). *Wayne: An abused child's story of courage, survival, and hope*. Gig Harbor, WA: Harbor Press.

Trueman, T. (2003). *Inside out*. New York: HarperTempest.

Magazines and Newspapers for Children, Teens, and Adults

Arts

ASK (grades 1–4) teaches about the arts in its many forms. Each issue has a different theme.

Dance Magazine (grades 9–12) reviews the latest dance news and performances. The exquisite action photographs are engaging and the text is accessible to high school and adult readers interested in dance.

Dramatics: The Magazine for Students and Teachers of Theatre (grades 9–12) contains a wide variety of drama activities, including warm-ups, storytelling, plays, and Readers Theatre.

Ladybug (pre-K–grade 1) includes poems, rhymes, and songs helpful for developing phonemic awareness, as well as knowledge about the world.

Spider (grades 1–4) has stories, poems, and activities for elementary-age children who have begun to read independently.

Fiction

Cricket (grades 4–9) includes stories, puzzles, and contests that get children excited and involved in reading and writing.

Highlights for Children (grades 3–6) has stories and entertaining activities for elementary-age children who have begun to read independently.

Literary Cavalcade (grade 9–adult) includes high-interest fiction and nonfiction literature for high school students. Among its regular features is the World of Words, which focuses on building a powerful vocabulary through a variety of vocabulary activities.

Multicultural Studies

Faces: People, Places, Cultures (grades 4–9) is a world culture magazine that teaches about the people and customs of different cultures around the world.

Skipping Stones (grade 2–adult) is a nonprofit magazine that focuses on multicultural themes that focus on the arts, writing, and nature.

Social Studies

Appleseeds (grades 3–6) contains social studies information based on themes that vary with each issue.

Calliope (grades 4–9) teaches history, background knowledge, and vocabulary in fun-filled ways. Each issue is theme-based and focuses on a different historical period.

Kids Discover (grades 1–9) teaches geography and history. Each issue has a different theme.

LibrarySparks (grades 3–9) includes history and social studies information in a colorful, lively format. It focuses on timely observances and celebrations (i.e., Women's History Month, the Wright Brothers, etc.).

National Geographic Explorer, Pioneer Edition (grades 2–3) uses exquisite illustrations and basic text to excite readers about worldwide diversity of peoples, places, and cultures.

National Geographic for Kids (grades 3–6) is famous for its gorgeous illustrations from around the world.

National Geographic (grade 7–adult) contains bright, vibrant photographs from around the world.

Scholastic News (grades 1–10) includes articles and current news stories written in lively prose.

TIME for Kids: Big Picture (K–1), *TIME for Kids: News Scoop* (grades 2–3), and *TIME for Kids: World Reports* (grades 4–6) include current news, sports, and entertainment stories. Games are also featured.

USA Today (grade 9–adult) presents daily news stories in a mature yet accessible format.

Weekly Reader (pre-K–grade 8) covers news stories.

Sports

Sports Illustrated for Kids (grades 3–10) reports the latest sports news in a format likely to engage children. The action-packed photographs are especially appealing.

Science and Nature

ASK (grades 1–4) contains scientific information presented thematically; each issue focuses on a different theme.

ChicaDEE (K–grade 4) contains articles with hands-on activities that will engage young children interested in science.

Click (pre-K–grade 2) is excellent for very young children curious about science.

Discover Magazine (grade 9–adult) reviews the latest scientific discoveries in a vibrant, appealing format that is enhanced by colorful pictures.

Kids Discover (grades 1–9) offers science information in a thematic presentation. Each issue has a different theme.

Muse (grades 4–9) contains articles with information on a wide variety of subjects, including space, genetics, lasers, computers, rain forests, physics, math, and visual arts.

OWL (grades 4–8) contains scientific information likely to fascinate students of all ages, but especially middle schoolers intrigued by science.

Ranger Rick (grades 2–8) focuses on animals in their natural habitats. It contains nature stories and information supplemented by colorful photographs likely to entice reluctant readers who are animal lovers.

Your Big Backyard (pre-K–grade 2) focuses on information about nature and includes animal stories.

Zoobooks (pre-K–grade 6) has information and attractive photographs about animals that will appeal to preschool and elementary-age children.

Alternative Texts: Picture Books for Young and Old

Adapted from Ivey, G. (2004, May). **Meeting the needs of struggling readers.** *Paper presented at the annual convention of the International Reading Association, Reno, NV.*

Billout, G. (2002). *Something's not quite right.* Boston, MA: David R. Godine. This picture book for grade 3–adult contains short captions that accompany the picture puzzles to be solved on each page. The book uses clever wordplay and unusual pairings of climate, subject, and place, and each page shows a painting with impossible juxtapositions. For example, the cover shows an ocean liner traveling right over a huge gorge. Another painting reveals a tank driving through a field of flowers without running over the flowers. The book is funny and is useful for teaching how to attend to details and solve logical puzzles. It is ideal for use as a story starter in which students write their own stories about their favorite pictures.

Branzai, S. (1997). *Grossology begins at home: The science of really gross things in your everyday life.* New York: Penguin. This book includes sections on "Toilet," "Ten Reasons Why You Shouldn't Kiss Anyone Except the Dog," "How to Talk to Your Dog," and "How to Talk to Your Cat." It contains easy, fun-to-do classroom experiments that teach science in a hilarious manner likely to delight even the most reluctant reader of any age, grades 3–12.

Cronin, D. (2004). *Diary of a worm.* New York: HarperCollins. This humorous book was selected as a Children's Choices book and covers hilarious "crises" such as a worm who eats his homework and other easy-to-relate-to themes. The book takes a lighthearted view of difficult situations and universal themes likely to appeal to children in grades 3–10.

Davies, N. (2003). *Surprising sharks.* Cambridge, MA: Candlewick. This informational book was a 2004 Children's Choices selection. It introduces various species of sharks, points out their distinguishing characteristics (such as the small size of the dwarf lantern shark), and addresses both the physical and behavioral traits that enable sharks to kill. Designed for early elementary children (grades 1–4), it may also appeal to older students who are interested in learning about sharks.

Dussling, J. (1998). *Slinky scaly snakes.* New York: DK Publications. This book is filled with wonderful pictures and lots of information about snakes and how they live. It includes details about the physical characteristics that make snakes unique and fascinating information about their daily habits. It is an easy-to-read book originally designed for grades 1–3; however, older students interested in snakes will likely find the text accessible and the information intriguing.

ADDITIONAL RESOURCES

Giblin, J. (1994). *Thomas Jefferson: A picture book biography*. New York: Scholastic. This biography presents information about the life of the third U.S. president, Thomas Jefferson, through the use of vivid pictures. Although it was written primarily for children in grades 1–6, older readers are likely to discover that the attractive illustrations convey important information about Jefferson's life.

Jackson, D. (2000). *The wildlife detectives*. Boston: Houghton Mifflin. This book describes how scientists at the National Fish and Wildlife Forensics Laboratory in Ashland, Oregon, analyze clues that enable them to catch and convict people responsible for crimes against animals. The book has a sixth-grade readability level yet is likely to appeal to older students in grade 7–adult who love animals and are interested in learning how scientists solve mysteries.

Maynard, C. (2000). *Sharks: Natural born killers? The facts behind the fiction*. London: Walker Books. This book is filled with numerous shark facts and photos and is part of an engaging "Informania Series" of high interest informational books with wide appeal. Written especially for children in grades 3–7, it is an excellent informational book for older students as well.

McDonald, M. (1990). *Is this a house for a hermit crab?* New York: Orchard Books. This informative book contains appealing, realistic pastel illustrations that make the text come alive. The book uses a narrative format with periodic repetition to teach about the habits of hermit crabs and the complex concept of symbiotic relationships. Written for children in preschool through grade 2, it is easily accessible and can be used with older striving readers who are interested in nature.

Pilkey, D. (1994). *Dog breath: The horrible trouble with Hally Tosis*. New York: Blue Sky Press. This amusing book is about Hally, the Tosis family dog, whose breath smells so bad that Mr. and Mrs. Tosis plan to give her away. Fortunately, they change their minds when Hally proves to be an invaluable watchdog. This humorous picture book is for grades 1–5 but will likely entice reluctant readers of all ages. Parents, friends, and teachers will laugh through this hilarious story as well.

Williams, Mo. (2003). *Don't let the pigeon drive the bus*. New York: Hyperion Books for Children. This is a 2004 Caldecott Honor Book written for children from preschool–grade 1. However, due to its silly humor, the appeal of this book can extend to grades 2–6. The book can be used for lessons on the art of persuasion, especially persuasive writing.

High-Interest Books

Elementary School

Bridwell, N. (2003). *Clifford the big red dog*. Alexandria, VA: Scholastic.

Bryant, A. (2004). *Berry yummy cookbook*. New York: Grosset & Dunlap.

Bryant, A. (2003). *Jack's party*. Minneapolis, Minnesota: Picture Window Books.

Burton, V.L. (2002). *Katy and the big snow*. Boston: Houghton Mifflin.

Cleary, B. (2001). *Henry and Beezus*. New York: Avon Books.

Cole, J. (1995). *The magic schoolbus*. New York: Scholastic.

Cole, J. (2004). *Lost in the snow*. New York: Scholastic.

Coman, C. (2004). *The big house*. Asheville, NC: Front Street.

Cooney, B. (1985). *Miss Rumphius*. New York: Puffin.

Dahl, R. (1994). *Matilda*. New York: A.A. Knopf/Random House.

Dahl, R. (1998). *Danny the champion of the world*. New York: Puffin.

D'Aulaire, I., & E.P. (1998). *Pocahontas*. Sandwich, MA: Beautiful Feet Books.

D'Aulaire, I., & E.P. (2005). *Norse gods and giants*. New York: New York Review Books.

Eastman, P.D. (1998). *Are you my mother?* New York: Random House.

Gannett, R.S. (1998). *Three tales of my father's dragon*. New York: Random House.

Giff, P. (1984). *The beast in Ms. Rooney's room*. New York: Dell.

Giff, P. (1986). *Snuggle doodles: The kids of the Polk Street School*. New York: Delacorte.

Giff, P. (1989). *In the dinosaur's paw*. New York: Delacorte.

Giff, P. (1998). *Friends and amigos*. Milwaukee, WI: Gareth Stevens Publishers.

Gwynne, F. (1989). *The king who rained*. New York: Simon & Schuster.

Hamilton, V. (1988). *Anthony Burns: The defeat and triumph of a fugitive slave*. New York: Knopf.

Hamilton, V. (1988). *In the beginning: Creation stories from around the world*. San Diego, CA: Harcourt, Brace, Jovanovich.

Hamilton, V. (1995). *Her stories: African American folktales, fairy tales, and true tales*. New York: Blue Sky Press.

Lindgren, A. (1999). *Pippi's extraordinary day*. New York: Viking.

Lindgren, A. (2001). *Pippi Longstocking in the park*. New York: Viking.

Lindgren, A. (2003). *Mio, my son*. Keller, TX: Purple House Press.

Lobel, A. (1970). *Frog and Toad are friends*. New York: Harper & Row.

Lobel, A. (1997). *Arnold Lobel Book of Mother Goose*. New York: Knopf.

Parish, P. (1999). *Amelia Bedelia*. New York: HarperFestival.

Provenson, A., & Provensen, M. (2001). *Our animal friends at Maple Hill Farm*. New York: Aladdin Paperbacks.

Rey, H. (1994). *Curious George*. Boston: Houghton Mifflin.

Sendak, M. (2003). *Where the wild things are*. New York: Harper Collins.

Seuss, Dr. (1958). *The cat in the hat comes back!* New York: Beginner Books.

Seuss, Dr. (1993). *Green eggs and ham*. New York: G. Schirmer.

Seuss, Dr. (2003). *The cat in the hat*. New York: Golden Books.

Sharmat, M. (2004). *Nate the great*. New York: Dell.

Silverstein, S. (1981). *A light in the attic*. New York: Harper & Row.

Steig, W. (1984). *The rotten bad island*. Boston: David R. Godine.

Steig, W. (1986). *Brave Irene*. New York: Farrar Straus Giroux.

Steig, W. (1995). *Sylvester & the magic pebble*. New York: Little Simon.

Steig, W. (1997). *Dr. DeSoto*. New York: Farrar Straus Giroux.

Steptoe, J. (1984). *The story of jumping mouse: A Native American legend*. New York: Lothrop, Lee, & Shepard Books.

Whelan, G. (1992). *Goodbye, Vietnam*. New York: HarperCollins.

Whelan, G. (2004). *Chu Ju's house*. New York: HarperCollins.

Whelan, G. (2005). *Listening for lions*. New York: HarperCollins.

Middle School–Adult

Babbitt, N. (1999). *Tuck everlasting*. Austin, TX: Holt, Rhinehart, & Winston.

Bartoletti, S. (1999). *No man's land: A young soldier's story*. New York: Blue Sky Press.

Blume, J. (2003). *Superfudge*. New York: Puffin.

Blume, J. (2004). *Freckle juice*. New York: Dell Yearling.

Blume, J. (2004). *Are you there, God? It's me, Margaret*. New York: Dell Yearling.

Bowen, G. (1994). *Stranded at Plymoth Plantation 1626*. New York: HarperCollins.

Byars, B. (1988). *The pinballs*. Santa Barbara, CA: ABC-Clio.

Carter, F. (1991). *The education of little tree*. Albuquerque, NM: University of New Mexico.

Coman, C. (1993). *Tell me everything*. New York: Farrar Straus Giroux.

Cook, K. (1997). *What girls learn*. New York: Pantheon.

Cooney, C. (1990). *The face on the milk carton*. New York: Bantam.

Cooney, C. (1992). *Flight #116 is down*. New York: Scholastic.

Cooney, C. (1993). *Whatever happened to Janie?* New York: Delacorte.

Cooney, C. (1994). *Driver's ed*. New York: Delacorte.

Cooney, C. (1995). *Night school*. New York: Scholastic.

Cooney, C. (1996). *The voice on the radio*. New York: Delacorte.

Cooney, C. (1997). *The Terrorist*. New York: Scholastic.

Cooney, C. (2000). *What Janie found*. New York: Delacorte.

Cooney, C. (2005). *Hit the road*. New York: Delacorte.

Curtis, C. (1995). *The Watsons go to Birmingham—1963*. New York: Delacorte.

Davis, T. (2003). *If rock & roll were a machine*. Spokane, WA: Eastern Washington University.

Dickens, C. (1992). *David Copperfield*. New York: Chelsea House.

Dickens, C. (2005). *Great expectations*. Philadelphia: Chelsea House.

Ellis, D. (2001). *The breadwinner*. Berkeley, CA: Publisher's Group West.

Fleischman, S. (2003). *The whipping boy*. New York: HarperTrophy.

Fleming, A.M. (2004). *Frederick Douglass: From slave to statesman*. New York: PowerKids Press.

Giff, P. (2004). *A house of tailors*. New York: Wendy Lamb Books.

Giff, P. (1982). *The gift of the pirate queen*. New York: Delacorte.

Giff, P. (1998). *Lily's crossing*. New York: Random House.

Giff, P. (2000). *Nory Ryan's song*. New York: Delacorte.

Giff, P. (2002). *Pictures of Hollis Woods*. New York: Wendy Lamb Books.

Grahame, K. (1989). *The wind in the willows*. New York: Aladdin.

Gutman, D. (1993). *Baseball's biggest bloopers: A baseball card adventure*. New York: Puffin.

Gutman, D. (2000). *Babe and me*. New York: Avon.

Haley, A. (1987). *Roots: The saga of an American family*. New York: Ballantine.

Hamilton, N., Brunelle, J.K., Scully, B., & Sherman, R. (2000). *Atlas of the baby boom generation: A cultural history of postwar America*. New York: Macmillan.

Hershey, M. (2005). *My big sister is so bossy*. New York: Wendy Lamb Books.

Kennedy, J.F. (2000). *Profiles in courage*. New York: Harper Perrenial.

Kidd, S.M. (2002). *The secret life of bees*. New York: Viking Penguin.

L'Engle, M. (1962). *A wrinkle in time*. New York: Bantam Doubleday Dell.

Lowry, L. (1989). *Number the stars*. New York: Bantam Doubleday Dell.

Myers, W.D. (1981). *Hoops: A novel*. New York: Delacorte.

Myers, W.D. (2004). *Monster*. New York: HarperTempest/Amistad.

Naidoo, B. (2001). *The other side of truth*. New York: HarperCollins.

Paulsen, G. (1994). *The car*. San Diego, CA: Harcourt Brace.

Paulsen, G. (1999). *Hatchet*. New York: Aladdin.

Paulsen, G. (2003). *Shelf life: Stories by the book*. New York: Simon & Schuster.

Paulsen, G. (2004). *Molly McGinty has a really good day*. New York: Wendy Lamb Books.

Quindlen, A. (1993). *Thinking out loud: On the personal, the political, the public, and the private*. New York: Fawcett Columbine.

Rowling, J.K. (1998). *Harry Potter and the Sorcerer's Stone*. New York: Arthur A. Levine.

Rowling, J.K. (1999). *Harry Potter and the prisoner of Azkaban*. New York: Arthur A. Levine.

Rowling, J.K. (2001). *Quidditch through the ages*. New York: Arthur A. Levine.

Rowling, J.K. (2003). *Harry Potter and the Order of the Phoenix*. New York: Arthur A. Levine.

Rowling, J.K. (2005). *Harry Potter and the half-blood prince*. New York: Arthur A. Levine.

Ryan, P.M. (2001). *Esperanza rising*. Austin, TX: Holt, Rinehart & Winston.

Sebold, A. (1999). *Lucky*. New York: Scribner.

Sebold, A. (2002). *The lovely bones: A novel*. Boston: Little Brown.

Soto, G. (1999). *Buried onions*. New York: HarperCollins.

Warner, G.C. (1991). *The boxcar children cookbook*. Morton Grove, IL: Albert Whitman & Co.

Warner, G.C. (1992). *The boxcar children: The amusement park mystery*. Morton Grove, IL: Albert Whitman & Co.

Warner, G.C. (1999). *The boxcar children: The basketball mystery*. Morton Grove, IL: Albert Whitman & Co.

Warner, G.C. (2002). *The boxcar children: The mystery of the mummy's curse*. Morton Grove, IL: Albert Whitman & Co.

Warner, G.C. (2003). *The boxcar children: The black widow spider mystery*. Morton Grove, IL: Albert Whitman & Co.

Warner, G.C. (2004). *The boxcar children mysteries: The clue in the corn maze*. Morton Grove, IL: Albert Whitman & Co.

Warner, G.C. (2005). *The boxcar children mysteries: The ghost of the chattering bones*. Morton Grove, IL: Albert Whitman & Co.

Wharton, E. (2005). *Ethan Frome*. West Berlin, NJ: Townsend Press.

White, E.B. (2006). *Charlotte's web*. New York: HarperCollins.

Winkler, H., & Oliver, L. (2003). *Hank Zipper, the world's greatest underachiever: I got a "D" in salami*. New York: Grosset & Dunlap

Winkler, H., & Oliver, L. (2003). *Hank Zipper, the world's greatest underachiever: Niagara Falls, or does it?* New York: Grosset & Dunlap

Winkler, H., & Oliver, L. (2004). *Hank Zipper, the world's greatest underachiever: Help! Somebody get me out of fourth grade!* New York: Grosset & Dunlap.

Winkler, H., & Oliver, L. (2004). *Hank Zipper, the world's greatest underachiever: Holy enchilada*. New York: Grosset & Dunlap.

Winkler, H., & Oliver, L. (2004). *Hank Zipper, the world's greatest underachiever: The night I flunked my field trip*. New York: Grosset & Dunlap.

Winkler, H., & Oliver, L. (2005). *Hank Zipper, the world's greatest underachiever: Summer school! What genius thought that up?* New York: Grosset & Dunlap.

Woodson, J. (2003). *Hush*. New York: Speak.

Wright, B.R. (1983). *The dollhouse murders*. New York: Holiday House.

Zusak, M. (2000). *Fighting Reuben Wolfe*. Norwood, South Australia: Omnibus Books.

Zusak, M. (2006). *Book thief*. New York: Alfred A. Knopf.

Readers Theatre Resources, K–Adult

Early Grades

Marx, P. (1997). *Take a quick bow: 26 short plays for classroom fun*. Glenview, IL: Good Year Books. This book is excellent for grades 2–4. It contains plays that support the curriculum for young children on a wide array of topics, including seasons, holidays, international folklore, U.S. history, the environment, equality and brotherhood, the arts, and science. In addition to emphasizing oral reading fluency, the book includes warm-up and follow-up activities to develop speaking, listening, researching, and writing skills.

Talbot, A.R. (1994). The Lost Cat *and other primary plays for oral reading*. Billerica, MA: Curriculum Associates. This collection of short plays (10–15 minutes each) is appropriate for young children in grades 1–4. The short plays deal with topics of interest to young children: cats, dogs, ghosts, robots, parties, etc. The book includes a teacher guide with ideas for writing and art activities that relate to the plays. The large print will appeal to young children learning to read, and the print format is easily reproducible so that each child has his or her own copy of the script.

Wolfman, J. (2004). *How and why stories for Readers Theatre*. Englewood, CO: Teacher Ideas Press. This book contains 40 Readers Theatre scripts based on motivating questions, such as How did the bee get his bumble? How do birds get their feathers? and Why is the bluebird blue? These scripts will appeal to children in grades 1–5 with various interests.

Intermediate Grades

Fredericks, A. (2001). *Silly salamanders and other slightly stupid stuff for Readers Theatre*. Englewood, CO: Teacher Ideas Press. This book has over two dozen reproducible scripts for grades 3–8. It includes humorous and unexpected twists to old fairy tales and legends. The activities focus on developing skills in listening, reading, speaking, and writing.

Jenkins, D.R. (2004). *Just deal with it! Funny Readers Theatre for life's not-so-funny moments*. Englewood, CO: Teacher Ideas Press. This is a book of humorous scripts for children in grades 4–8. It contains lots of funny episodes with creative solutions to life's everyday problems.

Laughlin, M.K., Black, P.T., & Loberg, M.K. (1991). *Social studies Readers Theatre for children: Scripts and script development*. Englewood, CO: Teacher Ideas Press. This rich resource is appropriate for children in grades 2–7. It focuses on American history and folklore and includes complete scripts of many American folk heroes. Scripts are arranged chronologically to fit with the history and social studies curriculum. One excellent feature is the inclusion of partial scripts; students do historical research and read historical novels in preparation for writing the completion of the started script. In addition, the book has directions for developing a Readers Theatre program that features eight novels from the Little House on the Prairie series by Laura Ingalls Wilder. Also included is an annotated bibliography of good historical fiction for children.

Laughlin, M.K., & Latrobe, K.H. (1989). *Reader's Theatre for children: Scripts and script development*. Englewood, CO: Teacher Ideas Press. This excellent collection of both completed and suggested scripts (to be completed by students) includes selections from literature that will appeal to children in grades 3–8. Completed scripts include *Treasure Island*, *The Wonderful*

Wizard of Oz, *A Christmas Carol*, *Heidi*, and *The Secret Garden*. Scripts to be completed by students include *After the Goat Man*; *The Get-Away Car*; *Thank-You, Jackie Robinson*; *How to Eat Fried Worms*; *Mail-Order Kid*; and *Charlotte's Web*. A useful annotated bibliography is also included.

Worthy, J. (2004). *Readers Theater for building fluency: Strategies and scripts for making the most of this highly effective, motivating, and research-based approach to oral reading*. New York: Scholastic. This book is appropriate for children in grades 3–6; in addition to providing practice in oral reading with engaging activities, it also has lessons for boosting comprehension, vocabulary, and writing skills.

Middle School–Adult

Blank, C., & Roberts, J. (1996). *Live on stage: Teacher resource book, performing arts for middle school*. New York: Dale Seymour Publications. This is an outstanding book for middle school students in grades 6–8 (or older). The book includes a wide array of creative improvisational activities that support literacy learning in highly engaging ways. It integrates games, activities, and dances and has lots of practical ideas for using Readers Theatre and other oral reading lessons. The book contains extension activities such as keeping a theater journal and researching performance genres from 15th-century comedy to modern film, dance, and theater. Included in this book are ways to use musical forms, dance and body movement, art, costumes, surveys, lists, writing ideas, etc.

Feyder, L., (Ed.). (1992). *Shattering the myth: Plays by Hispanic women*. Houston, TX: Arte Publico Press. This collection of contemporary plays questions established myths and is appropriate for students in grade 9–adult. The plays lend themselves to Readers Theatre and other dramatic venues, as well as to critical reading analyses. Included are complete scripts of prize-winning contemporary plays that can be performed. Plays include *Shadow of a Man*, about a 12-year-old Mexican girl who lives in Los Angeles and has secrets she can no longer tell her priest; *Simply Maria or the American Dream*, about a young girl who struggles when she fails to convince her family that she should attend college; *Miriam's Flowers*, about a 16-year-old Puerto Rican girl and her 7-year-old brother who live in the South Bronx; and *A Dream of Canaries*, about a militaristic society and political "disappearances."

Latrobe, K.H., & Laughlin, M.K. (1997). *Readers Theatre for young adults: Script and script development*. Englewood, CO: Teacher Ideas Press. This is a rich resource for teachers of late middle school and high school students, grade 7–adult. The book teaches concepts of theme, character, and drama and includes 12 reproducible scripts from classic literature. In addition, scenes from over 30 contemporary young adult novels have been adapted for Readers Theatre activities (for example, *The Pigman*, *Tex*, *The Other Side of Dark*, *Summer of My German Soldier*, *Wilderness Peril*, *My Life in Seventh Grade*, *Prairie Songs*, and *Z is for Zachariah*). Writing activities and an annotated bibliography in this book are helpful for developing background information and follow-up activities.

CHAPTER **2**

Bilingual Readers: Marvelous Mentors and Cultural Pride

ow do bilingual students surmount their difficulties learning to read and write in a new language? We know that the road to second-language reading varies from child to child (Cummins, 1994). Individual differences vary according to each child's unique learning style and culture of origin (Li & Zhang, 2004). Many bilingual students struggle with reading, yet some who struggle ultimately succeed. How do they do it? What factors account for their success? Clues to this puzzle are revealed through the experiences of two highly successful Latino Americans: Baruj Benacerraf, a Nobel Prize–winning immunologist, and Cruz Sanabria, an early childhood educator.

A Family That Mentored: Baruj Benacerraf's Story

Baruj Benacerraf was born into an affluent Jewish family in Caracas, Venezuela, so his first language was Spanish. Although he struggled with severe reading problems, he eventually learned to read and write in four languages: Spanish, French, Hebrew, and English, in that order. At the age of 5, he moved with his family to Paris and at 20, to New York City. Benacerraf struggled with reading from an early age, yet became a sophisticated reader, eventually becoming chair of the Department of Immunology and Pathology at Harvard Medical School. He discovered how to prevent organ transplant rejection—a discovery that has saved many lives and won him the Nobel Prize. How did he achieve such phenomenal success despite his reading difficulties? This question intrigued me.

My first interview with Benacerraf took place on a warm July day at his oceanside summer home in Cape Cod, Massachusetts. We sat outside on lawn chairs on a terrace overlooking the glistening waters of Vineyard Sound. As we spoke, Benacerraf's 10-year-old grandson occasionally ran over to ask his grandfather a question. Benacerraf spoke with enthusiastic pride in his voice, not only about his own accomplishments but also about those of his daughter, whose research with ultrasound technology enables doctors to diagnose fetal abnormalities early in pregnancy. Like Benacerraf, his daughter and grandson also struggled with severe reading problems.

I wondered what had enabled Benacerraf to surmount his reading difficulties. What I discovered was that, at each stage of development, he had marvelous mentors—at home, at school, and at work. At home, he had relatives who worked with him tirelessly and instilled in him a true affinity for reading.

I loved reading. Always! I read a lot! Reading sufficiently is one of my greatest pleasures.

Benacerraf's family mentors intuitively realized the benefits of a balanced approach to reading. They exposed him to the delights of compelling "real-life" books and simultaneously worked with him on sound–symbol relationships and phonological decoding skills. Luckily for Benacerraf, his cousin Suzanne lived with the family and tutored him daily. She taught him that letters and their combinations stand for certain sounds and, at the same time, she provided him with lots of good books. Suzanne began tutoring Benacerraf when he was 5 years old and continued with daily tutoring sessions until he was 12. Eventually, after years of continuous tutoring, reading finally clicked for him. And from then on he continued to improve.

> *From about 11 or 12, I surmounted my reading problem. And from 12 to 20, I got better and better at reading.*

Cultural Pride and Reading With Pleasure

Pride and pleasure were repeating themes in Benacerraf's life. He took pride in his multiple languages and cultures and took pleasure in his reading. His pleasure in learning to read fits with the themes of pleasure, fascination, and flow that inform the Interest-Based Model of Reading.

During his interviews, Benacerraf frequently alluded to pleasure and pride in his complex, multifaceted heritage: pride in person, family, extended family, and culture. His cultural pride was nurtured in a highly literate family that valued cultural history, the arts, sciences, and languages.

> *I have had the good fortune to be influenced by several distinct cultures and societies.... I am indebted to my French upbringing and education for my analytical skills.... My Jewish ancestry, and anti-Semitism and the necessity to flee Hitler when I was young, have fostered in me the feeling that I belong to a vulnerable group.... I felt immediately at home in the United States, a country of immigrants who have never forgotten their origins....*

With pride in his heritage, Benacerraf viewed his multiple cultures and languages as rich assets. Spurred on to capitalize on these assets by the high expectations of his family, he recollected that his mother was very demanding. She had high hopes for her son even though he struggled with reading. So she did everything possible to make reading enticing. I noticed a twinkle in his eyes and a playfulness in his voice as he recalled, "They bought me chocolate letters as an incentive to read!"

Family members also enticed Benacerraf to read by providing a wide variety of books in his favorite genre: biography. He was particularly interested in the lives of scientists and artists, so his mother and cousin Suzanne bought him lots of biographies.

> *I read about the lives of famous scientists. Famous scientists and artists, too. I had a special dictionary with pictures, and it told about the lives of famous people. Here, this was one of my favorites [handing me the book].*

Benacerraf's family mentors knew how to encourage him in reading. And, in addition to his family, he also had wonderful mentors at school and at work—people who took a special interest in helping him develop as a reader, writer, and scientist. A pivotal mentor was Rene Dubois, Benacerraf's examiner in science at the Lycee Français in Paris. Dubois continued to be an important mentor as Benacerraf's career evolved and both men emigrated to the United States. Benacerraf spoke with gratitude and admiration about this memorable mentor, who was a well-known scientist in his own right. Eventually the two men became not only colleagues but also lifelong friends.

Teachers Who Mentored: Cruz Sanabria's Story

After interviewing Baruj Benacerraf, I interviewed Cruz Sanabria, another Latino American who, like Benacerraf, struggled with severe reading problems but became an educator. Unlike Benacerraf, however, Sanabria was born in Spanish Harlem in New York City, the son of poor Puerto Rican immigrants. One of seven children, he was raised by a single mother who was a high school dropout. Although his mother worked hard and wanted the best for her son, transmitting a sense of cultural pride was a challenge due to her difficult financial circumstances. As a boy, Sanabria helped support the family with odd jobs that included a newspaper route. He became interested in reading newspaper comics and drawing his own cartoons.

Unlike Benacerraf, Sanabria did not have much family support. His mother loved him, but putting food on the table for seven growing children was a constant struggle for a poor single mother. Consequently, she was unable to encourage her son in his education, let alone help him with his reading problems or teach him about his culture. However, Sanabria got support at school from Mr. Tilman, his junior high school teacher. He remembered him vividly.

> *Mr. Tilman is a teacher I'll never forget. Mr. Tilman used the newspaper,*
> *which I was interested in from my paper route. And he got me psyched*
> *about reading by using comics and art, which fascinated me.*

Despite his teacher's best efforts at mentoring, Sanabria continued to struggle with reading and, after years of failure, dropped out of high school and joined the military. He was sent to fight in the Vietnam War and eventually returned home badly wounded—a disabled veteran. While Sanabria was recuperating from his injuries in a veterans' hospital, the hospital staff encouraged him to take high school equivalency courses. But Sanabria doubted his own ability to succeed. He lacked Benacerraf's pride in his culture and doubted his own academic ability. So at first he was reluctant to try taking courses for fear of failure. However, his mentors at the hospital gave him lots of encouragement, and gradually he gained courage and resumed his education, eventually earning a high school equivalency diploma (GED).

Afterward, he attended the University of Massachusetts in Boston, where he was fortunate to have wonderful professors who were truly marvelous mentors to Sanabria, encouraging him a great deal and helping him to complete college despite his ongoing financial and academic struggles. Later on, buttressed by Professor Susan Dubler's support, Sanabria continued his education even further. He attended graduate school at Lesley University in Cambridge, Massachusetts, and became an early childhood educator.

Mentors Who Mattered

Both Baruj Benacerraf and Cruz Sanabria had mentors who mattered. Despite differences based on class and family background, both of these striving readers had marvelous mentors who made a difference. In Sanabria's case, he could not rely on his family for help; instead, teachers and hospital mentors mattered most. In contrast, Bencerraf had the benefits of an educated, affluent family and had lifelong mentors at home, at school, and at work. For both men, however, mentors played vitally important roles in helping them to become skilled readers and successful professionals, a finding that fits with the Interest-Based Model of Reading. Mentoring support is a key component of the model.

What Teachers and Families Can Do

The case studies of Baruj Benacerraf and Cruz Sanabria suggest useful approaches for teaching reading to all students, and especially bilingual learners. Teachers, family members, reading specialists, and tutors can all play key roles in promoting bilingual students' ultimate success by taking the following steps:

1. Develop cultural knowledge and pride.
2. Find inspiring biographies.
3. Use informational texts.
4. Use the arts.
5. Become a marvelous mentor.

Develop Cultural Knowledge and Pride

Baruj Benacerraf had enormous pride in each of his languages and cultures. In contrast, many bilingual students experience a loss of cultural identity, painful cultural conflicts, and marginalization (Robinson & Howard-Hamilton, 2000). These problems can be ameliorated by acknowledging students' cultural backgrounds and encouraging them to develop curiosity, pride, and knowledge of their heritage. We can start by using informative texts that celebrate students' cultural backgrounds and promote respect. Two main goals are of paramount importance: to develop knowledge and pride in students' primary languages and cultures and, simultaneously, to teach them American English and culture.

FOLK TALES AND FOLK LITERATURE. Folk tales are a great place to begin cultural exploration. Folk tales provide universal themes, narrative power, and deep sociocultural underpinnings. To engage Latino students, parents and teachers can use Latin American folk tale collections such as *Jade and Iron: Latin American Tales From Two Cultures* (Aldana, 1996). This collection uses the vivid language and authentic imagery unique to each of the diverse Latino cultures represented. It could be used for small-group or whole-class discussions and activities that explore complex cultural concepts. For example, the Mexican tale "The Enchantress of Cordoba" could be used to explore concepts such as colonialism, imperialism, racism, and sexism. In introducing "The Enchantress," the teacher could present new vocabulary words and discuss their underlying concepts before students read the story; by preteaching vocabulary in this way, the teacher promotes optimal reading comprehension of this complex tale.

"The Black Ship," another story in *Jade and Iron*, is a suspenseful Nicaraguan tale about a ship that reaches an unexplored island. The crew discovers families suffering from food poisoning and, consequently, wrestles with a moral dilemma: Should they delay their journey and sacrifice their wages to help the sick, starving families, or should they protect their jobs and continue on, leaving the stranded families to die? There is a lot to consider and discuss in this short, well-told tale.

Also included in *Jade and Iron* are captivating Venezuelan folk tales, such as "Blanca and the Wild Man," about the disappearance of a 15-year-old girl. The unresolved question in this story is, Did Blanca run away from home, or was she abducted? A class discussion of students' answers and their reasons can help develop inferential reading skills and generate awareness of gender issues that transcend cultures. Thoughtful guidance in discussing these folk tales helps Latino and non-Latino students alike develop appreciation and respect for Venezuelan literature.

Reading folk tales can also foster strong home–school connections, intergenerational literacy, and bilingual growth. Together, parents and children can develop fluency, familiarity, and pride in reading in both languages by taking turns doing repeated readings in two languages. For example, after reading an English version of the Mexican tale "How the Rainbow Was Born" (see Delacre, 1996), students could be encouraged to read it to parents, grandparents, and siblings at home. In addition, students could take home Spanish-language texts, such as *El festival de cometas: The Kite Festival* (Torres, 2004), and read them with family members. Other good bilingual texts that students and families can share include *Arroz con leche: Popular Songs and Rhymes From Latin America* (Delacre, 1989), *Las Navidades: Popular Christmas Songs From Latin America* (Delacre, 1990), and *Diez deditos: Ten Little Fingers & Other Play Rhymes and Action Songs From Latin America* (Orozco, 1997). Parents, grandparents, and older siblings can be encouraged to read the text aloud in Spanish while the child reads the same text aloud to the family in English.

These approaches implicitly demonstrate respect for the richness of a student's native culture. By using folk literature in this way, we ascribe value to the child's first language and culture, as well as to English. Learning cultural pride and reading skills simultaneously can help bilingual students become skilled readers, thereby ending intergenerational cycles of low literacy—cycles that sometimes marginalize minorities from one generation to the next.

See Additional Resources (pages 59–63) for an annotated list of compelling cultural stories and websites from around the globe. It is organized by geographical region and includes books and websites with humorous, lighthearted tales as well as serious, philosophical stories. Many of the books on this list include exciting follow-up research activities.

OTHER CULTURAL RESOURCES. In addition to using folk stories to transmit traditional culture, we need to find books that provide deep cultural background and up-to-date information on a variety of cultural topics. Students need information about each culture's current customs, politics, geography, economics, social values, and beliefs. See Additional Resources (page 63) for recent series that contain rich information on culture, genealogy, history, and other related topics.

Find Inspiring Biographies

Baruj Benacerraf loved biographies, especially about scientists and artists. By immersing himself in this genre as a child, he engaged in lots of reading and became increasingly skilled. His avid reading in this genre of passionate, personal interest supports the Interest-Based Model of Reading. In his case, biographies provided the repetition and practice that were crucial to his fluency development.

Biographies provide a great way into reading for students of all ages and abilities. This genre is especially effective for introducing bilingual students to U.S. history and culture. By reading biographies about the lives of famous U.S. heroes, students become familiar with the history and social context of their adopted country. And, by reading biographies they also learn about other individuals who, like themselves, came as immigrants from other parts of the world, forging new identities in the United States.

One inspiring biography of a Latina scientist is *Scientist From Puerto Rico, Maria Cordero Hardy* (Verheyden-Hilliard, 1985). This easy-to-read book has large print and a controlled vocabulary and is appropriate for intermediate grades, middle school, and high school. Another excellent biography that will likely appeal to middle school and high school students is *Pride of Puerto Rico: The Life of Roberto Clemente* (Walker, 1988). Baseball player Roberto Clemente was both black and Latino and, consequently, endured painful prejudice and discrimination despite his fame. Yet, he emerged with enormous pride—pride in his athletic skill, his family, and his native Puerto Rico. This book poignantly recounts Clemente's disagreement with his father over his first job contract. While intergenerational conflicts such as Clemente's are common in U.S. culture, they go against the norms of Latino families, who expect obedience from a son. Teachers could use this father–son conflict as a springboard for discussion about cultural conflict, assimilation, and the challenge of defining one's identity as distinct from that of one's parents.

Another inspiring biography with appeal across grade levels K–adult is *Toussaint L'Ouverture: The Fight for Haiti's Freedom* (Myers, 1996). This story of the liberator of Haitian slaves is relevant to Haiti's political struggles today. The colorful tempera illustrations that accompany the narrative will appeal to Haitians and non-Haitians alike.

A list of biographies that span a wide variety of backgrounds, careers, and interests appears in Additional Resources (pages 64–67). This comprehensive list contains biographies appropriate for students at each grade level—elementary, middle grades, high school, and adult.

Use Informational Texts

Another way to build students' knowledge of their heritage is through nonfiction texts, which offer unique opportunities to learn about the world (Saul & Dieckman, 2005). Students of all ages can benefit from various kinds of informational texts—biographies, travel books, encyclopedias, search engines, cultural and historical websites, history books, and so forth. Fortunately, there are many engaging informational books about specific cultures. For example, *Cultures of the World: Venezuela* (Kohen, 1991) contains a wealth of information on Venezuelan geography, fauna and flora, history, business, politics, class structure, racism, Indian languages, Spanish, eating practices, and holiday rituals and customs. This book also contains photographs and maps of Venezuela, a glossary of Spanish terms, a "Quick Notes" section full of Venezuelan facts, and an index to help find information quickly.

Another excellent nonfiction book is *Haiti* (Hintz, 1998), which analyzes Haiti's history in a mature format appropriate for intermediate through high school students. Beautifully illustrated, *Haiti* covers controversial topics such as deforestation, the environment, and government land policies. Another excellent book for middle school students is *The Dominican Republic* (Rogers & Rogers, 1999). Among its attractions are a Spanish pronunciation guide and a list of common cultural superstitions. Readers are asked, "Have you heard of any of the following superstitions?" Using this question as a starting point, teachers can guide discussion and research on (a) the role of superstitions, (b) reasons for the persistence of superstitions, and (c) relationships between superstitions and traditional religious beliefs. In addition, teachers can encourage students to create their own research questions based on their personal curiosity and interests.

An overarching purpose of cultural research is to engage students in in-depth cultural explorations. Guided by the teacher in this process, bilingual students gain experience and skill in selecting and evaluating research materials. At the same time, they gain knowledge, pride, and respect for their culture of origin.

Use the Arts

Students also benefit from reading lessons that incorporate the arts. Cruz Sanabria's junior high teacher knew the power of art to spark his interests, so he used Sanabria's love of drawing and comics to engage him. Integrating the arts with reading lessons is effective at all levels, from preschool through college, because the arts can easily "hook" students and get them engaged in reading. All art forms are effective—drawing, crafts, painting, drama, dance, music, poetry, rhymes, finger plays, storytelling, creative writing, and so forth. The teacher does not need to be adept at drawing or any other art form to use art effectively. All that is needed is a desire to engage students and get them hooked on reading. (Figure 3 shows a book project bulletin board and a display of masks at the Lincoln School in Brookline, Massachusetts. As shown in Figure 3, the art of mask-making can be integrated with reading lessons about specific cultures.)

MUSIC. Incorporating music into reading lessons is a great way to get students excited about reading. Several books are available that demonstrate how to integrate reading and music. Some that feature music combine finger plays, rhymes, song, and dance, and some include texts in two languages. A good example is *Diez deditos: Ten Little Fingers & Other Play Rhymes and Action Songs From Latin America* (Orozco, 1997). The text is in Spanish as well as English and is excellent for preschool, primary, and intermediate grades. This book also includes sheet music, dances, colorful illustrations, and visual images of the hand and finger motions described. In addition, I also recommend *Arroz con leche: Popular Songs and Rhymes From Latin America* (Delacre, 1989) and *Las Navidades: Popular Christmas Songs From Latin America* (Delacre, 1990). Both books contain colorful illustrations, sheet music, and notes about the customs and history behind each song.

FIGURE 3
Integrating the Arts

DRAMA. Another way to integrate the arts and reading is through narrative mime theater. This exciting dramatic approach is described in detail in an excellent book, *Dramatizing Myths and Tales: Creating Plays for Large Groups* (Thistle, 1995). This practical guide gives directions for organizing and executing a drama, from start to finish. The book contains scripts for five multicultural myths (appropriate for grades 3–12). Each script contains cultural information and thought-provoking research and critical thinking activities to enrich children's experiences with this form of drama.

DANCE. The art of dance is another exciting way to engage students in multicultural reading. Dancing a story from start to finish enables children to learn sequencing skills and helps them resolve difficult feelings. Complex costuming is not necessary. Any small accessory that moves freely through the air will spark a child's imagination and help the child initiate and sustain body motions. For example, teachers and children can dance a wide variety of stories aided only by scarves to indicate a fairy godmother's wand, a pirate's headcover, and so forth.

Dramatizing Myths and Tales, mentioned previously, is an excellent book that describes how to perform simple dances from a variety of cultures and includes music to accompany each dance. I have used cultural folk dances from around the world with my own students across grade levels, preschool to high school. Students enjoyed learning the dances, developed socialization skills, and gained respect for the culture represented by each dance.

Audiotapes and CDs of favorite folk tales can also be used to help students reenact narratives through dance. After reading a story, the teacher and students can dance freely together, moving their bodies in ways that indicate the plot's unfolding action and each character's personality. Used in this way, dance is especially effective for retelling folk tales. One of my favorite tales for preschool and primary-age children is "The Three Billy Goats Gruff." This compelling story lends itself to dancing about anger, power, fear, and other strong emotions with which children struggle. This linking of fairy tales, dance, and drama is excellent for getting children excited about reading.

Become a Marvelous Mentor

Mentors mattered and were crucial to the success of Baruj Benacerraf and Cruz Sanabria. In Sanabria's case, teachers and hospital staff—not family members—were pivotal mentors. They helped him in several ways. First, they gave Sanabria personal attention—attention that was essential yet hard to come by at home in a family of seven needy children. Second, they believed that Sanabria was smart and capable of learning, and they communicated their belief to him. This in turn enabled Sanabria to believe in his own capabilities and attempt new challenges. Third, his junior high school teacher used engaging materials based on Sanabria's interests in art, comics, and newspapers; in this way, he motivated in Sanabria a desire to read. Fourth, mentoring teachers and hospital staff set the bar high, urging Sanabria to strive for lofty goals: a GED, and college and graduate degrees.

Between Benacerraf and Sanabria there were a variety of mentors, including teachers, parents, relatives, hospital staff, and peers who helped them to grapple with their difficulties and move on. What did these mentors do? They supervised, modeled, and guided; they provided interesting books, solid instruction, and plentiful practice in reading and writing. In addition, they encouraged Benacerraf and Sanabria to select challenging courses and materials, strive for high academic and career goals, connect with good teachers and tutors, and apply to appropriate educational programs.

Teachers and family members should do two things to help striving readers: Become a mentor who matters and enlist help from other mentors, including reading buddies, family members, and community mentors.

READING BUDDIES. Reading buddies make wonderful mentors and are proving to be a rich resource in many schools. Reading with an individual buddy is usually less threatening and overwhelming to a struggling reader than reading aloud in a group. With the reading buddies approach, a striving reader is paired with another student for practice, reinforcement, and enrichment. Usually, a buddy pair consists of a fluent and a less fluent reader who read together, taking turns in various ways. Frequently, one student reads while the reading buddy listens; then the two change places. For some reading buddies, choral reading is helpful and fun. In choral reading, two students read aloud in unison. The skilled reader models good pronunciation, intonation, prosody, and expression; when the less skilled reader falters, he or she can follow the skilled reader's model and learn to self-correct. After reading with a buddy, students can be directed to discuss and write about the text, then share what they wrote with each other by reading their reflections aloud.

I observed reading buddies in action at the Lincoln School. Each buddy pair was so deeply engrossed in reading that their time spent on task was virtually 100%. Reading with a peer enabled each child to practice and refine several skills at once: reading, discussing, writing, and interacting with one another. (Figure 4 shows reading buddies at the Lincoln School.)

FIGURE 4
Reading Buddies

FAMILY MENTORS. In addition to peers, family mentors are a superb resource for helping students with reading. Family involvement not only improves children's reading achievement scores but also improves their self-esteem and attitudes toward learning (IRA, 2002).

Family members can help by being positive reading role models themselves. For example, when the family's language of origin is different from English, the family demonstrates to the child that reading is valued by reading newspapers in their home language. The family can also provide daily opportunities for children to read about topics of their own choice. It is not necessary to buy lots of books and magazines (although that is helpful). Frequent trips to the public library can provide children with sufficient reading materials. Family involvement in children's reading should continue throughout school, including middle school and high school. Families can encourage their teenagers' enthusiasm for reading by seeking advice from local librarians and becoming familiar with popular young adult titles.

Usually, parents are the school's best partners, even though many parents have limited finances, time, education, and emotional resources. Parents are key mentors because they know the child best, can provide invaluable insights, and can oversee extra reading practice at home. To enlist the help of a family, teachers need to be sensitive to each family member and cultural group, and consider two key questions: (1) What do I need to know to ensure that I do not offend this family? and (2) How should I interact with parents whose views of parenting and education differ from my own?

A wonderful resource on family mentors is *Family-School Partnerships: Essential Elements of Reading Instruction in the United States* (IRA, 2002). This brochure provides valuable advice for teachers and other mentors, including an explicit reminder to respect the beliefs, lifestyles, and child-rearing practices of all families. Additional Resources (pages 67–68) contains additional mentoring resources for parents, teachers, and others.

COMMUNITY MENTORS. Teachers can also enlist the help of community mentors through programs such as Boys' and Girls' Clubs of America, Big Brothers Big Sisters, Literacy Volunteers of America, and senior citizen volunteers. These community mentors provide wonderful support for children of all ages, including middle school and high school students, who are at a stage when relationships with family members are changing. For some adolescents, it is easier to accept help from community mentors instead of the family.

Conclusion:
Be a Marvelous Mentor, Foster Cultural Pride

The bilingual readers in this study eventually became highly skilled readers in English. Their case studies suggest that a student's cultural heritage can provide a strong linguistic foundation on which to build English skills. By fostering cultural knowledge and pride, teachers help students view their multiple languages and cultures as rich assets, not deficits. By simultaneously developing cultural pride and reading skills, we can help bilingual students ultimately to achieve high levels of English literacy.

The bilingual readers in this study succeeded with help from marvelous mentors. This finding fits with the Interest-Based Model of Reading, of which mentoring support is a key component. Both Baruj Benacerraf and Cruz Sanabria had mentors who mattered. Without the mentoring of dedicated teachers, it is unlikely that either of them would have surmounted his reading difficulties. Marvelous mentors were the key to their success at all stages, helping them to develop into highly skilled readers and outstanding professionals. Benacerraf had help from wonderful family mentors, but Sanabria could not rely on his family for help. However, teachers filled the void for Sanabria.

Researchers know that a teacher's knowledge, actions, and relationships with students are crucial for helping students learn to read (Bond & Dykstra, 1967/1997; Paratore, 2004). We know that good mentors provide lots of materials on students' interests and regular opportunities for students to read and be read to. They model good reading behavior and read aloud to students regularly, not only in the early grades but also during middle school and high school—crucial periods when many U.S. students fall behind their counterparts in other industrialized countries (IRA, 2001, 2002). Students of all ages and abilities benefit both from being read to by a mentor and from reading themselves; this is especially the case for striving bilingual students, who need intensive practice both in listening while others read to them and in reading texts themselves.

Intensive instruction and practice enable bilingual students to succeed. Benacerraf developed into a skilled reader after seven years of daily, individualized instruction with his cousin Suzanne. His experience fits with what educators know about other bilingual students: Although they take only about one or two years to acquire social language skills (Gass & Selinker, 2001), they usually take much longer—between five and seven years, or even longer—to develop academic reading (Collier, 1992; Coppola, 2004; Cummins, 1994; O'Malley & Valdez-Pierce,

1996; Valdez-Pierce, 2003). The reason for this difference is that social or conversational English is much easier to learn than academic reading skills.

It takes longer to learn the complex skills of academic literacy—skills such as comparing, contrasting, informing, ordering, classifying, analyzing, justifying, persuading, problem solving, synthesizing, and evaluating (O'Malley & Valdez-Pierce, 1996). Learning academic literacy is not a natural process picked up easily and informally; rather, it is one that needs to be taught. It requires a great deal of effort by the student and the teacher. According to this study's results, the additional effort can ultimately have excellent outcomes.

Based on the results of these case studies, each teacher and family member can become a marvelous mentor. Mentoring requires not only dedication but also understanding the student's unique strengths, interests, and cultural and linguistic background. In addition, it requires understanding the student's specific needs and difficulties, both in terms of reading and the larger context of the student's life. A good mentor plans opportunities for students of all ages to talk about books with others, then react in writing to what they've read. But perhaps most important, a marvelous mentor believes in the student, has high expectations, and guides the student into challenging courses and careers. These issues are discussed further in chapter 3.

Folk Tale Books, Folklore Websites

Worldwide Tales

Adler, N. (1996). *The Dial book of animal tales from around the world*. New York: Dial. This book is likely to engage primary, intermediate, and middle school students, grades 1–8. Enhanced by colorful illustrations and border designs throughout the text, the book's compelling tales originated from a wide variety of cultures: Native American, Indian, Chinese, Australian, German, Thai, African, Canadian, and Brazilian.

MacDonald, M.R. (1992). *Peace tales: World folktales to talk about*. Hamden, CT: Linnet Books. This is a book for all grade levels, 1–adult. The collection of tales focuses on how to prevent and solve conflicts equitably and harmoniously. The short, often humorous vignettes from around the world present dramatic episodes and dilemmas useful for discussion and creative problem solving. The unique peacemaking techniques are excellent for dramatic reenactments, debates, and follow-up writing activities.

Mayo, M. (1993). *Magical tales from many lands*. New York: Dutton. This book recounts 14 diverse folk tales. Included are Zulu, Jewish, African American, and Turkish folk tales as well as many others from around the world. The stories are full of mystery and magic and will appeal to all grade levels, K–adult. The sensitive illustrations have a Chagall-like quality, the tales are entertaining, and historical notes about the origin of each tale make this an attractive collection.

Rosen, M. (Ed.). (1995). *South + north + east + west: The Oxfam book of children's stories*. London: Walker Books. This book has an appealing introduction by Whoopi Goldberg. The concise stories have universal themes and lots of humor, such as "Why Do Dogs Chase Cars?" This collection will appeal especially to intermediate and middle school children, grades 4–8. Its greatest strength is the multitude of cultures represented: the Middle East; Cyprus; Greece; Jamaica; England; Malta; Vietnam; North Africa; Central, Southern, and East Africa; West Africa; Northern Ghana; Zimbabwe; Korea; China; Indonesia; Dominican Republic; Brazil; Bolivia; Nepal; Mali; Botswana; India; and Bangladesh.

Latin American Tales

Aldana, P. (1996). *Jade and Iron: Latin American tales from two cultures*. Toronto, ON: Groundwood. This is a compelling collection for grade 2–adult with tales that range from precolonial oral traditions to modern folk stories. The artwork is authentic, and the introduction does an effective job of linking Latin America's history with unresolved conflicts that continue in the region today.

Barra, N.C. (2002). *Monica and the summer party*. Arlington, MA: The Intercultural Center for Research in Education. This is a large-print chapter book in the Sunflower Multicultural Story Book series. Written for elementary children, grades 1–6, each chapter tells a different story about a Latino immigrant family and shows how they integrate cultural practices from the old country with their new life in the United States. The book has a multicultural glossary useful for teaching key vocabulary.

Bunting, E. (1988). *How many days to America?* New York: Clarion. This is the story of a refugee family fleeing danger and upheaval from an ambiguous country, possibly Cuba or Haiti.

Appropriate for intermediate grades, middle school, and high school, the ambiguities in this story could be used for inferring and questioning at various developmental levels, grade 4–adult.

Crespo, G. (1993). *How the sea began*. New York: Clarion Books. This book presents a Taino creation myth appropriate for primary through middle school students, grades 1–7. Not only does this book use compelling language and colorful illustrations, it also has historical notes and a pronunciation guide that enables readers to pronounce and understand Spanish and Taino vocabulary.

Delacre, L. (1996). *Golden tales: Myths, legends, and folktales from Latin America*. New York: Scholastic. This is an outstanding collection with rich research notes that extend the reader's understanding of each story. Topics include a child who disobeys, a father–son conflict, the birth of the sea, and many others. It can be used across grade 2–adult.

González, L.M. (1997). *Señor Cat's Romance and other favorite stories from Latin America*. New York: Scholastic. In this engaging book, a Cuban author recounts popular, entertaining folk tales with universal themes: The power of sharing, the value of humor and wit, and the challenge of overcoming grief, to name just a few. The book is gorgeously illustrated and will appeal to students from the primary grades to middle school.

Jaffe, N. (1996). *The golden flower: A Taino myth from Puerto Rico*. New York: Simon & Schuster. This is a Native Indian folk tale that tells how the sparkling island of Puerto Rico originated from a pumpkin seed. The engaging text is accompanied by gorgeous illustrations likely to entice young children, pre-K–3.

Jimenez, F. (1998). *La mariposa*. Boston, MA: Houghton Mifflin. This K–3 picture book is compelling story about a migrant boy's struggle to learn English and get through school. It is adapted from Jimenez's *The Circuit* and will likely resonate with students beyond its intended audience. Bilingual students can relate to the struggles of the child in the story, and others will learn about the travails and joys of this migrant boy.

Malone, M. (1996). *A Guatemalan family*. Minneapolis, MN: Lerner. This book describes a journey between the two worlds of Guatemalan culture and American culture. English-language learners of all ages and grades, K–adult, are likely to identify with the joys, conflicts, and challenges of this immigrant family.

Pico, F. (1991). *The red comb*. Rio Piedras, Puerto Rico: Troll Associates. This story is set in 19th-century Puerto Rico. An award-winning book based on rich historical documents, it tells how two women plotted against the town's slave catcher and succeeded in saving a runaway slave. It is an excellent choice for the intermediate grades through middle school.

Soros, B. (1998). *Grandmother's song*. Brooklyn, NY: Barefoot Books. This book tells a poignant Mexican tale of intergenerational love. It is gorgeously illustrated and recounts a tale about a girl and her grandmother that is likely to engage students from the intermediate grades through adulthood. A poetic story of life and death, this compelling book addresses the continuity of life and meaning of human relationships.

Torres, L. (2004). *El festival de cometas: The kite festival*. New York: Farrar Straus Giroux. In this book, written in Spanish, the Columbian American author uses Spanish-only text to celebrate the beauty of the Spanish language. With lively illustrations, the book tells the story of a boy named Ferdinand, who wants to participate in a kite festival yet lacks the requisite kite. All of the stores are closed, so, with help from his grandparents, he creates his own kite.

This is a delightful book for the primary and intermediate grades and contains instructions on kite building that can be used as a wonderful extending activity.

Middle Eastern Tales

O'Connor, K. (1996). *A Kurdish family*. Minneapolis, MN: Lerner. This book describes an immigrant family from Kurdistan, with its unique culture and religion. The family emigrates to the United States and encounters a completely different culture and language. It will be of interest to middle school and high school students, as well as adults.

Sunami, K. (2002). *How the fisherman tricked the genie: A tale within a tale within a tale*. New York: Atheneum. This is a brightly illustrated Arabian story that will appeal to children from preschool through the intermediate grades. The author, who is part African American, part Japanese American, appeals to children's humor and silliness to tell this story with its universal message about good and evil.

African Tales

Janisch, H. (2002). *The fire: An Ethiopian folk tale*. Toronto, ON: Groundwood. This is a captivating Ethiopian tale of slavery and freedom retold by an Austrian writer and Mexican illustrator. The text and illustrations are dramatic and moving and will likely appeal to young and old alike, primary grades through adulthood.

Paye, W., & Lippert, M.H. (2002). *Head, body, legs: A story from Liberia*. New York: Henry Holt. This is a magical retelling of the creation story by a member of the Dan people of northeastern Liberia, who was trained as a storyteller by his grandmother. The animated story and cutout doll-like illustrations will appeal to children from preschool through the intermediate grades.

Raven, M.T. (2004). *Circle unbroken: The story of a basket and its people*. New York: Farrar Straus Giroux. This is a tale about love and cultural continuity for intermediate, middle school, high school, and adult students. Powerfully illustrated, the book reveals the preservation of the art of the sweetbaskets of South Carolina and Georgia through a moving story of the capture of West African slaves from what is now Sierra Leone and Senegal. This book celebrates sweet-basket art and contains historical information and a list of resources useful for research on this African American culture.

Chinese Tales

Fang, L. (1995). *The Ch'i-Lin purse: A collection of ancient Chinese stories*. New York: Farrar Straus Giroux. This book presents classic Chinese stories likely to appeal to students in grade 6–adult. With lively prose and historically accurate illustrations, this collection uses a chapter book format that gives it a mature appearance attractive to older students.

Li, C. (1966). *Stories from Liu Hu-lan's childhood*. Shanghai, China: Foreign Languages Press. This book tells the story of a 13-year-old revolutionary heroine during the Chinese People's War of Liberation (1945–1949). She fought valiantly on the side of the peasants against landlords and tyrants and refused to submit when she was captured. This series of illustrated tales will appeal to students from grade 4–adult.

Murphy, N. (1997). *A Hmong family*. Minneapolis, MN: Lerner. This book recounts the experiences of an immigrant family as they begin a new life in the United States. The book is likely to appeal to students of Asian heritage, who may identify with the experiences of this immigrant family. It is appropriate for middle school and high school students.

Japanese Tales

Houston, J.W. & Houston, J.D. (2000). *Farewell to Manzanar*. Austin, TX: Holt, Rinehart & Winston. This Pulitzer Prize–winning book recounts the haunting and beautifully told story of a Japanese American family's internment during World War II. The author was 7 years old when she and her family were uprooted from their home, imprisoned behind barbed wire, and forced to struggle to maintain a sense of basic human dignity. This page-turner is appropriate for grade 8–adult.

Mochizuki, K. (1993). *Baseball saved us*. New York: Lee & Low. This is a moving story about the Japanese internment camps in the United States during World War II. It is appropriate for students in grade 6–adult and can be used to discuss critical reading/thinking questions such as: Who is an American? How can we know if our government is right or wrong? What should we do if we disagree with our country's actions?

Say, A. (1993). *Grandfather's journey*. Boston: Houghton Mifflin. This book recounts a Japanese grandfather's two lives, one in Japan, the other in the United States. This story is appropriate for students in the primary grades through middle school and sheds valuable insight into the grandfather's ambivalence about his hybrid identity. When he is in the United States, he feels homesick for Japan; however, when he returns to Japan, he is homesick for the United States.

Uchida, Y. (1993). *The bracelet*. New York: Philomel. This is a masterful story about friendship appropriate for the intermediate grades through adulthood. Set in the context of the Japanese internment camps, it is beautifully told and raises thought-provoking questions that can be used to teach inferential comprehension skills.

Uegaki, C. (2004). *Suki's kimono*. Tonawanda, NY: Kids Can Press. This book will appeal especially to young children in grades K–3. It is about the importance of being yourself. Suki loves her blue kimono and plans to wear it to school despite what people may say. Her struggles and celebration of her identity are recounted in this charming story.

American Tales (United States)

Jagendorf, M.A. (1948). *New England bean pot: American folk tales to read and tell*. New York: Vanguard Press. These tales will appeal to readers of all ages, from the primary grades through adulthood. Written by a masterful, vivacious storyteller, this collection is excellent for both reading and oral retelling. The tales have universal themes that can serve as points of departure for follow-up drama or writing activities.

Indian Tale

So, M. (2004). *Gobble, gobble, slip, slop: A tale of a very greedy cat*. New York: Knopf. This is an Indian folk tale retold through gorgeous illustrations, lots of suspense, and repeated refrains. The story is about a greedy cat who eventually gets its comeuppance. It will appeal especially to young children, pre-K–grade 2.

Folklore Websites

The folklore websites listed below are great for various types of research projects. They present folk stories, historical background, and procedures for conducting oral histories and interviews. Folkloric websites also connect students with others in their culture through electronic bulletin boards and chat rooms. They're fun, interactive, and informative.

A Teacher's Guide to Folklife Resources for K–Adult Classrooms at www.loc.gov/folklife/
    teachers.html
City Lore at www.citylore.org
Doing Oral History at www.gcah.org/oral.html
Oral History and Interviews at www.cyndislist.com/oral.htm
Story Arts Online at www.storyarts.org
Urban Legends Reference Pages at www.snopes2.com

Genealogy, Culture, and History Books

Books About Genealogy (grade 4–adult)

Crowe, E.P. (2001). *Genealogy online* (5th ed.). New York: Osborne-McGraw-Hill.

Foner, N. (2000). *From Ellis Island to JFK: New York's two great waves of immigration*. New Haven, CT: Yale University Press.

Horowitz, L. (1999). *Dozens of cousins: Blue genes, horse thieves, and other relative surprises in your family tree*. Berkeley, CA: Ten Speed Press.

McClure, R. (2000). *The complete idiot's guide to online genealogy*. Holbrook, MA: Adams Media.

Mokotoff, G., & Blatt, W. (1999). *Getting started in Jewish genealogy*. Bergenfield, NJ: Avota.

Wolfman, I. (2002). *Climbing your family tree: Online and off-line genealogy for kids*. New York: Workman.

Visual Geography Series (grades K–6)

Behnke, A. (2003). *Afghanistan in pictures*. Minneapolis, MN: Lerner.

Taus-Bolstad, S. (2003). *Vietnam in pictures*. Minneapolis, MN: Lerner.

The Excavating the Past Series (grades 4–6)

Gaff, J. (2004). *Excavating the past: Ancient Egypt*. Chicago: Heinemann Library.

Hatt, C. (2004). *Excavating the past: Greece*. Chicago: Heinemann Library.

Hatt, C. (2004). *Excavating the past: The Viking world*. Chicago: Heinemann Library.

MacDonald, F. (2004). *Excavating the past: Ancient Rome*. Chicago: Heinemann Library.

Saunders, N., & Allan, T. (2004). *Excavating the past: Greece the Aztec empire*. Chicago: Heinemann Library.

World Art & Culture Series (grades 6–8)

Bingham, J. (2004). *African art & culture*. Chicago: Raintree.

Khanduri, K. (2004). *Japanese art & culture*. Chicago: Raintree.

Lewis, E. (2004). *Mexican art & culture*. Chicago: Raintree.

ADDITIONAL RESOURCES

Inspiring Biographies

Grades K–3

Adler, D. (1984). *Our Golda: The story of Golda Meir*. New York: Puffin.
Adler, D. (1992). *A picture book of Florence Nightingale*. New York: Holiday House.
Adler, D. (1993). *A picture book of Sitting Bull*. New York: Holiday House.
Adler, D. (1994). *A picture book of Abraham Lincoln*. New York: Scholastic.
Adler, D. (1994). *A picture book of Anne Frank*. New York: Scholastic.
Adler, D. (1994). *A picture book of George Washington*. New York: Scholastic.
Adler, D. (1994). *A picture book of Helen Keller*. New York: Scholastic.
Adler, D. (1994). *A picture book of Jackie Robinson*. New York: Scholastic.
Adler, D. (1994). *A picture book of John Fitzgerald Kennedy*. New York: Scholastic.
Adler, D. (1994). *A picture book of Martin Luther King, Jr.* New York: Scholastic.
Adler, D. (1996). *Lou Gehrig: The luckiest man*. New York: Harcourt.

Grades 4–8

Andronik, C. (1994). *Prince of humbugs: A life of P.T. Barnum*. New York: Atheneum.
Bornemann, K.S. (1999). *Franklin D. Roosevelt*. Springfield, NJ: Enslow.
Brallier, J. (2002). *Who was Albert Einstein?* New York: Grosset & Dunlap.
Brallier, J. (2002). *Who was Amelia Earhart?* New York: Grosset & Dunlap.
Brallier, J. (2002). *Who was Annie Oakley?* New York: Grosset & Dunlap.
Brallier, J. (2002). *Who was Benjamin Franklin?* New York: Grosset & Dunlap.
Brallier, J. (2002). *Who was Harriet Tubman?* New York: Grosset & Dunlap.
Brallier, J. (2002). *Who was Helen Keller?* New York: Grosset & Dunlap.
Brallier, J. (2002). *Who was Maria Tallchief?* New York: Grosset & Dunlap.
Brallier, J. (2002). *Who was Sacagawea?* New York: Grosset & Dunlap.
Brallier, J. (2002). *Who was Thomas Jefferson?* New York: Grosset & Dunlap.
Brallier, J. (2002). *Who was Wolfgang Amadeus Mozart?* New York: Grosset & Dunlap.
Bray, R. (1995). *Martin Luther King*. New York: Greenwillow.
Carrigan, M. (1994). *Carol Moseley-Braun: Breaking barriers*. New York: Children's Press.
Coleman, P. (1992). *Spies! Women in the Civil War*. New York: Shoe Tree Press.
Coleman, P. (1993). *Fannie Lou Hamer and the fight for the vote*. New York: Millbrook.
Coleman, P. (1994). *Mother Jones and the march of the mill children*. New York: Millbrook.
Coles, R. (1995). *The story of Ruby Bridges*. New York: Scholastic.
Connolly, P. (1991). *Coaching Evelyn: Fast, faster, fastest woman in the world*. New York: Harper.
Cooper, F. (1996). *Mandela: From the life of the South African statesman*. New York: Philomel.
Cooper, F. (1994). *Coming home: From the life of Langston Hughes*. New York: Philomel.
Copley, R. (2000). *The tall Mexican: The life of Hank Aguirre, all-star pitcher, businessman, humanitarian*. Houston, TX: Arte Publico.
Cox, C. (1999). *Mark Twain: America's humorist, dreamer, prophet*. New York: Apple Publishing.
Dahl, R. (1988). *Boy: Tales of childhood*. New York: Viking.
Demi. (2003). *Muhammad*. New York: Simon & Schuster.
Dean, W.M. (2001). *The greatest: Muhammad Ali*. New York: Scholastic.

Denewberg, B. (2002). *Stealing home: The story of Jackie Robinson*. New York: Scholastic.

Doherty, K. (1999). *William Bradford: Rock of Plymouth*. New York: 21st Century/Millbrook.

Dolan, S. (1999). *Michael Jordan: Basketball great*. Topeka, KS: Econo-Clad.

Fisher, L.E. (1994). *Marie Curie*. New York: Macmillan.

Fischer, L.E. (1995). *Gandhi*. New York: Simon & Schuster.

Franchere, R., & Thollander, E. (1970). *Cesar Chavez*. New York: HarperCollins.

Freedman, S. (1994). *Ida B. Wells-Barnett and the anti-lynching crusade*. New York: Millbrook.

Gherman, B. (1986). *Georgia O'Keefe: The "wideness and wonder" of her world*. New York: Aladdin.

Giblin, J. (1994). *Thomas Jefferson: A picture book biography*. New York: Scholastic.

Goldin, B.D. (1995). *Bat mitzvah: A Jewish girl's coming of age*. New York: Viking.

Goldstein, M.M., & Larson, J. (1994). *Jackie Joyner-Kersee: Superwoman*. New York: Lerner.

Goodall, J. (1996). *My life with the chimpanzees*. New York: Pocket Books.

Greene, C. (1991). *Elizabeth Blackwell: First woman doctor*. New York: Children's Press.

Heiligman, D. (1994). *Barbara McClintock: Alone in her field*. New York: Scientific American Books for Young Readers.

Horenstein, H. (1994). *My mom's a vet*. New York: Candlewick.

Hughes, L. (2000). *Nelson Mandela: Voice of freedom*. Lincoln, NE: iUniverse.com.

Hurwitz, J. (1997). *Helen Keller: Courage in the dark*. New York: Random House.

Hurwitz, J. (1989). *Astrid Lindgren: Storyteller to the world*. New York: Puffin.

Kamen, G. (1996). *Hidden music: The life of Fanny Mendelssohn*. New York: Atheneum.

Karnes, F.A., & Bean, S.M. (1995). *Girls and young women inventing*. New York: Free Spirit Press.

Katz, B. (2001). *We the people*. New York: HarperCollins.

Knudson, R.R. (1985). *Babe Didrikson: Athlete of the century*. New York: Puffin.

Krull, K. (1996). *Wilma unlimited: How Wilma Rudolph became the world's fastest woman*. New York: Harcourt.

Kunhardt, E. (1993). *Honest Abe*. New York: Greenwillow.

Levin, P. (1993). *Susan B. Anthony: Fighter for women's rights*. New York: Chelsea House.

Livingston, M.C. (1994). *Keep on singing: A ballad of Marian Anderson*. New York: Holiday.

McKissack, P., & McKissack, F. (1992). *Mary McLeod Bethune: A great teacher*. New York: Children's Press.

MacLeod, E. (1999). *Albert Einstein: A life of genius*. Tonawanda, NY: Kids Can.

MacLeod, E. (2001). *Alexander Graham Bell: An inventive life*. Tonawanda, NY: Kids Can.

MacLeod, E. (2002). *Lucy Maud Montgomery: A writer's life*. Tonawanda, NY: Kids Can.

MacLeod, E. (2003). *The Wright brothers: A flying start*. Tonawanda, NY: Kids Can.

MacLeod, E. (2004). *Helen Keller: A determined life*. Tonawanda, NY: Kids Can.

McMane, F., & Wolf, C. (1995). *Winning women: Eight great athletes and their unbeatable stories*. New York: Bantam.

McPherson, S.S. (1992). *I speak for the women: A story about Lucy Stone*. New York: Carolrhoda.

McPherson, S.S. (1990). *Rooftop astronomer: A story about Maria Mitchell*. New York: Carolrhoda.

Miller, W. (1995). *Frederick Douglas: The last days of slavery*. New York: Lee & Low Books.

Morgan, T., & Thaler, S. (1995). *Steve Young: Complete quarterback*. Minneapolis, MN: Lerner.

Norton, R.S. (1997). *Patriarch: George Washington and the new American nation*. Boston: Houghton Mifflin.

Parker, S. (1992). *Marie Curie and radium*. New York: HarperTrophy.

Pettit, J. (1996). *Maya Angelou: Journey of the heart*. New York: Lodestar.

Quackenbush, R. (1995). *Clara Barton and her victory over fear*. New York: Simon & Schuster.

Reef, C. (1992). *Jacques Cousteau: Champion of the sea*. Breckenridge, CO: Twenty-First Century Books.

Reeve, C. (1999). *Still me*. New York: Ballantine.

Ride, S., with Okie, S. (1986). *To space and back*. New York: Beech Tree.

Robinson, S. (2004). *How Jackie Robinson changed America: Promises to keep*. New York: Scholastic.

Rockwell, A. (2000). *Only passing through: The story of Sojourner Truth*. New York: Random House Children's Books.

Ryan, P.M. (2000). *Amelia and Eleanor go for a ride*. New York: Scholastic

Ryan, P.M. (2002). *When Marion sang: The true recital of Marion Anderson, voice of a century*. New York: Scholastic.

Sakurai, G. (1995). *Mae Jemison: Space scientist*. New York: Children's Press.

Sanford, W.R., & Green, C.R. (1993). *Billie Jean King*. New York: Crestwood House.

Siegel, B. (1995). *Marian Wright Edelman: The making of a crusader*. New York: Simon & Schuster.

Sobol, R. (1994). *Governor: In the company of Ann W. Richards, governor of Texas*. New York: Cobblehill.

Stanley, D., & Vennema, P. (1994). *Cleopatra*. New York: Morrow.

Stewart, M. (1996). *Hakeem Olajuwon*. New York: Children's Press.

Streissguth, T. (1995). *Rocket man: The story of Robert Goddard*. Minneapolis, MN: Carolrhoda.

Streissguth, T. (1999). *Jesse Owens*. New York: Lerner.

Sullivan, G. (2000). *Helen Keller*. New York: Scholastic.

Townsend, B. (1994). *Shaquille O'Neal: Center of attention*. Minneapolis, MN: Lerner.

Vare, E.A. (1992). *Adventurous spirit: A story about Ellen Swallow Richards*. New York: Carolrhoda.

Walker, P.R. (1988). *Pride of Puerto Rico: The life of Roberto Clemente*. San Diego, CA: Harcourt, Brace, Jovanovich.

Warhola, J. (2004). *Uncle Andy's: A faabbbulous visit with Andy Warhol*. New York: Putnam.

Yu, C. (2005). *Little Green: Growing up in the Chinese cultural revolution*. New York: Simon & Schuster.

Grade 9–Adult

Alland, A. (1974). *Jacob A. Riis: Photographer and citizen*. New York: Aperture.

Atkinson, L. (1985). *In kindling flame: The story of Hannah Senesh*. New York: Lothrop.

Ayer, E.H. (1992). *Margaret Bourke-White: Photographing the world*. New York: Silver-Burdett.

Baker, R. (1982). *Growing up*. New York: Plume/New American Library.

Bird, L. (1989). *Larry Bird drive: The story of my life*. New York: Doubleday.

Clayton, E. and Hodges, D. (1996). *Martin Luther King: The peaceful warrior*. Huntington Beach, CA: Archway.

Dyer, D. (1997). *Jack London*. New York: Scholastic.

Feinman, R. (1999). *The meaning of it all: Thoughts of a citizen scientist*. Cambridge, MA: Perseus.

Frank, A. (1967). *Anne Frank: The diary of a young girl.* New York: Doubleday.

Hall, B.E. (1998). *Tea that burns: A family memoir of Chinatown.* New York: Free Press.

Haskins, J. (1992). *I have a dream: The life and words of Martin Luther King, Jr.* Brookfield, CT: Millbrook Press.

Keller, H. (1988). *The story of my life.* New York: Signet Classics.

Levine, E. (1995). *Anna Pavlova: Genius of the dance.* New York: Scholastic.

Lyons, M.E. (1990). *Sorrow's kitchen: The life and folklore of Zora Neale Hurston.* New York: Scribner.

Malone, M. (1995). *Maya Lin: Architect and artist.* New York: Enslow.

Meltzer, M. (1999). *Carl Sandburg: A biography.* Breckenridge, CO: Twenty-First Century Books.

Meyer, S.E. (1990). *Mary Cassatt.* New York: Harry A. Abrams.

Niven, P. (2004). *Carl Sandburg: Adventures of a poet.* New York: Harcourt.

O'Connor, B. (1994). *Barefoot dancer: The story of Isadora Duncan.* New York: Carolrhoda.

Reef, C. (1992). *Jacques Cousteau: Champion of the sea.* Breckenridge, CO: Twenty-First Century Books.

Schraff, A. (1999). *Ralph Bunch: Winner of the Nobel Peace Prize.* Springfield, NJ: Enslow.

Senna, C. (1992). *Colin Powell: A man of war and peace.* New York: Walker.

Severance, J. (1999). *Einstein: Visionary scientist.* New York: Clarion Books.

Szymusiak, M. (1989). *The stones cry out: A Cambodian childhood.* New York: Farrar Straus Giroux.

Books and Websites for Marvelous Mentors

Compiled with the assistance of Pamela Redlener.

Books for Marvelous Mentors

Allington, R.L. (2001). *What really matters for struggling readers: Designing research-based programs.* New York: Addison-Wesley/Longman.

Armbruster, B.B., Lehr, F., & Osborn, J. (1991). *Put reading first: The research building blocks for teaching children to read.* Washington, DC: National Institute for Literacy.

Dudley-Marling, C., & Paugh, P. (2004). *A classroom teacher's guide to struggling readers.* Portsmouth, NH: Heinemann.

Dudley-Marling, C., & Rhodes, L.K. (1996). *Readers and writers with a difference: A holistic approach to teaching struggling readers and writers.* Portsmouth, NH: Heinemann.

Gaskins, I.W. (2005). *Success with struggling readers: The Benchmark School approach.* New York: Guilford.

Hall, S., & Moats, L.C. (1998). *Straight talk about reading: How parents can make a difference in the early years.* New York: McGraw-Hill.

Hall, S., & Moats, L.C. (2002). *Parenting a struggling reader.* New York: Broadway.

Morris, D. (2005). *The Howard Street tutoring manual: Teaching at-risk readers in the primary grades* (2nd ed.). New York: Guilford.

Shaywitz, S. (2005). *Overcoming dyslexia.* New York: Knopf.

Topping, K., & Ehly, S. (1998). *Peer-assisted learning.* Mahwah, NJ: Erlbaum.

Wood, J. (2004). *Literacy online: New tools for struggling readers and writers.* Westport, CT: Heinemann.

ADDITIONAL RESOURCES

Websites for Marvelous Mentors

LD Online: www.ldonline.org (information and links for parents and teachers of struggling readers)

Learning Disabilities Association of America: www.ldanatl.org (information and support to parents and teachers of struggling readers)

Reading Rockets: www.readingrockets.org (information about teaching reading to all kids, including those who struggle)

Schwab Learning: www.schwablearning.org (information for parents of struggling readers)

CHAPTER 3

Learning to Read Through Multiple Intelligences

o students learn reading through multiple intelligences? We know that a child may have strong ability in one subject yet, at the same time, show extreme weakness in another subject (Gardner, 1983; Piaget, 1952). Gardner's (1983, 1993) multiple intelligence theory explains how a child may show strong ability or "intelligence" in one content area or domain, such as spatial skills, yet weak ability in another skill, such as reading.

Gardner's idea is that schools tend to emphasize only a small number of a child's skills or intelligences, omitting many other important abilities, such as artistic intelligence, interpersonal intelligence, and others. The consequence is that by focusing almost exclusively on linguistic and mathematical intelligences, schools tend to overlook many children's talents and skills.

Fischer's (1980) skill theory helps to explain variation in how different children learn different types of skills (cf. Fink, in press; Fischer & Biddell, 1992, 1997; Fischer, Bullock, Rotenberg, & Raya, 1993; Fischer & Knight, 1990; Fischer, Knight, & Van Parys, 1993; Mascolo, Li, Fink, & Fischer, 2002). Fischer uses a ladder metaphor to represent traditional notions of reading development; the rungs of the ladder represent the linear, step-by-step skill development of many children as they learn to read. In contrast, Fischer uses a web metaphor to capture the variation and disparate abilities of some children as they learn to read. The web is not neat and linear but, instead, is complex and messy, showing the simultaneous forward and backward, upward and downward movement of some children as they learn to read. Fischer's notion of the web suggests that different children learn to read in different ways and provides a way to understand the alternative pathways taken by the highly successful readers who struggled and are the focus of this book. Nowhere is the theme of disparate, uneven abilities more evident than in the case history of Roy Daniels.

Disparate Abilities: Roy Daniels's Story

Despite lifelong struggles with reading, Roy Daniels became a world leader in science. He conducts research on cystic fibrosis, muscular dystrophy, and other devastating diseases and has written over 175 scientific articles. Daniels is Professor of Biochemistry and Genetics at Stanford University Medical School and one of the youngest members ever elected to the National Academy of Sciences. Yet despite these noteworthy achievements, he still has gaps in basic reading, writing, and spelling. His personal story reveals an unusual pathway to success.

I was intrigued to learn how Daniels's uneven abilities had developed in reading, science, and other subjects. Clearly, his early years did not foreshadow a stellar career in science.

I was at the bottom in reading skills and spelling skills. I was a very, very slow reader and couldn't read out loud or silently. It began in first grade and continued in second grade, third grade, and on and on and on....

Daniels repeated the first grade in a public school in rural Indiana, where he struggled continually with reading despite years of help from tutors. Eventually, he developed basic fluency when he was 11 years old. However, he continued to have difficulty identifying letters and their corresponding sounds and, to this day, has trouble distinguishing between letters that look alike such as *b, d, p, q, m,* and *n.* He compensates by printing in upper case.

Actually, I still print today. I print everything in capitals to help me tell the difference between letters like b *and* d.

Reading Advanced Texts About Passionate Interests

Despite his lingering weakness in the basics, Daniels was an avid science reader from an early age, voraciously reading science books and articles. He enjoyed doing this kind of reading.

You'd start reading a lot. Because you like it (grade 3 and up). You read science for—how things are put together. My interest in chemistry just came from—it started with my interest in airplanes in grade school...that quickly converted to propellant systems in seventh and eighth grades.

Daniels's reading development was propelled by an intense interest in science—what Winner (1996) calls a "rage to master" a subject (p. 4). Driven by his passionate interest, he read lots of advanced science books and journals despite his difficulties with visual–graphic and phonological decoding skills.

When I was a freshman in high school, I read quite a few college texts. I became fascinated with nitrogen chemistry, so I got organic chemistry textbooks. And I read all the journals, various aeronautic journals.

Daniels immersed himself in reading complex science texts, even as he continued to struggle with some basic reading skills.

Playing at Science Through Hands-On Activities

In addition to reading, Daniels also "played" at science, designing experiments, ordering chemical supplies, and creating his own science curriculum at home. He conducted intricate chemistry experiments in his basement laboratory when he was in elementary school.

> *I set up a lab in my basement and did experiments with compounds that I got from chemical supply companies.... That early experience was useful, building your own confidence by doing these things.*

Play of this type, based on innate curiosity, helps children at risk for failure to develop abstract concepts and literacy (Daiute, 1993; Daiute & Morse, 1993). When children play and create their own curriculum using toys, media, and artifacts of interest, their reading skills develop and grow (Daiute & Morse, 1993). This is precisely what happened to Daniels. He conducted science experiments in his spare time at home; in turn, his interest, confidence, and reading ability in science developed to higher and higher levels.

Benefiting From Sociocultural Support

Daniels immersed himself in scientific reading and experimentation at a time when the U.S. government was trying to attract young people to science. He vividly recalled the supportive sociocultural atmosphere when he was growing up.

> *After the Russians sent up Sputnik in a rocket, it became easier to go into science. Vans came around to schools and parks with lots of science books, including engineering and calculus books. So I borrowed a lot of very technical books and read them.*

Motivated by his own curiosity and a culture that valued science, Daniels read advanced science books well above his instructional reading level.

> *In grade school, a high school chemistry teacher got me a high school chemistry textbook, and when I was in high school, my biology teacher*

got me engineering and calculus books to read and put me in contact
with a biology professor at Eastern Illinois University.

Daniels benefited from the sociocultural support of his era, when traveling library vans carried enticing science books to his neighborhood. In addition, he benefited from teachers who mentored him, directing him to advanced books and magazines about chemistry, engineering, and calculus.

Developing a Schema

How did Daniels comprehend advanced chemistry, engineering, and calculus books? He became conversant with the schema of science and its specialized vocabulary, concepts, questions, and typical organization as a result of his extensive science reading. His avid science reading provided lots of drill and practice, which led to his schema familiarity. Upon encountering an unfamiliar word, Daniels drew on his deep knowledge of scientific schema. He relied to a great extent on context clues, which were relatively reliable due to his familiarity with science texts. His increasing wealth of scientific background information provided the scaffolds that supported his development of optimal scientific reading skills. In Stanovich's terms (1986), Daniels got "richer," or better at reading, as a result of lots of practice—practice that he enjoyed.

Developing Confidence

Daniels's fascination with science drove him at an early age to "do science" far above the level of his classmates. But despite his scientific ability, he had a hard time in school, especially in English classes. Some of his teachers were unaware of his abilities and saw only deficits. When he was in the eighth grade, Daniels took a timed group intelligence quotient (IQ) test that required reading. He scored in the "low normal" intelligence category, presumably due to his weak reading ability. Unfortunately, unitary notions of intelligence prevailed at the time; intelligence was conceptualized as a single trait that individuals either possessed or lacked. (Either you were smart or you were not smart. Period.) More complex, dynamic notions of intelligence were still in the future—for example, Gardner's (1983) theory of multiple intelligences. Gardner's theory acknowledges the coexistence of different types of intelligences at different levels within the same person. But when Daniels was in school, his guidance counselor focused on Daniels's score on a single IQ test; consequently, he thought Daniels was a slow learner, incapable of all abstract reasoning regardless of the subject. So he forbade Daniels to take elementary algebra, urging him to take shop instead, saying, "You can't be a chemist; you don't even qualify to be a chemist's assistant washing dishes. Your aptitude is not high enough even for that. With an IQ of 90, you'll never pass algebra. Forget the algebra, and major in shop."

Daniels's father was a carpenter and would have been happy to have his son major in shop—just like dad. Daniels's mother took in laundry to make ends meet. Both parents were loving, but they had only completed the eighth grade, so they didn't have the educational background to recognize their son's scientific talents. Nevertheless, Daniels was fascinated by science and knew that he wanted to go to college to become a scientist. Knowing that algebra was a requirement for college, he defied his guidance counselor, saying "'OK, I'll take shop, but I'm going to take the algebra class too'…. We argued, and then he said, 'OK, go and take it, and when you flunk out, I'm going to tell you I told you so.'"

Undaunted, Daniels borrowed a copy of the algebra textbook over the summer. He read it slowly and haltingly, in a manner typical of many striving readers when they encounter unfamiliar material. Reading the book in this slow, methodical manner, he gradually mastered the concepts. The result? He got a final grade of 95%—the highest grade in his algebra class.

What led Daniels to disregard the dire warnings of his guidance counselor, who was convinced he would fail algebra? The key was Daniels's self-confidence and an astute observation—early on he had noticed a disparity between his capabilities and the assessments of people in authority.

In grade school I could estimate in math and do approximations instantly, better than other kids. This gave me confidence. Yet people would tell me that I couldn't do it. Now that immediately questions their credibility. You begin to question their wisdom and trust yourself more.

While Daniels was learning to trust himself, several teachers focused narrowly on his ongoing problems with basic reading, writing, and spelling. Like the guidance counselor, they concluded that Daniels was not "college material," basically telling him that he would not succeed in college because the requirements for English were far too stiff, his IQ was too low, and so forth. They refused to write college recommendations for him.

Daniels's response was, "If you won't help me, then I'll apply myself," which he did. Confronted with the daunting prospect of facing the college admissions process alone, Daniels demonstrated the same kind of gritty persistence reported in other studies of successful readers who struggled but did not give up (Fink, 1998a, 2000b, 2002, in press; Gerber & Reiff, 1991; Margalit, 2003; Meltzer, 2004). He applied to a community college (where recommendations were not required), was accepted, and after attending for a few semesters, transferred to a four-year university. Ultimately, Daniels graduated from college, earning straight A's in all of his science courses.

Using Alternative Strategies

Daniels's record of straight A's in science—from grade school through college—reflects his interest and proficiency in scientific reading. In contrast, his grades were much lower in English and history (C's, B's, and F's). In these "noninterest" subjects, his reading skills remained rudimentary because he read a bare minimum in these content areas. Consequently, he lacked sufficient background knowledge to use the contextual schema of English or history effectively in the same way he did with science. So he had to use other strategies, especially visualization and retelling, to read, comprehend, and remember information in these noninterest subjects. Visualization strategies helped him to get by. In history, for example, Daniels saw in his mind's eye a sign with a number on it for the date of a significant battle.

> I'd actually stop and sit back and look away from the print. I'd imagine a sign with the date on it in front of me, and I'd see battles as they physically happened. In that way, I'd remember the order. People called it "daydreaming"; I was constantly accused of daydreaming!

Daniels's reading abilities fluctuated depending on the subject. He avoided doing most of the assigned reading in English and, as a result, got less practice and fell further and further behind. His avoidance of literature and resulting lack of familiarity with literary genres, in turn, resulted in his low English grades, even in college.

> I got an F in English Comp. in college. So I researched all the English teachers and figured one who would give me a passing grade, given my spelling problems.

Daniels passed English composition the second time around by using a problem-solving approach that Gerber and Reiff (1991) call "reframing." The reframing approach involves naming, facing, and acknowledging a problem, then creatively seeking an alternative solution. Daniels's habit of seeking viable positive alternatives worked well for him until graduate school, where he ran into a serious snag.

Using Accommodations

Daniels's goal was to become a scientist, so he applied to doctoral programs and took the Graduate Record Examination (GRE). The GRE consists of timed silent reading comprehension questions; even the chemistry section tests reading comprehension (see sample questions at www.ets.org/Media/Tests/GRE/pdf/Chemistry.pdf). The results of Daniels's GRE test revealed enormous discrepancies between his extremely high and low scores in different content areas.

Daniels scored in the highest (99.9th) percentile nationally in chemistry. In contrast, he scored in the lowest (16th) percentile in English. Based on his extraordinarily high chemistry score—the top 1% nationwide—Daniels was admitted to the California Institute of Technology with a full scholarship in the doctoral chemistry program. Once in the program, he excelled in science courses and experimental laboratory work; however, his language weaknesses continued to plague him. Although he took a course to prepare for the required French proficiency exam, he continually failed the exam. There were serious consequences.

> *They cut my scholarship and...told me not to come to the lab anymore.*
> *They told me I was going to flunk out of graduate school if I didn't*
> *pass the second-language requirement.*

So Daniels studied French full time and took the French exam again, but to no avail. At that point, though, Daniels's thesis advisor recognized Daniels's talent as an experimentalist and finally advocated for special accommodations for him in French.

> *He went to bat for me and convinced the graduate committee that I*
> *was an unusual circumstance, that I was a good experimentalist who*
> *couldn't pass the French test. He convinced them to let me do a*
> *translation project instead of the test. And they let me use a dictionary*
> *for the translation.*

Like other striving readers, Daniels could not read a foreign language accurately without the aid of a dictionary. However, with a dictionary by his side, he was able to translate a scholarly scientific article from French to English and, finally, pass the foreign-language requirement.

Without these accommodations, Daniels would have flunked out of graduate school. His dream of becoming a scientist would have been shattered, and we would not have benefited from his discoveries—discoveries that have spawned major advances in modern medicine.

Reading as an Adult

Today, Daniels reads at college and graduate school levels when using upper-level, meaning-making skills (e.g., Nelson-Denny Reading Test: vocabulary = grade 17.1, graduate school level; silent reading comprehension = grade 16.9, advanced college level). However, Daniels still has gaps in basic, lower level skills such as word recognition (out of context), word analysis, spelling, and oral reading, as shown by results on the Diagnostic Assessments of Reading With Trial Teaching Strategies (spelling = sixth-grade level; oral reading = eighth-grade level). (Figure 5 shows additional details of Daniels's reading profile of strengths and weaknesses.)

Daniels still moves his lips while reading silently the way children do when they are first learning to read. This slows him down considerably (Nelson-Denny Reading Rate SS = 181). His slow reading speed indicates poor integration of visual–graphic, phonological, and semantic, meaning-making skills. Daniels has not developed the seamless automaticity of most skilled readers; however, his overall functioning as a reader is high. He comprehends and writes at Stage 5 (Chall, 1983), the highest possible level, as his impressive publications attest. This suggests that Daniels developed his reading ability by following a developmental pathway different from that of most readers—an atypical web-like pathway.

An Alternative Pathway to Reading

According to traditional models of reading development, a child who follows a "normative" pathway climbs the sequential rungs of a ladder and moves progressively upward from lower level visual–graphic and sound-analysis skills to higher level semantic skills (including symbolic, abstract, and inferential meaning making). Later, the three elements of reading become integrated in an almost seamless

FIGURE 5
DAR Interpretive Profile

Student Roy D.   Date of Birth _____ Grade Not Applicable

DAR Administrator   Rosalie Fink   Teacher Not Applicable   (Adult)

DAR Test	DAR Level
Word Recognition	12
Word Analysis (Check if mastery is achieved.) √ Consonant Sounds -missed soft c √ Consonant Blends -missed drip √ Short vowel Sounds -missed short e & short u out of context; √ Rule of Silent *E* misread sit for set √ Vowel Digraphs √ Diphthongs √ Vowels with R √ Polysyllabic Words Pre-Reading Subtests: Simple matching task √ Naming Capital Letters √ Naming Lowercase Letters – confuses b/d √ Matching Letters √ Matching Words – very slow to figure out same or not the same; reported reading them twice to figure it out	
Oral Reading	8
Silent Reading Comprehension	12
Spelling See mistakes in spelling booklet	6
Word Meaning	12

1. For Word Recognition, Oral Reading, Silent Reading Comprehension, Spelling, and Word Meaning, enter the highest level for which the student achieved mastery.

2. For Word Analysis, check the subtests for which the student achieved mastery.

Note: See the TTS *Teacher's Manual,* especially "Part 2: Introduction to the Trial Teaching Strategies" And "Part 3: Preparing for Teaching," for information on reporting DAR results to students and Using results to plan and implement the TTS session with the student.

Subvocalized while spelling and reading silently.

fashion so reading becomes rapid, efficient, and automatic in the normative pathway (LaBerge & Samuels, 1974).

However, Roy Daniels did not follow this normative pathway; nor did one third of the individuals in this study. Instead, they developed reading through a different web-like pathway. For Daniels, skills did not become well integrated in a smooth, seamless fashion. For him (at least in unfamiliar reading situations), the elements of visual–graphic, sound-analysis, and meaning-making skills remain partly independent and only partly integrated.

For example, Daniels could not automatically distinguish between *horse* and *house* when I tested him. He strategized by reading them twice to make sure he was correct. And even now, he is not automatic in distinguishing between look-alike letters such as *b* and *d*. A strategy used by some individuals in this study is to scan the page for a familiar word, such as *but*, then match the *b* in *but* to the *b* in the unfamiliar word and decipher its letters. This circuitous alternative pathway reveals a lack of coordination and automaticity. In Daniels's alternative pathway, coordination and integration are lacking among the key components of reading when he reads texts that are not about science. Daniels still lacks automaticity when he reads unfamiliar material. In contrast, he reads with apparent ease, speed, and automaticity when reading science texts. His fluency as a reader depends on the content area.

Content Area–Dependent Fluency

Roy Daniels is fluent and comprehends scientific texts at the highest possible level due to the wealth of background knowledge from which he draws. However, in less familiar content areas, he shows clear evidence of dysfluency: an extremely halting, hesitant oral style; lack of appropriate expression; and frequent decoding errors. Is Daniels a fluent reader? It depends on the content area. He reads different types of texts with varying degrees of ease and automaticity. Daniels's fluency depends on the text, its interest to him, its structure, familiarity, concepts, and vocabulary. His fluency is variable, depending on the content area.

This finding of variable, or differentiated, reading ability in different content areas or domains extends Stanovich's (1986) notion of Matthew Effects to a within-the-individual analysis: The more a student reads in one content area, the "richer" or better the student's reading becomes in that content area. Daniels's content-variable fluency raises a new question: Should the concept of fluency be expanded to embrace a more flexible concept similar to the way that Gardner (1983) expanded the notion of intelligence to a more dynamic theory that includes multiple intelligences? Perhaps there are multiple fluencies. A more flexible, intra-individual notion of fluency might help us understand how children read personally appealing texts with more ease and skill than other texts. Fluency may not be simple, unidimensional, or static; rather, it may turn out to be a more complex, dynamic phenomenon that varies with the subject.

Daniels's case study argues for a more flexible notion of fluency that accounts for variability based on the content area. Currently, research is in progress to investigate the validity of this new, more flexible concept (see Fink, 2004a, 2004b). A more flexible concept could help raise educators' awareness of the enormous disparities that some students show in their ability to read different types of texts. Daniels shows dysfluent reading in English, history, and foreign languages. However, he reads and writes science materials at the highest possible level. In the domain of science, he is famous and has contributed—on a large scale—to world knowledge.

What Teachers and Families Can Do

Roy Daniels's story is relevant for other readers who struggle, not just budding scientists. Parents and teachers can promote resilience and success by working together and considering key aspects of Daniels's experience. Results from his case study support the Interest-Based Model of Reading. The results contain powerful lessons for teachers, guidance counselors, and families who want to help other striving readers:

1. Look for underlying abilities and multiple intelligences.

2. Create content area libraries in classrooms.

3. Use content area websites and CD-ROMs.

4. Encourage hands-on activities.

5. Consider content area–dependent fluency.

Look for Underlying Abilities and Multiple Intelligences

Parents, teachers, and other educators should look for underlying strengths and talents in each student. **We must not underestimate the abilities of striving readers**, who may show enormous discrepancies between their high and low skills. "Watering down" the curriculum to the student's lowest skill level in one subject (such as reading) may lead us to overlook the student's talent in another subject (such as science). To avoid this, we should encourage students to take challenging courses in all content areas, including higher level math and science. Reading difficulties such as Roy Daniels's may obscure a student's strengths in quantitative and scientific reasoning. Educators have a duty to provide access to stimulating upper level courses to all interested students, including those who struggle. Like Daniels, some students may surprise us if we give them a chance to try.

Create Content Area Libraries

To encourage striving readers like Roy Daniels to read about their interests, teachers should create their own content area libraries full of enticing materials at all readability levels. Trade books are an excellent place to start. A list of high-quality science trade books for students at different reading levels is included in Additional Resources (pages 86–88). The list specifies science books appropriate for elementary, middle school, and high school students and adults, and contains selections on a wide range of captivating science topics.

Outstanding titles for elementary school children include Balkwill and Rolph's *Gene Machines* (2002a), *Germ Zappers* (2002b), and *Have a Nice DNA* (2002c). These lively texts use humor and everyday situations to explain complex concepts about molecular biology and modern genetics. The language and illustrations communicate scientific ideas in ways that will amuse children and adults alike. Several of these books, although lighthearted, have a distinct ring of authenticity because they were written by real scientists. Some terrific examples include *The Space Place* (Sharman, 1997), by a female astronaut; *Planet Ocean* (Bett, 1997), by a marine biologist; and *Brainbox* (Rose & Lichtenfels, 1997), by a brain and behavior researcher. In addition, I recommend *The Big Book of the Brain: All About the Body's Control Center* (Farndon, 2000), which explains not only nerve cells and neurotransmitters, but also "getting nervous." I also suggest using *A Drop of Blood* (Showers, 2004), which contains amusing rhymes and comic characters that explain the function of blood. In addition, the book *Gorilla, Monkey & Ape* (Redmond, 2000) reveals the truth about monkey myths, people and primates, and gorilla family life. Colorful illustrations entice the reader and clarify each concept.

For middle school students, the Additional Resources list includes excellent books written by science teachers with extensive classroom experience. As a result, they are full of practical ideas and explicit instructions for teachers. Two superb examples are *Teaching the Fun of Science* (VanCleave, 2001) and *Scientific American: Great Science Fair Projects* (Rosner, 2000).

For high school students and adults, there are wonderful books on the list that capture the adventure of science and the magnetic pull of new discoveries. Included here are *Madame Curie: A Biography* (Curie, 1937/2001), about the only woman ever to win two Nobel prizes: one in physics and one in chemistry. This book contains a new introduction by award-winning science writer Natalie Angier, whose animated writing style is full of vivid metaphors. I also recommend *The Double Helix: A Personal Account of the Discovery of the Structure of DNA* (Watson, 1980). This vivid retelling of the discovery of DNA is full of suspense and reads like a mystery novel. Finally, *A Feeling for the Organism: The Life and Work of Barbara McClintock* (Keller, 1983) is an inspiring biography that tells about Nobel laureate McClintock's fascinating work with corn.

Use Content Area Websites and CD-ROMs

New technology offers great resources about every conceivable subject. One of the most exciting aspects of computer access to Web information lies in the wealth of new, up-to-date information that is now readily available with the click of a mouse. Quick and easy access to new information is a benefit in all content areas. However, it is especially helpful for students interested in science, a domain in which new discoveries occur daily at a truly mind-boggling pace. For this reason, the value of the World Wide Web cannot be overstated. Parents and teachers should guide students to take advantage of the wealth of new Web information. There is, of course, one caveat: Students need to be taught how to evaluate the quality and credibility of information provided by this wonderful new technology. Two good books to assist parents and teachers are *Literacy Online: New Tools for Struggling Readers and Writers* (Wood, 2004) and *Teaching With the Internet K–12: New Literacies for New Times* (Leu, Leu, & Coiro, 2004). (Figure 6 shows a teacher guiding a student as he conducts Internet research.)

For students and others interested in science, Additional Resources (pages 88–90) includes websites and CD-ROMs with up-to-date science information.

Encourage Hands-On Activities

Roy Daniels was into "doing science" by the age of 8. He conducted experiments that helped him develop reading skills, scientific thinking, experimental ability, and confidence. How can teachers engage other students in doing science? One of the best ways is through hands-on classroom demonstrations and experiments.

FIGURE 6
Teacher Guiding Student in Internet Research

The teacher does not need to be a science expert; all that is needed is a desire to engage students by exploring new activities.

Fortunately, there are excellent books available to guide teachers and students in fascinating, easy-to-perform experiments. One exciting resource for grades 4 and up is *Sports Science: 40 Goal-Scoring, High-Flying, Medal-Winning Experiments for Kids!* (Wiese, 2002). This book contains intriguing sports-related experiments that will engage most students, regardless of their skill level. Each easy-to-do experiment includes a list of simple materials, step-by-step procedures, and a concise explanation of the experiment's results. Also included are thought-provoking questions that guide critical thinking and interpretation of each experiment. For example, a chapter on brain signals and athletic practice poses the question, "If Michael Jordan was such a great professional basketball player, why did he have trouble playing professional baseball at the same level?" Students will be able to answer this intriguing question after conducting a simple experiment on themselves.

Another outstanding science book mentioned previously is *Teaching the Fun of Science*. Author Janet VanCleave's enthusiastic tone is exhilarating. This book is aligned with the National Science Education Standards (see Olson & Loucks-

Horsley, 2000) and packed with teaching tips, vocabulary words, extension activities, and reproducible projects. The author makes the scientific process fun by selecting intriguing topics (e.g., What would your weight be on different planets? What exactly is static electricity?). She shows teachers how to present the scientific method in an exciting way and how to organize experiments and set up collaborative science groups. Students learn not only science and reading skills but also interpersonal skills. Most of the materials needed for the experiments are easy-to-obtain household items. Other science supplies are easy to order through catalog suppliers and specialty stores (see Additional Resources, pages 90–91).

In addition, museums are great places for engaging students in the wonders of learning. Fortunately, many cities and suburbs have their own museums devoted to education in each content area, including science. Exhibits and programs in science museums are usually theme based and encourage hands-on activities. For example, the Dolan DNA Learning Center is a world class science museum in Cold Spring Harbor, New York. Masterminded by Nobel laureate James D. Watson, the Dolan Center runs a thoughtfully designed program with many facets: museum–school partnerships, school field trips, interactive exhibits, laboratory demonstrations, experiments, readings, videos, computer activities, and lectures. When I visited, I especially liked an exhibit called "The Genes We Share," which uses activity stations and demonstrations to engage children in exploring their own unique genome. In addition, I also observed children interacting at learning stations about human traits and human cells (e.g., color vision, fingerprints, "eye-dentification," and hair and cheek cells). Children were also involved in exhibits about identical twins, the human genome, family trees, human ancestors, and a model of DNA.

In addition to exhibits, science museums often have websites that contain a wealth of scientific information. Additional Resources (pages 91–92) includes an annotated list of science museum websites.

Consider Content Area–Dependent Fluency

As previously mentioned, today Roy Daniels reads highly technical science texts with excellent fluency and comprehension. On the other hand, he is less fluent when reading English or history books. Daniels's variable fluency suggests the need to expand the notion of fluency to a more flexible concept—a concept that accounts for variability based on text content and style.

How many people are fluent and can read physics texts with ease? Probably not many. Does this mean that overall they are not fluent readers? Probably not.

It simply means that they read some types of texts with better ease and understanding than others. Daniels may be less of an exception than we think; his wide skill disparities may be an extreme example of a common phenomenon: variable fluency based on the text's content area.

Teachers, families, and others who work with striving readers need to be aware that a student may be a fluent reader in one content area but a less fluent reader when presented with texts in a less familiar content area. An individual's reading ability may vary greatly, depending on the text. The subject and content of each text matters.

Conclusion:
Multiple Pathways to Reading Success

Roy Daniels's story fits the Interest-Based Model of Reading. His reading development was driven by his strong interest in and fascination with science; he read science texts avidly based on his intense desire to learn more about this subject of passionate, personal interest.

Daniels's story is a tale of multiple intelligences, disparate abilities, and multiple pathways to success. Daniels shows evidence of enormous strengths in science; at the same time, he shows ongoing weaknesses in some basic, lower level reading skills—weaknesses that remain with him into adulthood. Daniels demonstrates different levels of reading fluency, depending on the type of text that he reads. This result suggests the need for a new, expanded concept of fluency—one that accounts for variable fluency based on the content area of the text.

Results from Daniels's case study point to the need for family members and teachers to consider each student's multiple intelligences. Awareness of multiple intelligences can help ensure that striving readers' talents and abilities are not overlooked. Daniels was told not to take elementary algebra, to give up on his dream of becoming a scientist. As chapter 4 shows, other striving readers in the study were also discouraged from pursuing their dreams. Nevertheless they succeeded as readers and professionals, either by modifying their initial goals or by pursuing their goals in spite of what others told them.

Books for Science Lovers

Elementary Science Books

Ardley, N. (1991). *The science book of electricity*. San Diego, CA: Harcourt, Brace, Jovanovich.

Baldwin, R.F. (2003). *This is the sea that feeds us*. Nevada City, CA: Dawn Publications.

Balkwill, F., & Rolph M. (1993). *Cells are us*. Cold Spring Harbor, NY: Cold Spring Harbor Laboratory Press.

Balkwill, F., & Rolph M. (2002). *Enjoy your cells*. Cold Spring Harbor, NY: Cold Spring Harbor Laboratory Press.

Balkwill, F., & Rolph M. (2002). *Gene machines*. Cold Spring Harbor, NY: Cold Spring Harbor Laboratory Press.

Balkwill, F., & Rolph M. (2002). *Germ zappers*. New York: Cold Spring Harbor Laboratory Press.

Balkwill, F., & Rolph M. (2002). *Have a nice DNA*. Cold Spring Harbor, NY: Cold Spring Harbor Laboratory Press.

Berger, M. (2002). *Why I sneeze, shiver, hiccup, and yawn*. New York: HarperCollins.

Branley, F.M. (2000). *What the moon is like*. New York: HarperCollins.

Cerullo, M.M. (1993). *Sharks: Challengers of the deep*. New York: Cobblehill Books.

Cole, J. (1986). *Hungry, hungry sharks*. New York: Random House.

Darian, S. (2002). *Grandpa's garden*. Nevada City, CA: Dawn Publications.

Disney, W. (2003). *Finding Nemo: The ultimate sticker book*. New York: DK Publishing.

Duke, K. (1997). *Archaeologists dig for clues*. New York: Harper Books.

Dyson, M.J. (2003). *Home on the moon: Living on a space frontier*. Washington, DC: National Geographic.

Farland, D. (2002). *Jungle Jane*. Oxford, MA: Authentic Perceptions Press.

Fredericks, A. (2000). *Under one rock: Bugs, slugs, and other ughs*. Nevada City, CA: Dawn Publications.

Iverson, D. (2002). *My favorite tree*. Nevada City, CA: Dawn Publications.

Kerrod, R. (2002). *Our solar system: 100 questions and answers*. New York: Kingfisher.

Lavies, B. (1993). *A gathering of garter snakes*. New York: Dutton.

Martin, J. (1991). *Chameleons: Dragons in the trees*. New York: Crown.

Martin, J. (1998). *Tentacles: The amazing world of octopus, squid, and their relatives*. New York: Crown.

Pallotta, J. (1986). *The ocean alphabet book*. Watertown, MA: Charlesbridge.

Reed-Jones, C. (2002). *A tree in the ancient forest*. Nevada City, CA: Dawn Publications.

Rice, D. (2000). *Do animals have feelings?* Nevada City, CA: Dawn Publications.

Schmidt, V.E., & Rockcastle, V.N. (2002). *Teaching science with everyday things*. Dubuque, IA: Kendall/Hunt.

Showers, P. (2000). *What happens to a hamburger*. New York: HarperCollins.

Showers, P. (2000). *Where does the garbage go?* New York: HarperCollins.

Showers, P. (2004). *A drop of blood*. New York: HarperCollins.

Tate, S. (1991). *Tammy Turtle: A tale of saving turtles*. Nags Head, NC: Nags Head Art.

Tate, S. (1992). *Danny & Daisy: A tale of a dolphin duo*. Nags Head, NC: Nags Head Art.

VanCleave, J. (1993). *Microscopes and magnifying lenses: Mind-boggling chemistry and biology experiments you can turn into science fair projects*. New York: Wiley.

VanCleave, J. (2000). *Science around the year: Dozens of seasonal projects, loads of facts*. New York: Wiley.

Wiese, J. (2002). *Sports science: 40 goal-scoring, high-flying, medal-winning experiments for kids*. New York: Wiley.

Middle School Science Books

Atkins, J. (2000). *Girls who looked under rocks: The lives of six pioneering naturalists*. Nevada City, CA: Dawn Publications.

Bett, B. (1997). *Planet ocean*. London: Portland Press.

Billings, C.W. (1995). *Supercomputers: Shaping the future* (Facts on File). New York: Freeman.

Bortz, F. (1995). *Catastrophe! Great engineering failure—and success*. New York: Freeman.

Brandenburg, J. (1993). *To the top of the world: Adventures with Arctic wolves*. New York: Walker.

Cobb, V., & Cobb, J. (1993). *Light action! Amazing experiments with optics*. New York: HarperCollins.

Collins, M. (1994). *Flying to the moon: An astronaut's story*. Somerville, MA: Sunburst.

Farndon, J. (2000). *The big book of the brain: All about the body's control center*. New York: Peter Bedrick Books.

Goodall, J. (1996). *My life with the chimpanzees*. New York: Pocket.

Harbaugh, K. (2002). *Middle school science challenge*. Arlington, VA: National Science Teachers Association.

Isaacson, P.M. (1988). *Round buildings, square buildings, and buildings that wriggle like a fish*. New York: Knopf.

Kronstadt, J. (1990). *Florence Sabin: Medical researcher*. New York: Chelsea House.

Lauber, P. (1996). *Flood: Wrestling with the Mississippi*. Washington, DC: National Geographic Society.

Lindblom, S. (1991). *Fly the hot ones*. Boston: Houghton Mifflin.

Macaulay, D. (1988). *The way things work*. Boston: Houghton Mifflin.

Painter, M. (1997). *Satellite fever*. London: Portland Press.

Parker, S. (1995). *Thomas Edison and electricity*. New York: Chelsea House.

Patent, D.H. (1996). *Biodiversity*. New York: Clarion.

Pflaum, R. (1993). *Marie Curie and her daughter Irene*. Minneapolis, MN: Lerner.

Pringle, L. (1993). *Jackal woman: Exploring the world of jackals*. New York: Simon & Schuster.

Redmond, I. (2000). *Gorilla, monkey, & ape*. New York: Dorling Kindersley.

Rose, S., & Lichtenfels, A. (1997). *Brainbox*. London: Portland Press.

Rosner, M. (2000). *Scientific American science fair: Great projects*. New York: John Wiley & Sons.

Sharman, H. (1997). *The space place*. London: Portland Press.

Stille, D.R. (1995). *Extraordinary women scientists*. New York: Children's Press.

Streissguth, T. (1995). *Rocket man: The story of Robert Goddard*. Minneapolis, MN: Carolrhoda Books.

VanCleave, J. (2001). *Teaching the fun of science*. New York: Wiley.

Vare, E.A. (1993). *Women inventors and their discoveries*. Minneapolis, MN: Oliver Press.

Wadsworth, G. (1992). *Rachel Carson: Voice for the earth*. Minneapolis, MN: Lerner.

Yount, L. (1994). *Contemporary women scientists* (Facts on File). New York: Freeman.

High School and Adult Science Books

Curie, E. (2001). *Madame Curie: A biography*. New York: Academic Press. (Original work published 1937) deKruif, P. (2003). *The microbe hunters*. New York: Academic Press. (Original work published 1926)

Einstein, A. (2005). *The meaning of relativity*. Princeton, NJ: Princeton University. (Original work published 1948)

Ellis, R. (2003). *The empty ocean: Plundering the world's marine life*. Washington, DC: Island Press/Shearwater Books.

Garrett, L. (1994). *The coming plague: Newly emerging disease in a world out of balance*. New York: Penguin.

Garrett, L. (2002). *Betrayal of trust: The collapse of global public health*. New York: Penguin.

Head, T. (Ed.). (2006). *Conversations with Carl Sagan*. Jackson, MS: University Press of Mississippi.

Keller, E.F. (1983). *A feeling for the organism: The life and work of Barbara McClintock*. New York: Freeman.

Koprowski, H., & Oldstone, M.B.A. (Eds.). (1996). *Microbe hunters—Then and now*. New York: Academic Press.

Leopold, A., & Schwartz, C.W. (2000). *A sand county almanac and sketches from here and there*. New York: Ballantine Books.

Maddox, B. (2002). *Rosalind Franklin: The dark lady of DNA*. New York: HarperCollins.

Margulis, L., Matthews, C., & Haselton, A. (Eds.). (2000). *Environmental evolution: Effects of the origins and evolution of life on planet earth* (2nd ed.). Cambridge, MA: MIT Press.

Margulis, L., & Sagan, D. (1997). *The microcosmos: Four billion years of microbial evolution*. Berkeley, CA: University of California Press.

Miller, J., Engelberg, S., & Broad, W. (2001). *Germs: Biological weapons and America's secret war*. New York: Simon & Schuster.

Morowitz, H.J. (1992). *The thermodynamics of pizza*. New Brunswick, NJ: Rutgers University Press.

Pollen, M. (2002). *The botany of desire: A plants-eye view of the world*. New York: Random House.

Ryan, F. (1992). *The forgotten plague: How the battle against tuberculosis was won—and lost*. Boston: Little, Brown.

Sagan, C. (1997). *Billions and billions: Thoughts on life and death at the brink of the millennium*. New York: Random House.

Sagan, C. (2002). *Cosmos*. New York: Random House.

Sagan, D., & Margulis, L. (1993). *The garden of microbial delights: A practical guide to the subvisible world*. Dubuque, IA: Kendall Hunt.

Sayre, A. (1995). *Rosalind Franklin and DNA*. New York: Norton.

Watson, J.D. (1980). *The double helix*. New York: Atheneum. (Original work published 1968)

Watson, J.D. (2002). *Genes, girls, and Gamow: After the double helix*. New York: Knopf.

Science Websites and CD-ROMs

Science Websites

Global Warming International Center: www.globalwarming.net

This website includes up-to-date research results about numerous aspects of global warming, including the use of solar energy, hydrogen-powered automobiles, aviation, and so forth.

The website contains recent news articles about global warming worldwide; the information is advanced and most appropriate for students in grade 10–adult.

National Academies Press: www.nap.edu

This superb website provides a wealth of information and a wide array of excellent science books for students in grades K–12. A teacher's guide is available for each book in a new series sponsored by the National Science Foundation. The books form the literacy component of a science curriculum that integrates lessons in science, language arts, history, and social studies. Topics include: animal studies, ecosystems, electric circuits, experiments with plants, floating and sinking, food chemistry, land and water, magnets and motion, measuring times, microworlds, and others. Visitors to the website can view portions of the books online.

National Aeronautics and Space Administration (NASA): www.nasa.gov

This engaging website has information and lively activities designated for parents, teachers, and students (pre-K–adult). The site has vocabulary lessons, sound effects, cartoon characters in bright colors, and interactive games and activities that impart scientific information through hands-on learning experiences.

National Science Foundation: www.nsf.gov

This well-organized website has materials for parents and teachers of students in grade K–adult. Lessons and web resources are arranged by topic to make it easy to find resources of interest and create lessons and at-home activities. Resources include books, films, television programs, museums, and so forth. The wide array of topics cover Arctic and Antarctic science, astronomy and space, biology, chemistry and materials, computing, earth and the environment, engineering, mathematics, nanoscience, people and society, physics, and science education.

National Science Teachers Association: www.NSTA.org

This is an excellent website for teachers. Among its most useful features is an annually posted peer-reviewed list called NSTA Outstanding Science Trade Books for Students K–adult. Each book is annotated and listed by category (e.g., archaeology, anthropology, paleontology).

National Wildlife Federation: www.nwf.org

This interesting website contains information on diverse wildlife topics and features three nature magazines for students at all levels, pre-K–adult: *Wild Animal Baby* (preschool); *Your Big Backyard* (K–2); and *Ranger Rick* (2–adult). Teachers' guides are available for each grade level: pre-K, K–2, 3–5, 6–8, and 9–adult. The website is enticing and features a virtual girl who talks directly to website visitors while she appears to walk toward them. Magazine subscriptions are available online or from the National Wildlife Federation, PO Box 2038, Harlan, Iowa 51593.

Terrific Science: http://terrificscience.org

This website is for parents, teachers, and students in grades 1–12 and above. It contains many free resources, including a database of published Terrific Science activities linked to the National Science Education Standards. Materials and activities on this site teach key topics in science as well as scientific process skills. Included are a free searchable activity index, a lesson and lab exchange, and toy-based and literature-based science activities. In addition, there is a list of summer camps where activities focus on science.

The website also has a sales webpage—Terrific Science Books, Kits, & More—which lists books and kits with hands-on science activities designed to inform and excite children about science. For example, Terrific Science at Home Kits (grades 1–5) have three engaging science activities that introduce the science concept, connect the science to a storybook, and apply science concepts to a new challenge. These kits are appropriate for small-group activities and provide scientific explanations, assessment guides with answers, and children's instruction booklets with science journal pages. Another example is Instant Science Kits (grades 1–11), which are available in both Spanish and English. Each kit is designed for a different grade level and contains fun, reusable science toys, instructions for seven different experiments, extending activities using common household items, and scientific explanations.

Another feature of this website is its Integrated Science book series. Included here are books such as *Teaching Physical Science Through Children's Literature* (for grades K–4), which has reproducible pages that connect science and literature in 20 lessons using favorite children's stories. Another intriguing resource is the Toy-Based science book series (for grades K–9), which includes hands-on activities that explore the science behind toys and everyday materials. Titles include *Teaching Chemistry With Toys*, *Teaching Physics With Toys*, and *Investigating Solids, Liquids, and Gases With Toys*. This website also has a Real-World Science book series for grades 5–12 and a High School/College-Level book series.

CD-ROMs

Britannica Software. (1991). Compton's Multimedia Encyclopedia [Computer software]. San Francisco: Author.

Commonwealth Scientific and Industrial Research Organization. (1996). The Dynamic Rainforest [Computer software]. Clayton South, Victoria, Australia: Author.

Grolier Interactive/Scholastic. (1999). Grolier Multimedia Encyclopedia [Computer software]. New York: Author.

Scholastic. (1994). Scholastic's The Magic School Bus Explores the Human Body [Computer software]. Redmond, WA: Microsoft.

Scholastic. (1994). Scholastic's The Magic School Bus Explores the Solar System [Computer software]. Redmond, WA: Microsoft.

World Book. World Book Encyclopedia [Computer software]. Renton, WA: Topics Entertainment.

Science Supply Resources

Catalog Companies

Carolina Biological Supply Company
2700 York Road, Burlington, NC 27215; (800) 334-5551

Cuisenaire
10 Bank Street, PO Box 5026, White Plains, NY 10606; (800) 237-3142

Delta Education
PO Box 915, Hudson, NH 03051-0915; (800) 258-1302

Fisher Scientific—Educational Materials Division
485 South Frontage Road, Burr Ridge, IL 60521; (708) 655-4410; (800) 766-7000

Frey Scientific Division of Beckley Cardy
100 Paragon Parkway, Mansfield, OH 44903; (800) 225-3739

NASCO
901 Jamesville Avenue, PO Box 901, Fort Atkinson, WI 53538; (800) 558-9595

Sargent-Welch
911 Commerce Court, Buffalo Grove, IL 60089; (800) 727-4368

Showboard
PO Box 10656, Tampa, FL 33679-0656; (800) 323-9189

Ward's Natural Science
5100 West Henrietta Road, Rochester, NY 14586; (800) 962-2660

Stores

The Discovery Store
15046 Beltway Drive, Dallas, TX 75244; (214) 490-8299

Mineral of the Month Club
1290 Ellis Avenue, Cambria, CA 93428; (800) 941-5594; cambriaman@thegrid.net;
     www.mineralofthemonthclub.com

Nature Company
750 Hearst Avenue, Berkeley, CA 94701; (800) 227-1114

Nature of Things
10700 West Venture Drive, Franklin, WI 53132-2804; (800) 283-2921

World of Science
900 Jefferson Road, Building 4, Rochester, NY 14623; (716) 475-0100

Science Museum Websites

Adler Planetarium and Astronomy Museum, Chicago, IL
www.adlerplanetarium.org
     The site of this museum provides information about the solar system, space travel, and oth-
     er intriguing topics for children and adults.

American Museum of Natural History, New York, NY

www.amnh.org

   The site of this preeminent museum for research and education (which has over 32 million specimens and artifacts) has information about its famous dinosaur exhibit, educational programs, and field trips.

Boston Children's Museum, Boston, MA

www.bostonkids.org

   This site provides interactive, hands-on exhibits, children's activities, a teacher center, teaching kits, and much more.

Boston Museum of Science, Boston, MA

www.mos.org

   This site provides information about exhibits, workshops, movies, scientific materials, and more.

Dolan DNA Learning Center/Cold Spring Harbor Laboratory, Cold Spring Harbor, NY

www.dnalc.org/home.html

   This site has educational information about topics on genetics and gene expression. It provides a wide variety of online DNA resources as well as information about workshops, field trips, courses, and products.

Exploratorium, San Francisco, CA

www.exploratorium.edu

   The site of this fascinating San Francisco museum of science, art, and human perception provides interactive online exhibits, activities, websites, and more.

Frederick Phineas and Sandra Priest Rose Center for Earth and Science, New York, NY

www.fieldtrip.com/ny/27695101.htm

   This site is distinctive in that it features highly engaging high-tech exhibits.

Hayden Planetarium, New York, NY

www.haydenplanetarium.org

   The site of this enchanting planetarium teaches about the solar system, weightlessness in space, and a wide variety of other topics about astronomy and space.

Notebaert Nature Museum, Chicago, IL

www.chias.org

   This site offers information about nature and environmental science, midwestern U.S. environmental issues, Chicago's unique ecosystems, and the science of Grossology—the impolite science that children love. It uses recreated habitats, interactive river models, and more to make science come alive for children.

CHAPTER 4

Debunking Some Myths About Gender and Reading

Myths about gender and reading abound, not only in the popular culture, but also among educators. For example, many educators believe that girls who struggle with reading problems receive plenty of attention, whereas boys who struggle are frequently overlooked. In fact, research suggests just the opposite: Boys at all stages of schooling, preschool through graduate school, receive more attention from teachers, regardless of whether the teacher is male or female (American Association of University Women [AAUW], 1992; Maynard, 2002; Sadker & Sadker, 1994). Boys who struggle with reading receive more help (Shaywitz & Shaywitz, 2006).

So, do gender myths constrain reading development? Some answers are revealed in the results of my study, especially in the cases of three highly successful women: Susan Brown, a well-regarded filmmaker; Sylvia Law, an award-winning lawyer; and Florence Haseltine, a national leader in gynecology and women's health research. (Case histories of three men were the focus of chapters 2 and 3.)

Gender and Reading Experiences

Children develop concepts of gender early. By the age of 2 or 3, they already know most gender stereotypes and behave accordingly (Best et al., 1977; Carter & Levy, 1988; Haugh, Hoffman, & Cowan, 1980; Urberg, 1982). Most children act in gender-stereotyped ways, suggesting that being male or female is central to our core self-identity. Apparently, defining ourselves in terms of gender triggers a developmental process with major implications for our sense of who we are and which of our abilities and interests we choose to develop. Recently, reading researchers have been reconsidering traditional notions of gender that marginalize some children and limit the thinking of most people to constraining, stereotypical molds (Blackburn, 2003; Brozo, 2002; Dyson, 1997; Finders, 1997; Maynard, 2002).

According to researchers, boys' and girls' reading experiences differ in several ways (Brozo, 2002; Brozo, Walter, & Placker, 2002; Guzzetti, Young, Gritsavage, Fyfe, & Hardenbrook, 2002; Hardenbrook, 1997; Millard, 1997; Vogel, 1990; Young, 2000). First, more boys than girls are placed in special education due to reading difficulties (Brozo, 2002). On the other hand, girls who struggle with reading are more likely to be overlooked than boys (Shaywitz & Shaywitz, 2006). A review of the research literature shows that, for a girl with reading difficulties to get extra help, she has to have more severe problems than a boy (Vogel, 1990). Nevertheless, even though teachers at all grade levels pay more attention to boys (AAUW, 1992; Maynard, 2002; Sadker & Sadker, 1994), many boys are alienated by reading as it is taught in school. Many boys, in their desire to be considered "real boys," resist reading in the belief that reading is mostly "for girls" (Brozo, 2002).

As I conducted my research, I was curious about gender myths and the differences and similarities among the striving male and female readers in my study.

Differences in Text Choices

The results about gender fit the Interest-Based Model of Reading. Both the men and the women in my study were equally avid readers who read everything they could get their hands on about their favorite topics. However, the men and women preferred distinctly different types of texts. Their reading preferences followed traditional gender patterns (refer to Table 2 on page 9). Women, more often than men, noted the "pull" of fiction, especially novels about personal relationships. They were particularly drawn to romances, even when history was ostensibly the subject.

> *I remember reading many historical novels; I read those avidly, particularly about the Tudor and Stuart periods. Because mainly they were lovely love stories.*
> ANN L. BROWN (EDUCATIONAL RESEARCHER)

Men, more often than women, were drawn to factual, information-loaded materials found in nonfiction texts such as history books.

> *I always read history books. Beginning in grade school. And even today, I'm a [U.S.] Civil War buff. I love to read about the Civil War.*
> ROBERT KNAPP (GYNECOLOGIST)

Gender differences in reading preferences were evident even though reading test results showed no differences at all in skill levels: The men and women in my study became equally skilled readers, regardless of gender.

Pleasure Reading

The men and women also became equally engaged while reading—experiencing feelings of pleasure, amazement, and intense concentration. Regardless of gender, reading for them was a "flow" experience—a feeling of being carried away on a pleasurable current (Csikszentmihalyi, 1991).

I was amazed that I could be so locked in a book. It was like the discovery of how a book could take me somewhere different and take me into a world and characters that I could identify with.
PRISCILLA SANVILLE (ARTS EDUCATOR)

I loved stories; stories had the power to transport me!
A. McDONALD VAZ (WRITER)

However, more of the women than men read more than 10 books a year for pleasure—a result that fits with the habits of other skilled readers. On average, females of all ages read more books than their male counterparts (Finucci, Whitehouse, Isaacs, & Childs, 1984; Whitehead & Maddren, 1974).

Persistence and Empathy

Persistence and empathy were enduring personality traits for two thirds of these men and women. Regardless of gender, they believed their reading difficulties had led them to persist despite facing daunting obstacles. The trait of persistence—the ability to bounce back after failure—helped them succeed by enabling them to develop resilient attitudes and habits, try new solutions and accommodations, and ultimately develop their talents. Without the grit to persist, they probably never would have gone to college and graduate school, practiced demanding professions, or contributed books in their fields of expertise.

Regarding empathy, both the men and the women explained that they could empathize with others who struggle, because they had "been there" and, consequently, knew what it felt like. Very likely, this empathic trait helped them to forge strong interpersonal connections—connections that were important when they needed assistance from others.

Differences in Mentoring

During their elementary school years, both the men and the women in this study received help and support from teachers and parents (mostly from mothers). However, there were gender differences in mentoring from their extended families. Men in the study received academic help and guidance from extended family members such as grandparents, uncles, cousins, and so forth. In contrast, none of the women received help from relatives. There were other gender differences in mentoring as well, most dramatically after elementary school. Overall, the men had twice as many mentors as the women, beginning in middle school and extending to adulthood. In addition, men received more attention at home.

> *My brother has almost all the same learning problems that I have, but he got lots of attention. I didn't. My mother didn't even realize that I couldn't read until I was almost 11.*
> FLORENCE HASELTINE (GYNECOLOGIST)

> *It was kind of like the whole world revolved around my brother Bob, who was dyslexic. My mother spent so much time with him! She ignored my sister Arlene and me, even though we were both dyslexic, too.*
> KATHLEEN YELLIN (HOTEL MANAGER)

Differences in Expectations

Each man and woman in the study was asked what differences, if any, they thought they would have experienced if they had been of a different gender but had the same talents and the same reading difficulties. Results of the study showed that 93% of the women, compared to only 67% of the men, thought they would have been treated differently. Of the 30 women who responded, 28 believed that their home or school experiences would have been more positive. In contrast, of the 30 men who responded, only 20 men thought that being female would have made a difference (in most cases, a negative one). (Table 7 summarizes these results.)

TABLE 7		
Responses by Gender		

Question: Would being of a different gender with reading problems have made a difference?

	Women	Men
YES	28	20
NO	2	10

Fischer's exact test, $p = .021$

Overall, men believed that despite their struggles, others held high academic and career expectations for them, both at home and at school. One man's remarks about his mother's expectations were typical:

My sister was pressured to become a wife and mother, but I was the one that was going to succeed. My mother had me picked for being great.
S. CHARLES BEAN (NEUROLOGIST)

Women who struggled perceived lower academic and career expectations, which they attributed to gender. They thought they would have been pushed to achieve more if they had been boys.

My high school guidance counselor said that since my spelling was so bad, I could never be a secretary. Instead, he said I could be a receptionist, answering phones. He transferred me out of a more difficult college-prep English track to an easier one, because I was a girl.
TANIA BAKER (BIOCHEMIST)

My brother and I both had reading problems, but my mother pushed him to go to law school. She didn't push me.
MARLENE HIRSCHBERG (ARTS DIRECTOR)

I wondered whether the decade when they attended school had affected their concepts of gender. To find out, I analyzed responses by age and decade of school attendance. As the results in Table 8 show, there were no significant differences by age or by decade of school attendance.

Differences in Gender Assumptions

Despite differences in race, class, and ethnicity, researchers have shown that a girl's or a woman's prestige in U.S. society is measured primarily by her sexual attractiveness and potential for romantic success (Gray, 1999; Holland & Eisenhart, 1990; Lees, 1986; Lorber, 1994). Regardless of whether the message is explicitly stated or tacitly implied, girls often learn that focusing on femininity and "doing girl" is of utmost importance (Gray, 1999). Without being asked,

	TABLE 8	
	Responses by Decade and Age	

Question: Would being of a different gender with reading problems have made a difference?

	1960s–1990s	1940s–1950s
Response	Women age 26–40	Women age 41+
YES	16	12
NO	1	1
Response	Men age 26–40	Men age 41+
YES	5	15
NO	4	6

women in my study spontaneously reported that they had been "educated in romance"; that is, they were raised to believe that being pretty and popular mattered more than being smart. For women with brothers, this stood in sharp contrast to the emphasis in their brothers' upbringing.

> *I always got the sense at home that my academic career wasn't that important, wasn't as important as my brother's. I was social, and my parents expected me to marry well, marry a doctor (which I did). My parents focused on helping my brother become a doctor (which he did)—even though he wasn't a very good student earlier either.*
> TERRY BROMFIELD (SPECIAL EDUCATOR)

> *I was pretty as a child; I was constantly told I was pretty. And I was very, very successful; I won medals for dancing. So this was all that was expected of me. Academics was not expected of me.*
> ANN L. BROWN (EDUCATIONAL RESEARCHER)

Many women internalized the notion that "doing girl" was more important than "doing school." Apparently, one way to get through life was to excel at being exquisitely feminine.

I had the sort of body and beauty that carried me through. I mean, as a girl I was, you know, homecoming queen.
PRISCILLA SANVILLE (ARTS EDUCATOR)

I had other things going for me. I love to dance, so I took modern dance and ballet. And I was into fixing my hair and having boyfriends.
KATHLEEN YELLIN (HOTEL MANAGER)

Some women consciously used their femininity and social skills to avoid doing schoolwork.

A lot of what I call faking it, my manipulative ways of getting out of school assignments, were based on the fact that I was a girl. I could flirt my way through.
LEZLI WHITEHOUSE (SPEECH/LANGUAGE SPECIALIST)

I could get away with not doing schoolwork because of my personality, my friendliness. Teachers would kind of let me get by....
MELISSA HOLT (EARLY CHILDHOOD EDUCATOR)

Even families that espoused gender equity behaved according to gender stereotypes (intentionally or inadvertently). For example, Maureen Selig and her brother—white, privileged, upper middle class—both struggled with reading. As children, both were interested in science and raised in a science-oriented family. Selig's father was a doctor, and her husband, brother, and brother-in-law became doctors, too. Selig loved animals, was fascinated by science, and dreamed of becoming a veterinarian.

I wanted to be a vet, but my family discouraged me from taking science courses. But they encouraged my brother—even though we both had trouble reading. So I gave up on my dream of becoming a vet. I became a social worker instead. My family prides itself on being open-minded, but in reality we all have it; we're all part of the society. When a woman has difficulty academically, the family thinks it's OK 'cause

she'll go get married; someone will support her. So she's not encouraged
to fight the battle that a man would be kicked to do.
MAUREEN SELIG (SOCIAL WORKER)

Teachers and guidance counselors also had lower expectations for girls who struggled with reading. They made different assumptions for boys and girls—assumptions based on traditional male and female frameworks. Different women in the study responded to traditional female frameworks in various ways. Insight into their responses can be seen through the cases of three successful women: filmmaker Susan Brown, gynecologist Florence Haseltine, and attorney Sylvia Law.

A Traditional Framework: Susan Brown's Story

Filmmaker Susan Brown is from a well-known, affluent, African American, political family. Initially, she struggled with reading in public school, which she "hated intensely" because, no matter how hard she tried, she could not measure up and succeed. In her interview, Brown painfully recalled misspelling every single word on a third-grade spelling test. A friend of her mother's helped her study for the retest, but Brown failed again. And she continued to fail. Finally, at the beginning of fifth grade, she was sent to a private school. Although classes there were much smaller (only 4 to 14 children), Brown continued to struggle and, as the work got progressively harder in middle school, she was given private tutoring in reading.

Despite the extra tutoring, Brown was forced to repeat the eighth grade. She was devastated. Reeling from the humiliation of being left back at age 13, she was assessed by a reading specialist, who finally diagnosed her with dyslexia. The result was that Brown was given more tutoring in reading, this time a more intensive tutoring program.

Eventually, Brown attended an alternative private high school that emphasized activity-based education and learning academic subjects through the arts. For example, in a marine biology class, Brown learned scuba diving techniques and dove deep in the ocean, identifying plants and animals underwater. In another biology class, Brown dissected a cat to learn about the cat's intricate anatomy. Her biology teacher played popular music to help the students study, and Brown memorized the cat's anatomy by changing the words of a popular song to the names of the cat's body parts and their functions. Learning biology in this way was fun for Brown. She became fascinated by science—so fascinated that she thought she would become a scientist.

> *But I was told not to. My teachers discouraged me; they told me it*
> *would be too hard for me and I shouldn't bother trying.*

Brown listened to her teachers and followed their advice. She stopped taking science courses and gave up on her interest in a science career. Instead, she pursued another interest—babysitting.

> *I started babysitting and read to kids, and I discovered that I loved it.*
> *I'd ham up the stories, and kids loved my expression. And I loved*
> *reading to them!*

Reading to children fit with Brown's lifelong love of play acting and other imaginative activities. In fact, she was often immersed in the world of imagination.

> *I made up plays as a child and then I acted them out. And when I got*
> *a little older, I loved to read plays; I read lots of them—about 20, 30,*
> *even 40 plays. Plays were always easier for me to read 'cause I could*
> *visualize the characters and see the action happening.*

Fortunately, Brown's mother had nurtured her daughter's interests in imagination, drama, and the arts. When Brown was only 5, her mother enrolled her in a theater program and, from then on, Brown excelled in theater: She acted in plays throughout elementary school, middle school, and high school. When she got to college, Brown majored in theater at New York University and, in graduate school, majored in film at the University of Southern California. Consequently, after graduation, Brown was well positioned to launch a career in communications. She succeeded by developing her talents in the communication arts, accepting several good jobs in media and communication with companies such as Motown Records, Fox Emmy Awards, Walt Disney Television, and CBS Morning News. Brown had succeeded in the field of communication—a field more in keeping with a traditional female framework than science.

An Atypical Framework:
Florence Haseltine's Story

As I analyzed the interviews of women in the study, I noticed a pattern: Women who did not fit neatly into stereotypical molds of femininity succeeded at the highest levels. One example is Florence Haseltine, a stellar achiever in her field. Haseltine is a gynecologist with both an MD and a PhD; she is Director of the Center for Population Research at the National Institutes of Health and the recipient of many coveted medical awards. Haseltine founded the Society for the Advancement of Women's Health Research and is the coauthor of numerous books and articles such as *Woman Doctor* (Haseltine & Yaw, 1976), *The Woman's Guide to Good Health* (Gray, Haseltine, Love, & Mayzel, 1991), and *Reproductive Issues and the Aging Male* (Haseltine & Paulsen, 1994).

Haseltine's personality is charismatic: intense, intellectual, assertive, and caring. She is fiercely independent and courageous. From her early years in elementary school, Haseltine resisted stereotypical notions of femininity. A thread woven throughout her interviews is the theme of being an outsider, an oddball who continually struggled against feminine norms.

> *I was never proper or girlish. Never. I was sort of an odd duck in a lot of ways. Teachers used to put me in the back so I could play with the animals while other kids were working quietly. And I'd play with the snakes. In fifth grade, sixth grade, even in seventh grade, I'd play with snakes in the back of the room. People thought I was an oddball.*

As a girl Haseltine was intellectually curious and outspoken. In school she was considered odd—a girl bursting with energy and enthusiasm about atypical interests, interests in mathematics, animal biology, and human reproduction. From her earliest days in school she loved math and science and considered herself "a graph and table person." She was especially curious about how the human body works and was driven by an intense, intrinsic desire to pursue her scientific interests.

However, Haseltine's home circumstances were difficult. Although both parents were professionals (her father, an engineer; her mother, a French teacher), Haseltine's mother was chronically ill and frequently bedridden. Consequently, she was unable to care for herself or her family, which included four children:

three boys and a girl. Haseltine's father worked long hours. So, as the only girl among three brothers, Haseltine was expected to take on the traditional female role of family caretaker. This included nursing her ailing mother, who suffered frequent relapses. Whenever her mother was ill, Haseltine was responsible for all of the domestic household duties: She did the grocery shopping, she cooked the dinners, she cleaned the house, and she cared for her brothers.

Despite fulfilling these domestic roles and nurturing her family, Haseltine resisted traditional female norms early in childhood, even going by a boy's name—Paddy. She was interested in science, a nontraditional field for a girl, and she was encouraged by her junior high science teacher, Mr. Brewbaker. As she got older, her interests in science became more focused and more intense, and she won the Westinghouse Science Award in high school. She majored in science at the University of California at Berkeley and, after completing her undergraduate degree there, earned a doctorate degree in biophysics at the Massachusetts Institute of Technology (MIT). Then she earned a medical degree from the Albert Einstein College of Medicine and joined the faculty in the Department of Obstetrics and Gynecology at Yale University School of Medicine.

Haseltine faced many barriers to getting ahead as a woman in science. She had a hard time every step of the way but, undeterred, focused her efforts and became a trailblazer in the field of women's health.

I went to Congress and changed the law. It's called the National Institutes of Health Reauthorization Act. I sort of took that on as a crusade. The fact that women are now being included in clinical trials is a direct result of my effort. That was totally the result of what I did. But I had to fight hard to win.

Today Haseltine leads research programs in reproductive sciences, contraceptives, and reproductive products and procedures. She is the founding senior editor of the *Journal of Women's Health*. She is also a Weizmann Honored Scientist, and a member of the Institute of Medicine. In addition, she has received many other prestigious awards, including the American Woman's Medical Association Scientist Award. Haseltine attained the highest level of scientific achievement, working outside of a traditional female framework.

An Atypical Framework:
Sylvia Law's Story

Like Florence Haseltine, Sylvia Law did not conform to traditional female stereotypes. And, like Haseltine's achievements, Law's accomplishments are outstanding by any standard. Law is an internationally respected attorney and scholar in the fields of civil rights and health law. She holds impressive titles—she is the Elizabeth K. Dollard Professor of Law, Medicine, and Psychiatry and Director of the Arthur Garfield Hays Civil Liberties Program at New York University Law School. Law is the author of *Blue Cross: What Went Wrong?* (1974), which won *The New York Times* Outstanding Book Award. In addition to receiving other prestigious honors and awards, Law was inducted on October 8, 2005, into the U.S. National Academy of Arts and Sciences.

Throughout her school years, Law struggled with reading and schoolwork. Yet despite her reading difficulties, she was involved in many school activities: the drama club, the school newspaper, and the debating club. It was in these extracurricular activities that Law honed her writing and debating skills. Ultimately she excelled as a debator.

> *I was active in a lot of communicative activities and I was pretty good at those things, much better than at schoolwork. And I developed very strong debating skills of putting together your little index cards and figuring out your argument.*

Although she struggled with reading and did not get high grades, Law attributes her success to the help and encouragement of her high school debating coach. She also felt free from the constraints of female stereotypes.

> *Because I'm so big, I just knew I didn't fit the stereotype. There was NO WAY I could be what a girl was supposed to be like: petite and pretty and sociable. So I said, "Well, that's not me." You know, it's liberating not to fit the stereotype—to be so far from fitting it that there's no sense in trying. And so I was less disabled by those characteristic assumptions about the way women think and work than many people.*

Law resisted even trying to conform to gender stereotypes because she didn't think she could "make it" in the arena of traditional femininity. Convinced that she was too big to "look feminine," Law felt free to pursue her intellectual and civic interests, which were considerable. She is the author of numerous articles and books, including *The Rights of the Poor* (Law & Neuborne, 1973), "Family, Gender, and Sexuality: What the Founding Fathers Had to Say" (1987), "'Girls Can't Be Plumbers'—Affirmative Action for Women in Construction: Beyond Goals and Quotas" (1989), and *Law and the American Health Care System* (Rosenblatt, Law, & Rosenbaum, 1997). Today she is a well-known civil rights and health lawyer whose work influences U.S. public policy.

What Teachers and Families Can Do

Taken together, the results about gender and reading from this study should spur teachers and families to encourage *all* students to aim high, academically and professionally, regardless of their gender. In addition, these results underscore the need to find books that appeal both to boys and to girls.

The results about gender raise several important issues. The following approaches can help teachers and families to address unresolved gender issues that continue in the field of reading and in U.S. society:

1. Use critical literacy.
2. Use twin texts.
3. Use "target books" for boys and girls.
4. Share gender views.
5. Use youth-oriented topics.
6. Get students writing.
7. Celebrate with festivals.

Use Critical Literacy

Teachers and families can use critical literacy activities to expand students' ideas about gender and the world. Critical literacy leads students to analyze assumptions not only about reading, but also about the world in which they live. With critical literacy, students question the author's and their own assumptions about gender, race, religion, nationality, ethnicity, and so forth. As a result, students gain insights into the complexities and nuances of social relationships—insights that help them to forge their own evolving identities (Bean, 2004).

Based on this study's results, girls who enjoy romances should be encouraged to read this genre. However, we can help to change the way in which girls read romances by posing new, thought-provoking questions. For example, teachers can ask: What is meant by the conclusion, "She married the prince (or the doctor) and lived happily ever after"? Under what conditions did the woman live? The man? According to what assumptions? The discussions we engage in and the views of gender that we express affect both girls' and boys' developing views of themselves and their own life possibilities.

Table 9 shows critical literacy discussion questions that are open-ended and easily modified to fit different ages and developmental levels. In addition, students can also create their own discussion questions while working in pairs, small groups, or as a whole class. Involving students in devising their own questions is a great way to engage them in the reading–thinking process.

Use Twin Texts

According to the results of this study, students should be encouraged to read their favorite genres. But how can we expand their reading to include other genres as well? One excellent way is by using twin texts, which are great for facilitating broader reading experiences beyond the student's favorite genre. With twin texts, teachers help students find fiction and nonfiction books on a favorite topic, then guide them in reading both books consecutively. It's a good idea to start with the favorite genre, then follow with a book about the same topic in a different genre. When read as a pair in this way, twin texts simultaneously help students to deepen their knowledge and appreciate a new genre (Camp, 2000).

Use "Target Books" for Boys and Girls

Based on the gendered reading preferences of boys and girls, parents and teachers need to know which books will likely attract boys and which will likely attract girls. A superb resource that targets reluctant boy readers is *Guys Write for Guys Read: Boys' Favorite Authors Write About Being BOYS!* (Scieszka, 2005). *Guys Write* is a humorous book for all readers—young or old, male or female—and provides a great way to connect boys to men who love to read and write. This unique, down-to-earth book contains short pieces (about one to three pages each) written explicitly for boys by more than 90 favorite boys' authors. Each author

Romance Fiction and Fairy Tales

1. What is meant by the conclusion "She married a doctor (or prince, lawyer, scientist, artist, politician, business leader, etc.) and lived happily ever after"?

2. What was the quality of the couple's life 20 years later?

3. Under what conditions did the woman live? The man?

4. According to what assumptions did they live?

5. How fulfilling were their lives, and why?

6. Would the story have differed if it had concluded with the young man marrying a woman doctor? Would they have lived happily ever after? Why or why not?

7. How would the story have differed if two men or two women married? Do you think they would have lived happily ever after? Why or why not?

Novels

1. What character do you like most in this book? Why? How is this character like you or unlike you? In what ways are her or his experiences similar to or different from yours?

2. What is the main character's role in the plot of this story?

3. Which characters have the most power in this story? Which characters have the least power? Why?

4. Which characters are unseen or have no voice in this book? Why?

5. What views of the world do we see through the narrator of this story? Do you agree or disagree with this view? Why or why not?

6. How do characters in this book compare to other characters you've read about, seen, or heard in books, magazines, TV, radio, videos, CDs, movies, conversations, advertisements, etc.?

7. How do you feel about the ending of the book? Why? How might you change the ending if you were the author? Why would you change it in this way? How might this change in the plot alter the author's message?

8. What angers you about this book? Why? How would you change this aspect?

9. How would your parents, relatives, members of your church, synagogue, or mosque feel about this book?

10. Why do you think the author wrote this book? What was his or her purpose? Did she or he succeed? How? What is the main theme or idea overall? Do you agree with this message? Why or why not?

11. As a result of reading and discussing this story, what did you learn that you didn't know before? What else would you like to learn about this or a related topic? Did any of your ideas change? How? As a result of reading? As a result of listening to your classmates' interpretations? Explain.

The protocol for novels has been adapted from Harper, R., & Bean, T. (2004, May). *What's hot—and what should be hot—for the reading specialist.* Paper presented at Institute 11 of the annual convention of the International Reading Association, Reno, NV.

lists three books he has written and one entertaining "random fact" about his own life.

Two excellent books about both boys' and girls' reading preferences are *Great Books for Boys: More Than 600 Books for Boys 2–14* (Odean, 1998) and *Great Books for Girls: More Than 600 Books to Inspire Today's Girls and Tomorrow's Women* (Odean, 1997). Both books include lots of recommended titles, detailed annotations, and appropriate grade levels. They are organized by genre, making it easy to find books that match the reading preferences of most boys and girls.

Many of the suggested books present boys and girls with alternative visions of boyhood and manhood, girlhood and womanhood. *Great Books for Boys* is a compilation of books selected with the purpose of raising boys who love to read and are active and assertive as well as compassionate and cooperative. *Great Books for Girls* contains books about heroines who are not passive but instead are active, creative, articulate, and intelligent; they meet challenges, resolve conflicts, and engage in adventurous, active quests. In addition to Odeon's collections, I also recommend *Guidelines for a Gender-Balanced Curriculum in English* (National Council of Teachers of English, 1998), a brochure filled with interesting activities that promote gender development in boys and girls, men and women.

Share Gender Views

After students select their books, teachers can plan activities to help students formulate their own views of gender. This can be accomplished by reading, thinking, writing, and dramatizing issues presented in the texts. It is a good idea to have students share their diverse interpretations with one another. By sharing, students explore their own developing views and learn to respect and consider viewpoints different from their own. (Table 10 describes activities that encourage consideration of a wide range of gender perspectives.)

A disturbing finding from this study was that many women were ashamed of their favorite genre—romances—which they denigrated as "trashy novels." Is there value in reading this genre? According to Radway (1991) the answer is unequivocally "Yes." Radway argues that romance novels are reader friendly and help break down important barriers to reading—barriers that otherwise deter reluctant readers. Romances are easily accessible and understandable due to their simple vocabulary, standard syntax, and familiar language style. In addition, romances promote the development of sensitivity to others' feelings, a "care perspective" important for helping boys as well as girls learn to negotiate relationships in their own lives (Gilligan, 1993).

TABLE 10
Gender Balance Activities

Activity 1: Ask students to tell, write, or dramatize how the events or outcome of a story would have been affected if the character were of a different gender. For example, if Rumplestiltskin had assigned a task to the miller's son rather than the daughter, what would the task have been? If the boy named Caleb had been the older sibling in *Sarah, Plain and Tall* (MacLachlan, 1985), how might things have been different? In *What Girls Learn: A Novel* (Cook, 1997), if Tilden had been a boy, how would he have reacted if Uncle Rand had betrayed him in a similar way to the way he betrayed Tilden the girl? What, if any, different consequences would have resulted?

Activity 2: Locate fiction in which girls or women are active characters; locate fiction in which boys or men are sensitive caregivers. Have students discuss whether these characters appeal to them or not, and why. Discuss what would change if the girls and women were passive, and the boys and men were active. Would the characters be more or less appealing, and why? Engage boys and girls in comparing the characters in their original and imagined versions, and have them discuss which character in which version they would most like to be, and why.

Activity 3: Give voice to a minor character who was silent in an original text by asking students to retell, rewrite, or dramatize the events or outcome of a story through the eyes of the minor character. For example, rewrite parts of *Sarah, Plain and Tall* to show what Papa thought about Sarah and her suitability for the family. In "The Three Little Pigs," what did the mother of the three little pigs think about her sons' encounters with the world?

Activity 4: Have students reverse the gender roles in television commercials and magazine advertisements. Is a bathroom cleanser still perceived as a high-quality product if a *man* dances around the clean sink or toilet? Is a car still worth buying if a *man* leans on it? Will he wear a skimpy outfit and flip his hair during his sales pitch?

Activity 5:

1. Write down the title of your favorite book.

_____

2. Write down the name and gender of the main character.

_____

3. Check any attributes in the following list that describe that character.

☐ achieving	☐ curious	☐ passive
☐ adventurous	☐ dependent	☐ persevering
☐ aimless	☐ docile	☐ problem solver
☐ athletic	☐ fearful	☐ self-respecting
☐ autonomous	☐ incompetent	☐ spiritless
☐ caring	☐ ingenious	☐ victim
☐ creative	☐ object of ridicule	*(continued)*

110

TABLE 10 (continued)
Gender Balance Activities

4. Add any other attributes of this character that are not listed already.

5. Describe this character's attributes to a partner by retelling a story incident.

6. Discuss how the story might change if the main character were of a different gender.

Activity 6: Have students put themselves in the role of a minor character and discuss how they would feel if they were that character. For example:

1. Ask students to imagine themselves as Nick in *What Girls Learn: A Novel* (Cook, 1997). Describe Nick's situation as he tries to become part of his new family. Ask students, How would you feel if you were entering into a blended family? What challenges would you face if you were in Nick's situation? How did Nick deal with these challenges? What might you have done differently? Explain why.

2. Ask students to image themselves as Uncle Rand in *What Girls Learn: A Novel*. Ask students, How did Uncle Rand win and then lose Tilden's trust? How would you feel if you were Tilden and you had been betrayed in this way? What actions could you take if this were you? Why might you want to tell an adult what Uncle Rand did? What might be the results if you did or didn't tell somebody about this?

Activity 7: Have students put themselves in the role of a major character and discuss how they would feel if they were that character. For example, ask students to imagine themselves as Farah in *The Story of My Life: An Afghan Girl on the Other Side of the Sky* (Ahmedi, 2005). Describe Farah's situation at key points and key places in the story—in Afghanistan, in Germany, and finally in the United States. Ask students to discuss how they would feel if they were Farah at these different turning points in different countries. What challenges does Farah face at each point and how does she negotiate each challenge? How might you have reacted differently if you were Farah? Explain.

Adapted from Prosenjak, N. (1999, February). *Reading across the grain of gender*. Paper presented at the annual meeting of the Colorado Council of the International Reading Association, Denver, CO.

According to researchers, boys as well as girls yearn to develop sensitivity (Kindlon & Thompson, 1999; Pollack, 1998), which can be enhanced by reading and analyzing romantic fiction. But how can teachers address boys' yearning for sensitivity in view of boys' preferences for nonfiction? One approach could be to select riveting nonfiction in the form of compelling biographies. Because many biographies explore relationships with mentors, family, and friends, this "back-door approach" could expose boys to literature that helps them, too, develop sensitivity in their personal relationships.

Use Youth-Oriented Topics

Another good way to lure both boys and girls into reading is through books and magazines on topics of concern to them—topics such as making friends, getting along with parents and siblings, sexuality, adoption, suicide, kidnapping, death of a parent, school violence, terrorism, abuse, and so forth. Students relate to these issues, which make them powerful entry points to reading for even the most reluctant readers. Additional Resources (pages 119–123) includes annotated lists of books on sensitive issues faced by students today.

Get Students Writing

Involving students in writing is an excellent way to complement the reading program, because writing about a text improves comprehension and retention of the material. Writing is also extremely effective for promoting engagement. Teachers can choose from numerous types of writing activities, including community bookmaking, poetry, and a variety of other shared writing experiences. Additional Resources (pages 123–124) includes a list of books about how to teach various kinds of writing. (Figure 7 shows children engaged in writing at the Lincoln School in Brookline, Massachusetts.)

COMMUNITY BOOKMAKING. Community bookmaking is an exciting way to engage reluctant readers—as a class, with the entire school, or in after-school programs. For example, The Gorilla Press, a nonprofit organization for students K–12, conducts community bookmaking projects that engage inner-city children in writing and illustrating their own theme-based books. To create a book about justice, for instance, students (ages 9–13) observed a court in session; interviewed a judge; read about the criminal justice system; and researched, wrote about, and illustrated their personal views of justice. The result of this project was a book written and published by and for children—*What's Fair? What's Just? What's the Difference?* (Fink, 2000). The book includes the children's poems, essays, stories, photographs, and artwork.

Another Gorilla Press project used the powerful story *Danny the Champion of the World* (Dahl, 1998) as a springboard for writing and art. After reading the book, each child contributed original art and written work: poems, stories, autobiographies, essays, journals, murals, sculptures, paintings, drawings, collages,

FIGURE 7
Children Engaged in Writing at the Lincoln School

three-dimensional installations, and so forth. In May 2005, the StarArte Gallery in New York City held a reception and exhibited the children's artwork and writing. I attended the reception and observed the students' expressions of pride as they showed their artwork and writing to friends and family members. Each student who participated was presented with an individual award plaque during the reception. (See Figure 8 for photographs of this Gorilla Press event.) This project will be aired on public television, and a new book based on the project is being created: *Danny the Champion of the World Project: Art, Cars, Dreams, and Pheasants* (Fink, in preparation; for details, see www.gorillapress.com).

POETRY. Poetry is another exciting way to get students writing. Poetry lends itself both to in-school and out-of-school topics. Hartman (1997) found that African American boys who were failing *in school* lived rich literate lives *outside of school* by reading the Bible in church and listening to rap music at the mall. As educators,

FIGURE 8
Gorilla Press Reception at the StarArte Gallery in New York City

we need to tap into the rich reading opportunities in students' out-of-school lives. Striving readers are likely to get hooked on the enticing rhythms of "cool" raps, so we should encourage them to compose rap poems of their own, as well as other forms of poetry on topics of interest. Rap and other poetic forms are terrific ways to engage students in the power of language because of their rhythms, sounds, and multiple meanings. See Additional Resources (pages 124–125) for a list of poetry books and collections.

SHARED WRITING. After writing poems (or any genre), students benefit from peer writing conferences, usually held in short, 15-minute share sessions (Graves, 1994). During share sessions, students (1) read their written work aloud, (2) listen carefully to one another reading, and (3) give and receive constructive feedback, which is useful for revising and editing. This approach helps students develop both skill and confidence as writers and is appropriate across ages and grade levels (e.g., grade 3–adult). I have used this approach in my own teaching for all kinds of writing—narratives, essays, Readers Theatre, plays, poems, and so forth. (Table 11 presents a share session guide that can be used for all types of writing.)

TABLE 11
Writing Share Session Protocol

---

1. Listen: The writer reads her poem aloud while others listen.

2. Remember: The listener tells the poet everything that he remembers from listening or tells the part in the poem that he likes best (and the reason why he likes it).

3. Reminder: The listener tells the writer that what she wrote reminded him of another story, another poem, etc. (This encourages students to make text-to-text connections, enhancing comprehension.)

4. Striker: The listener tells the writer what was most striking about the poem. "What struck me was...." Students may comment on a vivid word, discuss its part of speech, discuss its meaning, etc.

5. Questioner: The listener asks the writer specific questions for clarification. "Questions that I have are...." (Such questioning helps the writer pinpoint what is unclear and needs revision.)

Adapted from Graves, D.H. (1994). *A fresh look at writing*. Portsmouth, NH: Heinemann.

Celebrate With Festivals

Poetry festivals (and celebrations for other genres) are great ways for students to share their favorite texts and original written work with friends and family. Festivals can have two components. In the first component students "perform" by reciting a favorite poem, accompanied by personally selected toys, gestures, songs, dances, videos, props, and so forth. In the second component, students perform a self-written poem on a topic of personal choice, which they read aloud to the audience. Each reading can be followed by a share session with the author and include immediate feedback from classmates and members of the audience. In addition to performing, children can also be encouraged to display their poems on bulletin boards (see Figure 9).

I observed a poetry festival in Evie Weinstein-Park's fourth-grade class at the Soloman Schecter School in Newton, Massachusetts. These fourth graders wrote and recited poems about a whole range of topics: riding a two-wheeler for the first time, emulating a baseball star at bat, frolicking in the grass with a pet, feeling ambivalent toward a brother or sister, feeling sad about a grandparent's death, and so forth. During their poetry performances, the children's engagement and enthusiasm were contagious, and each family's delight in their child's accomplishment was palpable. From my observations, girls and boys alike were equally engaged in all aspects of the festival—reading, writing, and performing.

FIGURE 9
Bulletin Board Display of Student Poetry

Conclusion: What's Gender Got to Do With It?

Several key findings about gender and reading resulted from this study. First, no reading skill differences were found between the men and women; regardless of gender, these striving readers read avidly about a topic in their area of interest—a result that supports the Interest-Based Model of Reading. However, differences were found in their favorite topics and genres, which followed traditional gender patterns. Women tended to prefer fiction, whereas men tended to prefer nonfiction. Yet there were many exceptions; women such as Ellen Corduan read lots of nonfiction, particularly U.S. Civil War history books; on the other hand, men such as S. Charles Bean read lots of poetry. Consequently, we cannot assume that boys necessarily will be drawn to nonfiction or that girls will be drawn to fiction; rather, each child's reading desires should be considered individually.

A second result was that men and women in this study showed similar personality traits, namely, persistence and empathy, which were central to the core self-concept of two thirds of these striving readers, males and females alike. This result indicates the need for parents and teachers to emphasize persistence and nurture it in students. In addition, it is important to encourage both males and females to pursue fields in which empathy is an asset (e.g., education, psychology, social work, and medicine).

Third, mentors were important regardless of gender—a result that also supports the Interest-Based Model of Reading. However, there were significant gender differences in mentoring: Boys overall had twice as many mentors as girls—beginning in middle school and extending into adulthood. This was the case at home, at school, and in the workplace.

Fourth, this study found that scientifically oriented striving readers were told not to take courses in science, mathematics, or technology. Seven women and one man were explicitly steered away from taking these courses. One explanation given was that their lagging reading skills would prevent them from succeeding, especially in science. The fact that women had this experience more often than men raises questions about why Susan Brown and Maureen Selig were discouraged from pursuing science. Was it because of their difficulties with reading? Was it because of stereotypical notions of masculinity and femininity? Was it due to a combination of myths about striving readers as well as gender myths? These questions remain a challenge for future studies. However, it was disturbing to learn that most of the striving readers in this study gave up on their dreams of becoming scientists (see chapter 3 for details about one of the exceptions, Roy Daniels).

Finally, there were different assumptions and higher expectations for boys than for girls based on traditional gender frameworks. This was the case both at home and at school. However, Florence Haseltine and Sylvia Law were both resisters and did not fit neatly into a traditional female framework. Both were among the highest achievers in the group of successful women who struggled with reading; their writings have been cited nationally and internationally. While resisting traditional feminine expectations, they developed a strong sense of themselves as change agents—individuals whose actions influence not only their own life circumstances, but also the circumstances of the world around them.

Many of the findings about gender and reading raise difficult questions for educators and families. First, how can we engage boys and girls in reading through their preferred interests and genres without promoting gender stereotypes? Second, how can we dissuade boys from believing that reading is mainly a "girl thing"? Third, how can we expand both boys' and girls' views about gender to include more flexible, imaginative views, both of literacy and life? These are important questions raised by this study. I hope that further research will provide more complete answers to these intriguing questions. In the meantime, some answers to these questions may lie in the ways in which we approach reading. A student's gender conceptualization and world knowledge can be expanded through alternative teaching approaches that focus both on text choices *and how texts are read and discussed.*

This study emphasizes the importance of helping each boy and each girl choose the right book—one that matches the student's reading interest, level, and desire. But in addition to finding "just right" books, we also need to create new ways to discuss books. By asking new kinds of questions and discussing literature differently, we can help both boys and girls to consider fulfilling new ways to imagine themselves and their own life possibilities.

Books on Topics of Kids' Concerns

Adapted from Lesesne, T.S. (2004, May). Matching adolescents to books. Presentation at the annual convention of the International Reading Association, Reno, NV.

Absent Father

Trueman, T. (2004). *Cruise control*. New York: HarperTempest. In this engaging story, a boy who is a talented basketball player copes with feelings of anger and helplessness due to two difficult problems: a father who deserted the family and a brother who is dysfunctional due to severe cerebral palsy.

Abuse

Jones, P. (2004). *Things change*. New York: Walker. This is a riveting story about a teenage girl (apparently a perfect student and obedient daughter) and her relationship with an exciting, new, fun-to-be-with boyfriend—who eventually becomes abusive. The novel deals with the widespread reality of dating violence by presenting a balanced view of the abuser as a sympathetic character. The tension mounts as the girl struggles first to keep, then to free herself of, her abusive boyfriend as she simultaneously wrestles with her changing relationships with her parents and her best friend.

Adoption

Yansky, B. (2003). *My road trip to the pretty girl capital of the world*. Chicago: Cricket Books. This story is about a boy who makes plans to travel to meet his birth parents. Taking his father's car, he heads toward Texas, picking up an interesting array of characters along the way: a man who claims to be Elvis, two bums, and an abused young wife. Each of his experiences increases the suspense as he searches for his birth parents.

Death of a Parent

Cook, K. (1997). *What girls learn: A novel*. New York: Pantheon. This book deals with the silencing of girls. It is a coming-of-age novel about a stepfamily and an adolescent girl whose mother has terminal cancer. The poignant story is a page turner that addresses family relationships and difficult subjects (e.g., menstruation, sexuality, cancer, divorce, family secrets, sexual abuse, and death).

Divorce

Appelt, K. (2004). *My father's summers: A daughter's memoirs*. New York: Henry Holt. This series of prose poems focuses on issues of divorce and remarriage and its effects on the author. The author tells personal stories and reflects on her life growing up in Houston, Texas, from the age of 11 to the age of 18 (and beyond).

Lion, M. (2004). *Swollen*. New York: Wendy Lamb. This book is about divorce and a young girl's complex feelings about the pregnancy of her father's new girlfriend.

Feelings and Friendship

Bendell, N. (2002). *The feelings book: The care and keeping of your emotions*. Middleton, WI: American Girl, LLC. This book explores a wide range of feelings that kids face—joy, sadness, anger, stress, excitement, and fear. In addition, it offers tips and advice for dealing with these complex emotions.

Criswell, P.K. (2003). *A smart girl's guide to friendship troubles: Dealing with fights, being left out, and the whole popularity thing*. Middleton, WI: American Girl, LLC. This book explores when and how to speak up without hurting a friend's feelings, how to resolve conflicts and make up after an argument with a friend, what to do if your friend deserts you for the popular crowd, and so forth.

Kidnapping/Mystery

Cooney, C.B. (1994). *The face on the milk carton*. New York: Bantam Books. This is a page turner about kidnapping, adoption, parents, siblings, and identity. The story is unforgettable and difficult to put down due to the author's vivid descriptions and dialogue. This is the first in a series of realistic sagas that begin with Janie's mysterious recognition of herself: The face of the missing child on the milk carton is hers!

Cooney, C.B. (1995). *Whatever happened to Janie?* New York: Bantam Books. In this sequel to *The Face on the Milk Carton*, the love and needs of two different families—the Johnsons and the Springs—compete as Janie's saga continues.

Rape

Sebold, A. (1999). *Lucky*. New York: Scribner. This fascinating book tells a fast-paced story that provides psychological insight into how a rape affects not only the youngster who is victimized, but her entire family and all of their relationships. A page turner, this book is a compelling commentary on gender issues today.

Sexuality and Adolescence

Blackstone, M., & Guest, E.H. (2000). *Girl stuff: A survival guide to growing up*. Orlando, FL: Harcourt. This excellent guide is chock-full of insights, advice, and important information about adolescence in its many aspects. For example, the book addresses questions such as, How can I resist sexual pressure? What makes a good friend? How do I know whom to trust? What percentage of the population is gay?

Fenwich, E., & Walker, R. (1994). *How sex works: A clear, comprehensive guide for teenagers to emotional, physical, and sexual maturity*. New York: Dorling Kindersley. This book deals with the physical and emotional changes of puberty, relationships, sexual feelings and intercourse, sexually transmitted diseases, pregnancy and parenthood, sexual abuse, sexual harassment, and rape.

Mayle, P. (1975). *What's happening to me?* Don Mills, ON: Musson. This is a guide to puberty for boys and girls. Written in an entertaining, reader-friendly style, the book uses humor and rich language to teach about "bumpy chests," "getting hairy," changing voices, erections, periods, pimples, wet dreams, masturbation, and more.

Mayle, P. (1973). *Where did I come from?* Don Mills, ON: Musson. This gem of a book tells the facts of life through lively text and humorous cartoon illustrations. It teaches not only what happens physically during sex, but also what happens emotionally. The book communicates in a funny, warm, nonpreachy way that love and deep personal relationships are key aspects of sexual relationships.

Same-Sex Relationships

Levithan, D. (2003). *Boy meets boy*. New York: Alfred A. Knopf. This story deals with the complexities of a romantic relationship between two teenage boys.

Schizophrenia

Myers, A. (2000). *Ethan between us*. New York: Walker. Ethan is a talented pianist who imagines that he received his musical training from a long-dead 19th-century composer. This story about Ethan, a gorgeous boy who is easy to talk to, deals with schizophrenia, truth, and friendship. When the truth about Ethan is revealed, friendship emerges as the key theme of the novel.

Trueman, T. (2003). *Inside out*. New York: HarperTempest. This story revolves around events surrounding a robbery by two teenage boys. It is told from the perspective of a boy with schizophrenia, who eventually is held hostage by the boys who committed the crime.

School Shootings

Prose, F. (2003). *After*. New York: HarperCollins. This riveting book deals with students grieving. In the aftermath of a nearby school shooting, a grief counselor comes to Central High School and enacts harsh measures. Students who fail to comply mysteriously seem to disappear.

Serial Killing

McNamee, G. (2003). *Acceleration*. New York: Wendy Lamb. This compelling story is about a 17-year-old boy named Duncan. He has a summer job working in the Lost and Found of the Toronto Transit Authority. One day he discovers a serial killer's diary in the subway and sets out to find the killer.

Suicide

Mack, T. (2003). *Birdland*. New York: Scholastic. This book deals with a tongue-tied 14-year-old boy named Jed, who struggles to understand his older brother Zeke's suicide. During his Christmas break from school, Jed films a documentary about his neighborhood in the East Village in New York City. Jed is continually reminded of his brother, who was an aspiring poet.

Runyon, B. (2004). *The burn journals*. New York: Alfred A. Knopf. This book tells the vivid true story of the author's failed suicide attempt at the age of 14, when he set himself on fire. Runyon shares his feelings and experiences during his recovery, which included painful skin grafting, rehabilitation, psychotherapy, and the struggle to have a normal life.

War

Ahmedi, F., with Ansary, T. (2005). *The story of my life: An Afghan girl on the other side of the sky*. New York: Simon Spotlight Entertainment. This is a fast-paced, first-person memoir of a girl who loses her leg when a mine explodes. It recounts the experiences of an Afghan girl's coming of age amidst the chaos of war. Set initially in Afghanistan, the action moves to Germany and the United States, where the girl and her mother begin a new life in a new culture. This riveting book was voted America's #1 story of 2005 in a contest on ABC's *Good Morning America*. It is an inspiring 21st-century American immigrant story rich with details about the Taliban and Afghanistan.

Kids' Books on Sexism, Heterosexism, and Racism

Adapted from Moffat, L. (2004, May). **Boys and girls in the reading club: Conversations about gender and reading in an urban elementary school.** *Poster presentation at the 49th Annual Convention of the International Reading Association, Reno, NV.*

Sexism

Bridges, S.Y. (2002). *Ruby's wish*. San Francisco: Chronicle Books. This story is set in China. At a time when few girls are taught to read or write, Ruby dreams of going to the university with her brothers and her male cousins.

Browne, A. (2001). *Piggybook*. St. Paul: Minnesota Humanities Commission. This story is about Mrs. Piggott, who unexpectedly leaves her family. The result is that her demanding family begins to realize how much she did for them.

McCully, E. (1998). *Beautiful warrior: The legend of the Nun's kung fu*. New York: Arthur A. Levine. This legend is about two unlikely kung fu masters whose skill in martial arts ultimately helps to save their lives.

U'ren, A. (2001). *Pugdog*. New York: Farrar Straus Giroux. This story is about a boy named Mike who discovers, to his surprise, that his rough-and-tumble puppy is a female. He tries to make her into a dainty dog.

Zolotow, C. (1972). *William's doll*. New York: Harper & Row. This is the story of William, who wants a doll very badly. When his father gives him a basketball and a train, William still wishes to have a doll.

Heterosexism

de Haan, L., & Nijland, S. (2002). *King and King*. Berkeley, CA: Tricycle Press. In this story, a queen insists that a prince get married and take on the responsibilities of being king. However, as the search for a suitable mate is conducted, the search does not turn out as expected.

de Haan, L., & Nijland, S. (2004). *King and King and family*. Berkeley, CA: Tricycle Press. In this story, King Lee and King Bertie take a honeymoon trip to the jungle and bring home an unexpected surprise.

Elwin, R., & Paulse, M. (1990). *Asha's mums*. Toronto, ON: Women's Press. This is a story about Asha on her school field trip. Asha has two mothers in her family, and as the plot unfolds, the developing relationship between Asha and her two moms is explored.

Newman, L. (2000). *Heather has two mommies*. Boston: Alyson Wonderland. This is the story of Heather, who feels bad when she goes to her playgroup, because she has two mommies but no dad. However, she eventually stops feeling bad when she learns that what matters most of all in any family is that all of the people love one another.

Simon, N. (2003). *All families are special*. Norton Grove, IL: A. Whitman & Company. In this story, the students in Mrs. Mack's class describe their own families—big or small, living together or apart, with two moms or no mom. In the end they learn why all families are special regardless of where they are or who is in them.

Skutch, R. (1995). *Who's in a family?* Berkeley, CA: Tricycle Press. This book is all about families and tells a story that shows what is most important in any family.

Willhoite, M. (1990). *Daddy's roommate*. Boston, MA: Alyson Wonderland. This story tells about a young boy and his father. They discuss the divorced father's new home in which he and his gay roommate share meals and chores—playing, laughing, loving, and living together.

Racism

Gaikesheyongai, S. (2004). *The seven fires: An Ojibway prophecy*. Toronto, ON: Sister Vision Press. In this legend, seven prophets come to Anishinabe at a time of peace. They foreshadow the future in seven prophecies about elders and young people, light-skinned and dark-skinned people, who live together but are divided by distrust, misunderstanding, and fear. The prophecies are handed down from one generation to the next, until finally the story is retold differently—ending this time by telling how it is possible for people of all races to live together in peace.

Hamanakas, S. (1994). *All the colors of the Earth*. New York: Morrow Junior Books. This book is written in verse. It reveals that, despite numerous outward differences, children everywhere are essentially similar—all children are lovable.

Hoffman, M. (1991). *Amazing Grace*. New York: Dial Books for Young Readers. This is the story of Grace, who is told by a classmate that she cannot play the part of Peter Pan in the school play. Why? Because she is black. However, Grace discovers that she can do anything she wants to do if she is determined enough.

Katz, K. (1999). *The colors of us*. New York: Henry Holt. This book is about the richness of human variation and diversity; it is specifically about various skin colors, various foods, and diverse things found in nature. The story is told through the eyes of 7-year-old Lena and her mother, who together observe the wide variations in the color of their own friends' skin.

Keshig-Tobias, L. (1991). *Bird talk*. Toronto, ON: Sister Vision Press. This is a story about the feelings of a young Native American girl whose classmates tease her because she is different.

Littlechild, G. (1993). *This land is my land*. Emeryville, CA: Children's Book Press. This book is about a Native American boy who grew up in Canada. Using both the text and his own paintings, the author describes the experiences of the Indians of North America in general, as well as his own personal experiences growing up as a Plains Cree Indian boy in Canada.

Books on Teaching Writing

Allan, K.K., & Miller, M.S. (2005). *Literacy and learning in the content areas: Strategies for middle and secondary school teachers* (2nd ed.). Boston, MA: Houghton Mifflin.

Anderson, C. (2000). *How's it going? A practical guide to conferring with student writers.* Portsmouth, NH: Heinemann.

Buss, K., & McClain-Ruelle, L. (Eds.). (2000). *Creating a classroom newspaper.* Newark, DE: International Reading Association.

Calkins, L.M. (1994). *The art of teaching writing.* Portsmouth, NH: Heinemann.

Culham, R. (2003). *6 + 1 Traits of writing.* New York: Scholastic.

Davis, J., & Hill, S. (2003). *The no-nonsense guide to teaching writing.* Portsmouth, NH: Heinemann.

Fletcher, R. (2004). *Poetry matters: Writing a poem from the inside out.* South Hadley, MA: Arrowpoint.

Fletcher, R., & Portalupi, J. (2001). *Writing workshop: The essential guide.* Portsmouth, NH: Heinemann.

Graves, D.H. (1994). *A fresh look at writing.* Portsmouth, NH: Heinemann.

Haven, K. (2004). *Get it write! Creating lifelong writers from expository to narrative.* New York: Teacher Ideas Press.

Heard, G. (1989). *For the good of the earth and sun: Teaching poetry.* Portsmouth, NH: Heinemann.

Heard, G. (1999). *Awakening the heart: Exploring poetry in elementary and middle school.* Portsmouth, NH: Heinemann.

Indrisano, R., & Paratore, J.R. (Eds.). (2005). *Learning to write, writing to learn: Theory and research in practice.* Newark, DE: International Reading Association.

Lane, B. (1993). *After the end: Teaching and learning creative revision.* Portsmouth, NH: Heinemann.

McClure, A.A., & Kristo, J.V. (Eds.). (1994). *Inviting children's responses to literature.* Urbana, IL: National Council of Teachers of English.

Noyce, R.M., & Christie, J.F. (1989). *Integrating reading and writing instruction in grades K–8.* Boston: Allyn & Bacon.

Peregoy, S., & Boyle, O. (2005). *Reading, writing, and learning in ESL* (4th ed.). Boston: Allyn & Bacon.

Robb, L. (2003). *Brighten up boring beginnings and other quick writing lessons.* New York: Scholastic.

Robb, L. (2004). *Nonfiction writing from the inside out: Writing lessons inspired by conversations with leading authors.* New York: Scholastic.

Robb, L. (2005). *Making revision matter: Strategies for guiding students to focus, organize, and strengthen their writing independently.* New York: Scholastic.

Tompkins, G.E. (1994). *Teaching writing: Balancing process and product* (2nd ed.). New York: Macmillan College.

Poetry for Boys and Girls

Bernier-Grand, C. (2004). *Cesar: Si, se puede!/Yes, we can!* New York: Marshall Cavendish.

Curtis, C. (2004). *I took the moon for a walk.* Cambridge, MA: Barefoot Books.

Fleishman, P. (1988). *Joyful noise: Poems for two voices.* New York: Harper & Row.

Fletcher, R. (2001). *Relatively speaking: Poems about family.* New York: Orchard Books.

Frost, H. (2004). *Spring through the universe: A novel in poems from Room 214.* New York: Farrar Straus Giroux.

Grandits, J. (2004). *Technically it's not my fault: Concrete poems*. New York: Clarion Books.

Grimes, N. (2003). *Bronx masquerade*. New York: Dial.

Hopkins, L.B. (1999). *Lives: Poems about famous Americans*. New York: HarperCollins.

Medina, T. (2002). *Love to Langston*. New York: Lee & Low.

Mora, P. (2000). *My own true name: New and selected poems for young adults*. Houston, TX: Arte Publico.

Nelson, M. (2001). *Carver: A life in poems*. New York: Front Street.

Nye, N.S. (2002). *19 varieties of gazelle: Poems of the Middle East*. New York: Greenwillow.

Panzer, N. (Ed.). (1994). *Celebrate America in poetry and art*. New York: Hyperion Books for Children.

Pollock, P. (2001). *When the moon is full: A lunar year*. New York: Little Brown.

Sword, E.H. (Ed.). (1995). *A child's anthology of poetry*. New York: HarperCollins.

Whitman, W. (1993). *Leaves of grass*. New York: Modern Library.

Williams, V.B. (2001). *Amber was brave, Essie was smart*. New York: Greenwillow.

ADDITIONAL RESOURCES

CHAPTER 5

Identifying
Striving Readers

H ow can teachers identify students at risk for reading problems as early
as possible? We know that early identification followed by early intervention instruction is effective for preventing reading failure (Flippo,
1997; Foorman et al., 1997; Torgesen, 2004). So teachers need to know

how to identify at-risk children as early as possible in order to intercept problems before they become compounded. In addition, teachers also need to know how to spot older students with reading problems. Fortunately, reading researchers have found effective approaches for identifying striving readers at all ages and stages of development, K–adult (Torgesen, Rashotte, Alexander, Alexander, & MacPhee, 2003).

Predicting Early Reading Difficulties

Several factors predict early reading difficulties effectively. In a kindergarten study, Ritchey (2004) reported correlations among three unique predictors:

1. The child's knowledge of initial literacy skills.
2. The child's rapid automatized naming, or RAN, ability—the ability to name letters quickly and automatically.
3. The child's school behavior.

These three categories of predictors are useful for identifying preschool- and elementary-age children with reading difficulties. Teachers can take several steps to consider whether a child is experiencing early reading difficulties. First, note the child's skill level on each literacy task; then, consider how the child's current literacy skills fit with or deviate from the norm. Second, in light of research showing that slow reading speed is a key indicator of the most severe reading difficulties (Fink, 1998a, 1998b; Wolf & Katzir-Cohen, 2001; Wolf & Obregon, 1997), observe the length of time it takes the child to complete each literacy task accurately. Observe, for example, whether the child takes an inordinate length of time to name letters, read words and sentences, read and comprehend a passage, and so forth. Third, evaluate the child's behavior. The following questions are useful as a behavioral guide:

- While listening to a story, does the child focus attention appropriately?
- How attentive is the child during reading and writing activities?
- Does the child frequently "act out" or play the role of class clown?

In addition to this behavioral framework, look for other indicators that are often, *but not always*, associated with early reading difficulties (Shaywitz, 2003):

- Delay in speaking (e.g., not speaking in phrases until approximately 2 years old or later).

- Pronunciation problems (e.g., idiosyncratic pronunciation past 5 or 6 years old).

- Word retrieval problems (e.g., difficulty finding or expressing the precise word; using a similar-sounding word instead).

- Poor alphabet knowledge (e.g., weak letter recognition).

- Difficulty discerning phonemes (e.g., trouble distinguishing and associating specific sounds with specific letters or groups of letters).

- Insensitivity to rhyme (e.g., difficulty learning nursery rhymes).

- Family history of reading difficulties.

Although no single observation or factor alone is sufficient to conclude that a child is at risk for reading problems, when taken together, these factors point to the likelihood of early reading difficulties.

Looking for Specific Indicators

Teachers, reading specialists, tutors, and parents should look for specific indicators whenever a reading difficulty is suspected. It is important to distinguish between the myths that surround reading problems versus the realities. For example, letter and word reversals do not necessarily indicate that a child will struggle with reading. In reality, many children—skilled readers as well as those who struggle—go through a normative developmental period when they reverse letters that look alike (but differ in orientation and directionality). These include letters such as *b*, *d*, *p*, and *q*. In addition, children may reverse words that look alike (but differ in letter position), such as *was* and *saw*. Typically, this normative developmental period extends from about age 3 or 4 to about age 7 or 8.

What factors are indicative of reading problems beyond the earliest years? There are three main types of problems typical of older striving readers. Based on my own teaching experience, as well as mounting research evidence (Shaywitz, 2003; Snow & Strucker, 2000), the following indicators are characteristic of older striving readers from the intermediate grades through adulthood:

1. Lack of sufficient internal vocabulary (insufficient number of words stored in memory).

2. Inability to read with fluency—that is, accurately, quickly, smoothly, and with appropriate expression, intonation, and comprehension.

3. Difficulty understanding and remembering text content.

Any one of these problems represents cause for concern, especially beyond the third grade. Taken together, these three indicators suggest that a student is striving to learn to read but having trouble.

Whenever teachers or parents suspect a reading problem, they should take preventive action immediately. If there is any doubt that a young child is at risk for reading difficulties, it is better to err on the side of overidentification rather than overlook a problem that could be dealt with easily and effectively if caught early. Moreover, parents and teachers who find that an older student is struggling with reading should take immediate action. A lot can be done to reverse reading difficulties in adolescence and adulthood. Despite myths to the contrary, research on adolescents and adults has, in fact, shown that it is never too late to overcome a reading problem (Allen, 1995; Fink, 1995/1996, 1998a, 1998b, 2002, 2004a, 2004b; Rawson, 1968, 1995; Reiff, Gerber, & Ginsberg, 1997).

Using Appropriate Assessments

Appropriate assessment instruments can help to identify and analyze reading difficulties at all ages and stages. The key to successful assessment lies first in selecting appropriate assessment instruments, then using them wisely.

Recently, teacher-administered assessments have been developed to measure early reading abilities in a variety of areas: letter knowledge, letter–sound association, phonemic awareness, syllable decoding, passage-reading fluency, and passage-retelling ability. Some popular K–3 assessments, such as the Dynamic Indicators of Basic Early Literacy Skills (DIBELS), include computerized programs to simplify the management of assessment data (Good & Kaminski, 2002; Wireless Generation, 2004).

Some of these instruments appear to be adequate for assessing phonological skills but may be less effective for assessing the complex skills of reading comprehension and metacognition. Furthermore, these instruments may not be sufficient for diagnosing and assessing the child with the most profound reading difficulties. This caveat indicates how important it is for teachers to make referrals to the school reading specialist when in doubt about an individual child.

A reading specialist is likely to administer several diagnostic assessments, including informal reading inventories (IRIs), qualitative reading inventories (QRIs), and diagnostic reading assessments (DRAs). These instruments have several advantages. First, they are administered individually and can determine both the level and type of instruction likely to be most beneficial for each student. Second, they provide estimates of each student's independent reading level, instructional reading level, and frustration reading level. Detailed knowledge of each of these levels makes planning instruction easier and more effective:

- The independent level is the level at which a student reads independently without teacher assistance with nearly perfect oral reading and comprehension (oral reading accuracy = 99% or more correct; comprehension accuracy = 90% or more correct).

- The instructional level is the level at which a student profits most from teacher-directed instruction (oral reading accuracy = 95–98% correct; comprehension accuracy = 75–89% or higher).

- The frustration level is the level at which reading materials are too difficult for a student to succeed with ease (oral reading accuracy = 90% or less correct; comprehension accuracy = 50% or less correct).

Another advantage of many informal instruments is that they span the developmental trajectory, K–adult, so they are effective for use at all levels, including elementary school, middle school, high school, and above. Many of them offer a balanced approach to assessment through equivalent emphasis on basic decoding skills and the complex skills of comprehension and metacognition.

Teachers can create their own IRIs, QRIs, and DRAs, but this is very time-consuming. Fortunately, there are several effective instruments available commercially. One widely used assessment is the Qualitative Reading Inventory–III (Leslie & Caldwell, 2001). This instrument attends to factors such as the reader's prior knowledge, the text structure (narrative or informational), and the mode of comprehension (oral or silent). Another example is the Informal Reading-Thinking Inventory (Manzo, Manzo, & McKenna, 1995), which takes into account the reader's prior knowledge, engagement with literacy tasks, and metacognitive abilities.

For help with implementing a well-balanced approach to assessment and instruction, I recommend *Reading Assessment and Instruction: A Qualitative*

Approach to Diagnosis (Flippo, 1997). This excellent book contains numerous checklists and forms that enable thorough, concise record keeping. It also suggests specific types of questions to help teachers conduct informal qualitative assessments on their own (see sample assessment questions in Table 12). Careful consideration of each of these questions is time-consuming yet extremely worthwhile. The questions can help teachers gain valuable insights that enhance in-depth assessment of each student's reading strengths and needs. These insights then provide key information—information useful for planning effective instruction.

During the assessment process, teachers should try to observe students and engage them in a dialogue about their own literacy processes. Observations and dialogues should focus not only on phonological decoding, word identification, and literal comprehension skills but also on critical and inferential comprehension and metacognition. Through observation, discussion, and questioning, the teacher can assess each student's evolving literacy skills, attitudes, interests, and strategies, then tailor instruction accordingly. The best instruction uses new information from periodic formal and informal assessments to guide each student's literacy program.

TABLE 12
Sample Questions for Qualitative Reading Assessment

1. Can the student give reasons to support his or her answers to comprehension questions?
2. What follow-up procedures does the student use to facilitate comprehension?
3. To what extent is the student aware of his or her metacognitive strategies for comprehension monitoring?
4. When the student realizes that comprehension is momentarily lagging, how effective is the student in going back to the text to find relevant information?
5. What strategies does the student use to regain understanding?
6. How well does the student use information from the text to support answers?
7. Does the student use general impressions or specific excerpts from the text?
8. Does the student understand the connotation of specific words as they are used in particular contexts?
9. Does the student use prior knowledge to support answers?
10. Does the student consider whether or not the author substantiates claims?
11. To what extent do the student's personal feelings about the topic influence responses, and is the student aware of the effect of his or her own feelings and perspectives on the interpretation?

Adapted from Flippo, R.F. (1997). *Reading assessment and instruction: A qualitative approach to diagnosis*. Fort Worth, TX: Harcourt Brace.

Conclusion: Good News About Engagement and Test Scores

Teaching the next generation of readers is a challenging task. We can succeed in this task by involving students in decisions about their own learning. After assessing their reading skills, we should enlist students to help locate materials that reflect their interests as well as their instructional levels. Through their interests, students become more deeply engaged in reading, which leads them to read more and more and become increasingly skilled. The good news from research is that reader engagement leads to better outcomes in all respects—including higher scores on state-mandated tests (Guthrie, 2004).

Having high expectations for students is important, but how will we know whether students have met our expectations? How can their reading achievement be assessed accurately? Standards-driven accountability through testing is one way, and I am not arguing against testing; however, a single test score alone should *never* be used as the sole indicator of satisfactory performance. Ongoing formal and informal assessments should also be used—and used in equal measure. Otherwise, students who struggle will continue to be left behind, and talented striving readers such as Baruj Benacerraf, Florence Haseltine, and others in this book will likely be overlooked. The stories of resilience and success in this study tell us that we *can* do a better job of identifying, assessing, and teaching students who struggle. With our help, striving readers really can succeed.

Conclusions
and Implications

The striving readers in this book told poignant tales of struggles and frustrations—struggles that resulted in resilience and success. Their odysseys provide critical insights into the learning process of striving readers who overcame their reading difficulties, eventually becoming highly skilled readers. Results from their cases led to the Interest-Based Model of Reading, which has five components: (1) a passionate, personal interest that spurs sustained reading; (2) avid, topic-specific reading; (3) deep schema knowledge; (4) contextual reading strategies; and (5) mentoring support. Each element of the model has specific implications, as does each result of the study. What are the main results and implications?

Passionate, Personal Interests and Intrinsic Motivation

First, when it comes to teaching, the power of a reader's passionate, personal interest cannot be overstated. Interest is a generative force for all kinds of learning, especially learning to read. A child who is curious about a topic of personal interest has intrinsic motivation to pursue reading because reading offers a route into learning about the topic. Research shows that this type of intrinsic motivation, driven by internal curiosity, is the most powerful kind of motivation—far more powerful and long-lasting than external motivators such as grades or prizes (Deci, 1992; Ryan & Deci, 2000; Schiefele, 1992). Internal motivation driven by personal curiosity is a powerful force that teachers and parents can use to propel learning forward. We know that a young child's curiosity about the world is boundless; all children have an innate curiosity and desire to learn. (Just observe a toddler exploring the intricacies of a single leaf from a tree!) We need to harness each child's natural curiosity in an effort to inspire reading. To accomplish this we should use alluring, enticing texts. The personal relevance of reading materials for each student provides the key to that student's success.

The Power of a Familiar Schema

A second result was that the power of a familiar schema is key for promoting deep comprehension. This finding, too, has important teaching implications. A key result from this study was that these striving readers ultimately became highly skilled readers—albeit three to four years later than their peers. How did they learn to read? Through schema familiarity based on avid reading about a favorite topic or genre. Schema familiarity provided the scaffolds that enabled them to develop increasingly higher levels of reading skills. This connection between schema familiarity and progress in reading opens the door to a new understanding of how children who struggle can learn to read not only at a basic level but also at a very high level.

Nonlinear Developmental Pathways and Balanced Teaching

Third, results of the reading tests revealed other important findings: Two thirds of these individuals never mastered spelling, and one third of them did not master spelling or other phonological decoding skills. Yet, they all became skilled readers—scoring at the highest levels in silent reading comprehension and vocabulary. Many followed nonlinear developmental pathways in which phonological decoding skills, visual-graphic skills, and semantic skills were only partially integrated.

Results from this study agree with other research that shows that not all children learn to read in the same way, and not all follow a traditional pathway in which the components of reading are highly integrated and seamless (Fink, in press; Fischer & Knight, 1990; Mascolo et al., 2002). What does this mean for teaching? A large body of research has established that most children benefit from structured lessons in systematic phonics and other language skills (Adams, 1990; Hall & Moats, 1999; Moats, 2000; Pressley, 1998; Snow et al., 1998; Torgesen, 2004; Torgesen et al., 2003). Yet, according to the results of this study, different children may benefit to differing degrees. Despite years of instruction in systematic language lessons, one third of the men and women in this study remained weak in phonological decoding skills. Nevertheless, they became excellent text comprehenders. This result suggests that, while phonological decoding ability is very important, it does not in itself ensure reading success—nor does it preclude reading strategies from developing. Therefore, phonics should be taught systematically and explicitly; phonics should not be discarded. However, other approaches should accompany the teaching of phonics and be given equal time. And, other approaches should be included from the very beginning—in kindergarten and the primary grades. We need to offer truly balanced teaching, which means providing equal time for solid skills instruction and rich experiences with authentic texts. Otherwise, some children will continue to be left behind—forever marginalized "on the outside looking in" (Purcell-Gates, 1991).

Time for Silent Reading

The striving readers in this study read a lot on their own—silently. Many elementary classrooms emphasize oral reading, which is an important skill. However, we should not overlook the importance of silent reading. Silent reading is essential for developing reading fluency and self-esteem. Children quickly learn by observation that the adults around them read silently (not orally) most of the time. How many adults do you know who read aloud regularly once their children are independent readers? Probably not many. What this means for practice is that we should plan sufficient time each day for silent reading practice, both at home and at school.

A New Notion: Content Area–Dependent Fluency

One surprising new result from this study was the discovery that reading speed and fluency can be highly sensitive and variable depending on the content area, topic, and genre. For some students, fluency is content area dependent and may remain noticeably lower in a less familiar content area, or domain. This was clearly the case for Roy Daniels, who showed evidence of differentiated reading ability in science and math compared to English and history. Daniels reads different types of texts with variable ease or difficulty. Even today, his fluency depends on the text and its interest to him, and its structure, familiarity, concepts, and vocabulary. This finding of differentiated reading ability in different content areas extends Stanovich's (1986) notion of Matthew effects to a within-the-individual analysis: The more a student reads in one content area, the "richer" or better he or she becomes reading in that domain.

Daniels's content area–dependent fluency raises a new question: Should the concept of fluency be expanded to embrace a more flexible concept similar to the way that Gardner (1983) expanded the notion of intelligence to a more dynamic theory that includes multiple intelligences? Perhaps there are multiple fluencies. A more flexible, intra-individual notion of fluency might help us to understand how students read personally appealing texts with more ease and skill than other texts. Fluency may not be simple, unidimensional, or static; rather, it may turn out to be a more complex, dynamic phenomenon that varies with the domain. More research is needed to explore this intriguing possibility further.

Marvelous Mentors and Policy

According to this study, the role of mentors cannot be overemphasized. The striving readers in this book attribute much of their success to support from dedicated mentors at school—teachers who took a special interest in them. Clearly, supportive mentors are crucial if striving readers are to succeed. But excellent mentoring requires extra time for teachers and specialists to spend with each student. And more time implies low student–teacher ratios, which leads inevitably to funding issues. We know that additional money alone will not teach a child to read; however, only with adequate funding can we provide the small classes in which mentoring has a chance to develop and thrive.

Psychologists Robert Brooks and Samuel Goldstein (Brooks, 2001; Brooks & Goldstein, 2001) say that each child needs at least one charismatic adult who connects, encourages, and believes in the promise of that child's talents and strengths. For a good mentor to emerge for each student, small classes are a necessity. Small classes enable rich human connections to take root and grow; in contrast, overcrowded classes inhibit deep connections from being forged.

Even with superb mentors, it took Nobel laureate Baruj Benacerraf 10 years to become proficient in English reading. Like him, most English-language learners take at least 5 to 7 years—or longer—to learn academic literacy. This reality is frequently overlooked when we adhere to outmoded deficit models that view language and cultural differences as problems instead of assets. Benacerraf's experience suggests just the opposite: Linguistic and cultural diversity are assets that educators can use to spur students' development of strong English reading. The case of Benacerraf and other case studies in this book lead to a powerful conclusion: Diversity can provide rich schematic background on which to build literacy. This suggests that we need flexible policies that encourage teachers to integrate reading materials from each student's culture of origin.

The Power of Play and Hands-On Activities

Another implication of the study relates to the role of play in learning to read. Roy Daniels "played" at science, conducting his own experiments in his basement at home. Susan Brown created her own scripts, enacting dramas of her own design. Researchers know that these kinds of play experiences are crucial for young children's cognitive development and that rich play experiences promote the development of background information that promotes literacy (Daiute, 1989; Daiute & Morse, 1993). Creative play activities help children build rich background knowledge and exploratory habits of mind. These, in turn, form the cornerstone, the very foundation, on which strong reading is built. But policies that mandate highly prescriptive programs in preschool, kindergarten, and the primary grades preclude play from the curriculum. Consequently, children's innate curiosity is curtailed, and spontaneous, "playful" reading development is cut short.

Rich play experiences from grade school to high school were pivotal to the striving readers in this book, helping them gradually to develop high reading levels. Playful activities involving the arts and sciences helped support their increasingly sophisticated reading and writing. What this means for policy is clear: We need to integrate reading lessons with multiple forms of the arts and sciences for students at all ages and stages of development. To meet each student's learning needs, we should encourage all forms of activity-based learning—experiments, demonstrations, field trips, song, dance, choral reading, Readers Theatre, drama, poetry, story writing and storytelling, drawing, painting, and working with clay. We should not abandon holistic approaches such as these for one-size-fits-all prescripted methods. There is no "magic wand" for reading instruction; different children learn to read in a variety of ways. Consequently, teachers must be prepared with a variety of strategies in order to meet the needs of all learners.

Hands-on, activities-based approaches are crucial for teaching in the expanding information economy in the United States, where curiosity, inquiry, and alternative ways of problem solving are highly valued. Policies that fail to emphasize these higher level thinking aspects of reading are counterproductive. The reason why is apparent: Not only will our children be ill-equipped to compete globally, but they will be deprived of the richness and thrill of creative inquiry.

Conclusion: Striving Readers CAN Succeed!

The high expectations of marvelous mentors helped the striving readers in this study to succeed at top levels—becoming leaders, thinkers, and writers in extremely demanding professions. Many became famous in their fields. The policy implications here are clear: Parents, teachers, administrators, and policymakers should have high expectations for all students. All students need the opportunity to learn a solid body of knowledge and engage in the critical thinking habits that lead to creative work.

Throughout the study of these inspiring men and women, I was struck by how deeply engaged they were in their reading. And I was struck by their profound emotions about their learning experiences. Apparently, learning to read in our highly literate society is a developmental process fraught with emotion. Teaching reading is not only about finding "the right" cognitive methods, but also about matters of the heart—passion, a burning desire to know, a tender bond between a teacher and a student.

The stories of these remarkably successful men and women send a resounding and powerful message: Striving readers *can* learn to read well, even if they learn differently from others. But success doesn't come easily; teaching reading and learning to read present enormous challenges to everyone involved. I hope that this book helps teachers, parents, and others to instill in each student the belief, "I CAN succeed; I can do it, too!"

Background and Design of the Study

This appendix reviews the literature on striving readers and traces the design of my study, which included 66 successful adults who were striving readers from across the United States.

What We Know About Teaching Striving Readers

Researchers have long recommended specific approaches for teaching reading to students who struggle, namely, highly structured, systematic methods that entail step-by-step lessons in specific language knowledge and skills (Adams, 1990; Chall, 1983; Cox, 1983; Hall & Moats, 1999; Knight, 1986; Moats, 2000; Tallal, 2000; Torgesen, 2004; Wilson, 1992). Highly structured approaches, sometimes called systematic or explicit phonics, are often emphasized in the early grades until students demonstrate mastery of phonological decoding and other basic skills. However, highly structured methods have also been used successfully with older children and adults (Greene, 1996, 2002; Torgesen et al., 2003; Wilson, 1992). Consequently, Catone and Brady (2005) have suggested that structured, systematic instruction may be needed for older students more frequently than was previously thought.

Many researchers recommend balancing explicit skills instruction with opportunities for students to practice reading authentic, meaningful texts. This means that in addition to teaching specific skills and subskills systematically, teachers should also provide a variety of good books and sufficient time for students to read them (Chall, 1983, 1996; Flippo, 1998; Guthrie, 2004; Guthrie & Alvermann, 1999; Guthrie & Wigfield, 1997; Hinchman, Alvermann, Boyd, Brozo, & Vacca, 2003/2004; Roller, 1996; Snow et al., 1998; Vail, 1991; Weaver, 1998; Wilson, 1992).

In addition, multisensory methods are also highly recommended, especially for teaching reading to students who struggle. Multisensory methods entail simultaneous instruction in the use and association of three sensory channels—visual, auditory, and kinesthetic/motoric. The rationale for multisensory instruction is that each sensory input provides additional reinforcement that many students need in order to develop mastery. Several widely used multisensory programs are available commercially, including the Orton-Gillingham Approach (Orton Dyslexia Society Research Committee, 1994), Language! (Greene, 2002), the Wilson Reading System (1992), and Starting Over (Knight, 2002).

In addition to these approaches, audio- and videotapes, books on tape, and computer-assisted programs have been used effectively with striving readers. Assistive technology and media have two primary goals for readers who struggle: (1) remediation in the student's areas of deficit and (2) provision of alternative means of access to subject matter content (Brooks, 1995; Meyer & Rose, 1998; Tallal, 2000; Wood, 2004).

A large body of research attests to the effectiveness of these approaches with young children. Moreover, research on striving readers beyond the third grade has been growing steadily. Best practices for teaching striving middle school and adolescent students is receiving increasing attention among reading researchers and teachers (Cassidy & Cassidy, 2004/2005; Catone & Brady, 2005; McCormack & Paratore, 2003; Moore, Alvermann, & Hinchman, 2000; Roller, 1996). There is also increasing interest in adults who struggle with reading yet ultimately succeed. Several studies reveal that some struggling readers show resilience and eventually achieve spectacular success, both in literacy and in life (Bruck, 1990; Fink, 1992, 1993, 1995/1996, 1998a, 1998b, 2000a, 2000b, 2002, 2003a, 2003b, in press; Gottfredson, Finucci, & Childs, 1983; Lefly & Pennington, 1991; Rawson, 1968; Vogel & Reder, 1998; Vogel, Vogel, Sharoni, & Dahan, 2003).

What contributes to the resilience of these readers? What strategies do they use to overcome their reading difficulties? These questions were the driving force behind the study described in this book.

In designing this study, I did not set out to focus on the role of students' interests in developing reading skills; in fact, none of the initial questions focused on interest. However, my study ended by doing just that because individual interest emerged from the data as a powerful and unexpected result that could not be ignored. In 1913, Dewey studied the powerful role of personal interest in promoting all kinds of learning. Since then, others have found that the influence of interest is "particularly salient when students are in the process of developing their reading skills" (e.g., Renninger, 1992, p. 391; cf. Alexander, 2002). In a recent study, Reeves (2004) concluded that students require above all else "something that is interesting" in developing reading skills (p. 240).

Identifying Participants for the Study

To conduct the study for this book, I interviewed and tested men and women from across the United States who had struggled with severe reading difficulties yet became highly successful, both as readers and as professionals. All but one individual gave me permission to use his or her real name in the hope of inspiring others who have trouble learning to read.

I used professional referrals and distributed notices at professional conferences in order to select the 66 striving readers who participated in the study. Prospective participants were screened in preliminary telephone interviews for exclusionary criteria, such as a history of inadequate schooling or poor vision. Their profiles of language-based difficulties were recorded and analyzed based on retrospective face-to-face interviews conducted individually with each participant. A case history was taken that included a family history of reading struggles and a personal history of diagnosis and special assistance for reading difficulties. Data from interviews, questionnaires, and reading and psychological assessments were used to identify common themes.

The study compared reading development in two groups of highly successful adults: one group was successful and had struggled with reading, whereas the other group (the comparison group) was equally successful but had not struggled. Equal numbers of males and females were included in an effort to move away from the tendency of previous research to focus disproportionately on boys and men (Fink, 1998a, 1998b, 2000a, 2000b, 2003a; Shaywitz, Towle, Keese, & Shaywitz, 1990; Vogel, 1990; Vogel & Walsh, 1987).

I made a conscious attempt to identify individuals who had struggled with reading yet succeeded in a wide array of careers that require extensive reading.

Therefore, the sample was not random but rather was selected based on the following factors: level of educational and career achievement, field of expertise, gender, age, and socioeconomic level. Participants were considered "successful" (1) if they demonstrated professional competence recognized by peers in an area of expertise that requires sophisticated reading and demands extensive training, skill, and responsibility and (2) if they supported themselves financially.

Defining Striving Readers

The choice of selection criteria met two definitions of striving readers: (1) the International Dyslexia Association (IDA) research definition of dyslexia, and (2) the Responsiveness to Intervention (RTI) definition of a striving reader. The IDA definition (Orton Dyslexia Society Research Committee, 1994), which is being considered for modification, maintains the classic notion of an "unexpected" reading problem or "discrepancy" between the person's potential (often measured by the Full Scale IQ) and his or her actual reading achievement (often measured by standardized diagnostic reading assessments) (Clark, 2003; Gresham, 2001; Keogh, Torgesen, & Chapman, 2004; Lyon, Shaywitz, & Shaywitz, 2003). The IDA conceptualizes a striving reader as demonstrating unexpected

> difficulties in single word decoding, usually reflecting insufficient phonological processing abilities...manifest by variable difficulty with different forms of language, often including, in addition to problems reading, a conspicuous problem with acquiring proficiency in writing and spelling. (p. 4)

The RTI definition (Gresham, 2002) identifies students as striving readers "if their academic performances in relevant areas do not change in response to a validated intervention implemented with integrity" (pp. 480–481). In my study, all 66 participants in the group of striving readers had failed to respond to validated interventions in reading, and had had difficulties learning to decode single words and/or learn adequate reading and spelling skills through at least the third grade. Participants in my study between age 26 and 50 had been diagnosed with reading difficulties by reading specialists using established assessment instruments; for those older than 50, educated when documentation was less common, a case history of early and continuing difficulties in reading unfamiliar words, spelling, and writing constituted the "diagnostic signature" of a striving reader (Shaywitz, Fletcher, & Shaywitz, 1994, p. 7). Men and women in the study described in this book were matched for types and severity of reading problems and concomitant traits, as shown in Table A1.

TABLE A1
Self-Reported Problems of Successful Striving Readers*

Problem**	Males	Females	Total***
Single word decoding	29	30	59
Spelling	30	29	59
Discrepancy	26	27	53
Diagnosis/remediation	25	25	50
Letter identification	23	23	46
Writing	25	24	49
Slow reading and/or writing	28	26	54
Memory	26	26	52
Laterality (left-right distinction)	16	22	38
Second language	27	28	55
Fine motor (i.e., illegible handwriting)	19	17	36
Familial dyslexia	22	26	48

*Mean number of problems per participant:

	Males	Females
Mean # of problems (SD)	9.9 (1.3)	10.0 (1.3)
Range	6–12	8–12

**There were no significant differences between males and females (t = 0.30, p = .767).

***Data not available for b participants.

Age, Class, and Achievements of Participants

Research suggests that self-report of childhood reading difficulties by adults is both valid and reliable (Decker, Vogler, & DeFries, 1989; Finucci et al., 1984; Gilger, 1992; Lefly, 1997; Lefly & Pennington, 2000). Moreover, accuracy and reliability are higher for middle-aged, normal-achieving, or high-achieving individuals (Gilger, 1992). All participants in the study described in this book were high achievers, and most were middle-aged. The mean age of the striving readers was 45 (range = 26–75); the mean age of the comparison group was 51 (range = 33–62). Males and females were matched for age.

Many participants in this study were outstanding professionals in the top echelons of their fields. Despite their reading difficulties, all participants except one had graduated from four-year colleges or universities. (One individual had attended but did not complete college.) Of the readers who struggled, 6 earned medical degrees, 18 doctoral degrees, 4 law degrees, 21 master's degrees, and 17 bachelor's degrees.

The matched comparison group included individuals who had not struggled with reading but were high achievers comparable to the striving readers. Due to limited resources, the comparison group was limited to 5 men and 5 women. Of the participants in the comparison group, 1 earned a medical degree, 5 doctoral degrees, 1 law degree, and 3 master's degrees. Like those who had struggled, participants in the comparison group also succeeded in fields that demand sophisticated, complex reading skills.

Diversity of Participants

The majority of participants were white, middle-class citizens from all regions of the United States, including 18 states and the District of Columbia. Most participants had been raised in middle to upper middle class families, although a few came from working class origins. A small number of African Americans and Hispanics participated, but their numbers were not proportionately representative of minorities in the U.S. population. An attempt was made to locate more members of minorities; however, finding them proved difficult, presumably because minorities are still not proportionately successful in our society due to ongoing discrimination (Gadsden, 1991; Ladson-Billings, 1994). Participants earned salaries that indicated middle to high socioeconomic status.

Procedures and Instruments Used in the Study

I conducted detailed, face-to-face interviews (3–9 hours each) with each individual. Interviews were guided by interview questions conducted in a semi-structured, open-ended format, shown in Table A2.

Carol Gilligan's clinical interview methodology was used—an approach in which the interviewing researcher follows not only her own research agenda and prepared questions, but also the agenda, needs, questions, language patterns, and cues of the interview subject (Attanucci, 1988). In keeping with Gilligan's approach, I encouraged the men and women to diverge from my questions, follow their own tangents, and tell their stories in their own words (Attanucci, 1988).

Whenever possible, interviews took place in the naturalistic setting of each person's home or workplace, where participants recollected their reading and learning history in a developmental framework, school grade by school grade,

TABLE A2
Learning Interview Schedule

1. As a child having trouble learning to read, as a student later on, and as an adult with dyslexia today, what special learning strategies have you used to help with reading, studying, and professional tasks? I'm very interested in finding out what learning strategies or tricks you developed that stand out for you as having been particularly useful.

2. Tell me about your struggles, obstacles you faced, and learning strategies that worked for you that you feel led to your present success.

3. What is your earliest memory of learning differently from other children?

4. Tell me about preschool (if you attended), kindergarten, and elementary school.

5. What tasks were particularly difficult for you in elementary school, and what specific strategies did you use to master skills such as reading? Writing? Spelling? Learning multiplication tables? Others?

6. How did your early teachers respond to your learning difficulties?

7. Tell me about your family. How did your parents respond to your learning problems?

8. When you were in elementary school, how did other children react to your learning problems?

9. Tell me about your struggles during adolescence. What schools did you attend? Do any courses stand out as having been particularly troublesome?

10. What specific learning strategies did you use to get through English class, social studies, math, science, foreign language?

11. What special services, if any, did you receive during school?

12. What were your experiences with IQ tests and achievement tests? With SATs and GREs?

13. Tell me about your relationships with your parents, teachers, and other students during middle school and high school. How did you feel about yourself during this period?

14. Were there people who were particularly helpful to you? Tell me about them.

15. Tell me how you decided to go to college. Why did you decide to go? Was it expected in your family? How did you choose your college? What was the application process like for you? Did teachers encourage you or discourage you? Tell me about it.

16. What were your experiences getting through all the required (and other) courses in college? What specific learning strategies did you use during college?

17. Why did you decide to go to graduate school? How did you get through the required courses? Were there particular courses or exams that stand out as having been stumbling blocks? How did you get through them?

18. What particular strategies do you use in your work as a professional today?

19. What, if any, differences do you think you would have experienced if you had had the same talents and abilities and the same reading struggles but been of a different gender?

Adapted from Fink, R.P. (1995/1996). Successful dyslexics: A constructivist study of passionate interest reading. *Journal of Adolescent & Adult Reading, 39*(4), 270.

content area by content area. Typical questions included, "What is your earliest memory of learning differently from other children?" and "What specific strategies did you use for reading, writing, spelling, multiplication tables, history, science, and so forth, in first grade, second grade, etc.?" Care was taken to avoid asking questions in a manner likely to influence responses.

Each interview was audiotaped and transcribed in its entirety by a trained transcriber in order to preserve rich descriptive detail and ensure accuracy. Interview transcripts were coded according to multiple dimensions of cognitive and affective development, including experiences of humiliation and frustration in learning, experiences of jubilation and joy in learning, topic(s) and type(s) of first books read, ages and circumstances of early memories of reading, and relationships with key people.

To check for reliability, data were coded and analyzed by two independent psychologists trained at the Harvard Graduate School of Education. Transcripts were analyzed for topics and genres of self-selected reading and ages of basic fluency development. Intercoder reliability for the topic/genre variable was 90%; intercoder reliability for the age variable was 100%.

To verify interview information, additional biographical data were collected from various sources. These included a detailed curriculum vita from each participant; diagnostic, school, and clinical reports, when available; information from parents and spouses, when available; information from public sources such as *Who's Who in America*; and journal articles, book chapters, full-length books, and works of art created by each participant.

Reading and Psychological Measures and Assessments Used in the Study

I individually administered formal and informal tests and assessments (see Table A3). The same assessments were administered to individuals who had struggled with reading and individuals in the comparison group.

The Adult Reading History Questionnaire

The Adult Reading History Questionnaire (ARHQ) was administered to assess the severity of each individual's reading difficulties and gain further insight into each participant's reading development, habits, and attitudes (Lefly, 1997; Lefly & Pennington, 2000). The ARHQ is highly correlated with adult diagnostic criteria in Pennington's familial dyslexic sample ($r = .61-.73$; $p < .001$) (Lefly &

TABLE A3
Reading Assessments

1. The Diagnostic Assessments of Reading With Trial Teaching Strategies (DARTTS) (Roswell & Chall, 1992). This is an untimed, nationally normed instrument that spans beginning through advanced reading levels (ceiling = 12th grade) and assesses a person's relative strengths and weaknesses in reading. It was selected to help ascertain whether each participant's reading profile was "jagged" or smooth.

2. The Nelson-Denny Reading Test of Vocabulary, Reading Comprehension, and Reading Rate, Form H (ND) (Brown, Fishco, & Hanna, 1993). This is a college-level reading test that measures reading ability through postgraduate levels. It is a timed, nationally normed test designed to provide an objective ranking of student ability in vocabulary development, silent reading comprehension, and reading rate.

3. The Pig Latin Test (adapted from Lefly, 1997). This informal instrument contains 48 items administered in an untimed format. It assesses awareness of phonemic elements and the ability to manipulate phonemes and syllables, along with other phonological skills.

4. The Florida Nonsense Passages (adapted from Gross-Glenn, Jallad, Novoa, Helgreen-Lempesis, & Lubs, 1990). This is an informal instrument that entails reading nonsense words embedded in otherwise meaningful paragraphs. It assesses decoding, oral reading speed, and oral reading accuracy.

5. The Graded Nonword Reading and Spelling Test (Snowling et al., 1996). This is an untimed measure of the ability to read and spell novel letter strings. Initially designed for use with children, it is considered suitable for adults who struggle with reading.

Pennington, 2000). Lefly and Pennington used a cutoff point of .30 to indicate the presence of reading difficulties. In this study, all of the striving readers had ARHQ scores above .30, indicating that they had experienced severe reading difficulties (Mean = .60, SD = .09, range = .38–.82).

Self-in-Relationship Interview Protocol

Monsour's (1985) self-in-relationship interview protocol was individually administered to each participant. This instrument analyzes the individual's core self-concept (Calverley, Fischer, & Ayoub, 1994; Fischer & Kennedy, 1997). In using this protocol, the individual first constructs a brief self-portrait by naming five key personal traits of personality, behavior, and character. Next, the individual produces five terms that describe the self in relation to important people (such as the mother, father, romantic partner, friend, colleague, etc.). Finally, the individual selects five adjectives from the previously produced list that reflect the enduring self, the "real me, the core me, the lasting self."

Guiding Questions of the Study

The following questions guided the study:

1. How, when in development, and under what conditions do highly successful professionals who struggled with reading develop reading skills?

2. What reading levels do they ultimately achieve?

3. Do they continue to show jagged profiles of reading strengths and weaknesses? If so, are there any discernible patterns in their profiles?

4. How do the reading profiles of striving readers compare with those of a matched comparison group?

5. Do the experiences of males and females who struggle with reading differ? If so, what are the differences?

6. What behaviors and characteristics should teachers look for to help identify striving readers in their classrooms?

7. What instructional methods, materials, and strategies are helpful for teachers to use with striving readers with differing interests at different ages?

8. What are the implications of the results of this study for theory; research; home, classroom, and clinical practice; and administrative and policy decisions?

REFERENCES

Adams, M. (1990). *Beginning to read: Thinking and learning about print*. Cambridge, MA: The MIT Press.

Alexander, P. (2002, December). *Profiling the developing reader: The interplay of knowledge, interest, and strategic processing*. Paper presented at the annual meeting of the National Reading Conference, Miami, FL.

Allen, J. (1995). *It's never too late: Leading adolescents to lifelong literacy*. Portsmouth, NH: Heinemann.

American Association of University Women (AAUW). (1992). *How schools shortchange girls: A study of the major findings of girls and education*. Washington, DC: AAUW Educational Foundation.

Attanucci, J. (1988). In whose terms: A new perspective on self, role, and relationship. In C. Gilligan, J.V. Ward, & J.M. Taylor (Eds.), *Mapping the moral domain: A contribution of women's thinking to psychological theory and education* (pp. 201–224). Cambridge, MA: Harvard University Press.

Bean, R.M. (2004). *The reading specialist: Leadership for the classroom, school, and community*. New York: Guilford.

Best, D.L., Williams, J.E., Cloud, J.M., Davis, S., Robertson, L., Edwards, J., et al. (1977). Development of sex-trait stereotypes among young children in the United States, England, and Ireland. *Child Development, 48*, 1375–1384.

Blackburn, M.V. (2003). Boys and literacies: What difference does gender make? *Reading Research Quarterly, 38*(2), 276–287.

Bond, G.L., & Dykstra, R. (1997). The cooperative research program in first-grade reading instruction. *Reading Research Quarterly, 32*(4), 348–427. (Original work published 1967)

Brooks, H.M. (1995). *Uphill all the way: Case study of a nonvocal child's acquisition of literacy*. Unpublished doctoral dissertation, Harvard Graduate School of Education, Cambridge, MA.

Brooks, R.B. (2001). Fostering motivation, hope, and resilience in children with learning disorders. *Annals of Dyslexia, 51*, 9–20.

Brooks, R.B., & Goldstein, S. (2001). *Raising resilient children*. Chicago: Contemporary Books.

Brown, J.I., Fishco, V.V., & Hanna, G. (1993). *Nelson-Denny Reading Test, Form H*. Chicago: Riverside.

Brozo, W.G. (2002). *To be a boy, to be a reader: Engaging teen and preteen boys in active literacy*. Newark, DE: International Reading Association.

Brozo, W.G., Walter, P., & Placker, T. (2002). "I know the difference between a real man and a TV man": A critical exploration of violence and masculinity through literature in a junior high school in the 'hood. *Journal of Adolescent & Adult Literacy, 45*, 530–538.

Bruck, M. (1990). Word-recognition skills of adults with childhood diagnoses of dyslexia. *Developmental Psychology, 26*(3), 439–454.

Burns, P.C., Roe, B.D., & Ross, E.P. (1992). *Teaching reading in today's elementary schools* (5th ed.). Boston: Houghton Mifflin.

Calverley, R.M., Fischer, K.W., & Ayoub, C. (1994). Complex splitting of self-representation in sexually abused adolescent girls. *Development and Psychopathology, 6*, 195–213.

Camp, D. (2000). It takes two: Teaching with twin texts of fact and fiction. *The Reading Teacher*, *53*(5), 400–408.

Carter, V.C., & Levy, G.D. (1988). Cognitive aspects of early sex role development: The influence of gender schemas on preschoolers' memories and preferences for sex-typed toys and activities. *Child Development*, *59*, 782–792.

Cassidy, J., & Cassidy, D. (2004/2005, December/January). What's hot, what's not for 2005. *Reading Today*, *22*(3), p. 1.

Catone, W.V., & Brady, S.A. (2005). The inadequacy of individual educational program (IEP) goals for high school students with word-level reading difficulties. *Annals of Dyslexia*, *55*(1), 53–78.

Chall, J.S. (1983). *Stages of reading development*. New York: McGraw-Hill.

Chall, J.S. (1994). Patterns of adult reading. *Learning Disabilities: A Multidisciplinary Journal*, *5*(1), 29–33.

Chall, J.S. (1996). *Stages of reading development* (2nd ed.). Fort Worth, TX: Harcourt Brace.

Clark, C.T. (2003). Examining the role of authoritative discourse in the labeling and unlabeling of a "learning disabled" college learner. *Journal of Adolescent & Adult Literacy*, *47*, 128–135.

Cohen, S. (2003). *The mysteries of Internet research*. Fort Atkinson, WI: Upstart Books.

Collier, V.P. (1992). A synthesis of studies examining long-term language minority student data on academic achievement. *Bilingual Research Journal*, *16*(1, 2), 187–212.

Coppola, J.M. (2004, January). *Teaching English language learners*. Presentation at the winter meeting of the Massachusetts Association of College and University Reading Educators, Framingham, MA.

Cox, A.R. (1983). Programming for teachers of dyslexics. *Annals of Dyslexia*, *33*, 221–233.

Csikszentmihalyi, M. (1991). Literacy and intrinsic motivation. In S.R. Graubard (Ed.), *Literacy: An overview by 14 experts* (pp. 115–140). New York: Hill and Wang.

Cummins, J. (1994). The acquisition of English as a second language. In K. Spangenberg-Urbschat & R. Pritchard (Eds.), *Kids come in all languages: Reading instruction for ESL students* (pp. 36–62). Newark, DE: International Reading Association.

Daiute, C. (1989). Play as thought: Thinking strategies of young writers. *Harvard Education Review*, *59*, 1–23.

Daiute, C. (1993). *The development of literacy through social interaction* (New Directions in Child Development Source Book). San Francisco: Jossey-Bass.

Daiute, C., & Morse, F. (1993). Access to knowledge and expression: Multimedia writing tools for children with diverse needs and strengths. *Journal of Special Education Technology*, *12*, 1–35.

Deci, E.L. (1992). The relation of interest to the motivation of behavior. In K.A. Renninger, S. Hidi, & A. Krapp (Eds.), *The role of interest in learning and development* (pp. 43–70). Hillsdale, NJ: Erlbaum.

Decker, S.N., Vogler, G.P., & DeFries, J.C. (1989). Validity of self-reported reading disabilities by parents of reading-disabled and control children. *Reading and Writing: An Interdisciplinary Journal*, *1*(4), 327–331.

Dewey, J. (1913). *Interest and effort in education*. Boston: Houghton Mifflin.

Dyson, A.H. (1997). *Writing superheroes: Contemporary childhood, popular culture, and classroom literacy*. New York: Teachers College.

Farstrup, A.E. (2005, January 28). Presentation at annual winter meeting of the Massachusetts Association of College and University Reading Educators, Framingham, MA.

Finders, M.J. (1997). *Just girls: Hidden literacies and life in junior high*. New York: Teachers College.

Fink, R.P. (1992). Successful dyslexics' alternative pathways for reading: A developmental study (Doctoral dissertation, Harvard University Graduate School of Education, 1992). *Dissertation Abstracts International*, F4965.

Fink, R.P. (1993). How successful dyslexics learn to read. *Teaching Thinking and Problem Solving, 15*(5), 1, 3–6.

Fink, R.P. (1995/1996). Successful dyslexics: A constructivist study of passionate interest reading. *Journal of Adolescent & Adult Literacy, 39*(4), 268–280.

Fink, R.P. (1998a). Literacy development in successful men and women with dyslexia. *Annals of Dyslexia, 48*, 311–346.

Fink, R.P. (1998b). Successful dyslexics: Studies of gender, interest, and literacy development. In L. Hoffman, A. Krapp, K.A. Renninger, & J. Baumert (Eds.), *Interest and learning: Proceedings of the Seon Conference on Interest and Gender* (pp. 402–407). Kiel, Germany: IPN - Leibniz Institute for Science Education at the University of Kiel.

Fink, R.P. (2000a). Gender and imagination: Gender conceptualization and literacy development in successful adults with reading disabilities. *Learning Disabilities: A Multidisciplinary Journal, 10*(3), 183–196.

Fink, R.P. (2000b). Gender, self-concept, and reading disabilities. *Thalamus, 18*(1), 15–33.

Fink, R.P. (2002). Successful careers: The secrets of adults with dyslexia. *Career Planning and Adult Development Journal, 18*(1), 118–135.

Fink, R.P. (2003a). Mastery of literacy and life: Individual interests and literacy development of successful adults with dyslexia. In S.A. Vogel, G. Vogel, V. Sharoni, & O. Dahan (Eds.), *Learning disabilities in higher education and beyond: An international perspective* (pp. 339–370). Timonium, MD: York Press.

Fink, R.P. (2003b). Reading comprehension struggles and successes: Case study of a leading scientist. *The Primer, 31*(2), 19–30.

Fink, R.P. (2004a, July). *Resilience and success: A surprising path to the National Academy of Sciences*. Paper presented at the 28th Annual Conference of the International Academy for Research in Learning Disabilities, Ann Arbor, MI.

Fink, R.P. (2004b, March). *Domain-dependent fluency: A reader's alternative pathway to the National Academy of Sciences*. Paper presented at the 35th Annual Conference of the Massachusetts Reading Association, Sturbridge, MA.

Fink, R.P. (in press). What successful adults with dyslexia teach us about children. In K.W. Fischer, J.H. Bernstein, & M.H. Immordino-Yang (Eds.), *Mind, brain, and education in reading disorders*. Cambridge, England: Cambridge University Press.

Finucci, J.M., Whitehouse, C.C., Isaacs, S.D., & Childs, B. (1984). Derivation and validation of a quantitative definition of specific reading disability for adults. *Developmental Medicine and Child Neurology, 26*, 143–153.

Fischer, K.W. (1980). A theory of cognitive development: The control and construction of hierarchies of skills. *Psychological Review, 87*, 477–531.

Fischer, K.W., & Biddell, T.R. (1992). Cognitive development in educational contexts: Implications of skill theory. In A. Demetriou, M. Shayer, & A. Efklides (Eds.), *Neo-Piagetian theories of cognitive development: Implications and applications for education* (pp. 9–30). London: Routledge.

Fischer, K.W., & Biddell, T.R. (1997). Dynamic development of psychological structures in action and thought. In R.M. Lerner (Ed.), *Handbook of child psychology: Vol. 1. Theoretical models of human development* (5th ed., pp. 467–561). New York: Wiley.

Fischer, K.W., Bullock, D.H., Rotenberg, E.J., & Raya, P. (1993). The dynamics of competence: How context contributes directly to skill. In R. Wozniak & K.W. Fischer (Eds.), *Development in context: Acting and thinking in specific environments* (Jean Piaget Society Series on Knowledge and Development, pp. 93–117). Hillsdale, NJ: Erlbaum.

Fischer, K.W., & Kennedy, B. (1997). Tools for analyzing the many shapes of development: The case of self-in-relationships in Korea. In E. Amsel & K.A. Renninger (Eds.), *Change and development: Issues of theory, method, and application* (pp. 117–152). Hillsdale, NJ: Erlbaum.

Fischer, K.W., & Knight, C.C. (1990). Cognitive development in real children: Levels and variations. In B. Presseisen (Ed.), *Learning and thinking styles: Classroom interaction* (pp. 43–67). Washington, DC: National Education Association.

Fischer, K.W., Knight, C.C., & Van Parys, M. (1993). Analyzing diversity in developmental pathways: Methods and concepts. In R. Case & W. Edelstein (Eds.), *The new structuralism in cognitive development: Theory and research on individual pathways* (Contributions to Human Development Vol. 23, pp. 33–56). Basel, Switzerland: S. Karger.

Flippo, R.F. (1997). *Reading assessment and instruction: A qualitative approach to diagnosis.* New York: Harcourt Brace.

Flippo, R.F. (1998). Points of agreement: A display of professional unity in our field. *The Reading Teacher, 52*(1), 30–40.

Flippo, R.F. (Ed.). (2001). *Reading researchers in search of common ground.* Newark, DE: International Reading Association.

Foorman, B.R., Francis, D.J., Beeler, T., Winikates, D., & Fletcher, J.M. (1997). Early interventions for children with reading problems: Study designs and preliminary findings. *Learning Disabilities: A Multidisciplinary Journal, 8,* 63–71.

Fountas, I.C., & Pinnell, G.S. (1999). *Matching books to readers: Using leveled books in guided reading, K–3.* Portsmouth, NH: Heinemann.

Fountas, I.C., & Pinnell, G.S. (2001). *Leveled books for readers, grades 3–6: A companion volume to guiding readers and writers.* Portsmouth, NH: Heinemann.

Gadsden, V. (Ed.). (1991). Literacy and the African-American learner: The struggle between access and denial. *Theory Into Practice, 31*(4) [Special edition].

Gardner, H. (1983). *Frames of mind: The theory of multiple intelligences.* New York: Basic Books.

Gardner, H. (1993). *Multiple intelligences: The theory in practice.* New York: Basic Books.

Gass, S.M., & Selinker, L. (2001). *Second language acquisition: An introductory course* (2nd ed.). Mahwah, NJ: Erlbaum.

Gerber, P.J., & Reiff, H.B. (1991). *Speaking for themselves: Ethnographic interviews with adults with learning disabilities.* Ann Arbor: University of Michigan.

Gilger, J.W. (1992). Using self-report and parental-report survey data to assess past and present academic achievement of adults and children. *Journal of Applied Developmental Psychology, 13,* 235–256.

Gilligan, C. (1993). *In a different voice: Psychological theory and women's development* (Reissue ed.). Cambridge, MA: Harvard University Press.

Good, R.H., & Kaminski, R.A. (Eds.). (2002). *Dynamic indicators of basic early literacy skills* (6th ed.). Eugene, OR: Institute for the Development of Educational Achievement.

Gottfredson, L., Finucci, J., & Childs, B. (1983). *The adult occupational success of dyslexic boys: A large-scale, long-term follow-up* (Report #34). Baltimore: Johns Hopkins University Press.

Graves, D.H. (1994). *A fresh look at writing.* Portsmouth, NH: Heinemann.

Gray, J.H. (1999, April). *"Maybe...She was a down-low girl": How young adolescent students construct understanding of online peers.* Paper presented at the Annual Meeting of the American Educational Research Association, Montreal, QC.

Gray, M.J., Haseltine, F., Love, S., & Mayzel, K. (1991). *The woman's guide to good health.* Yonkers, NY: Consumer Reports Books.

Greene, J.F. (1996). LANGUAGE! Effects of an individualized structured language curriculum for middle and high school students. *Annals of Dyslexia, 46,* 97–121.

Greene, J.F. (2002). *Language! A literacy intervention curriculum.* Longmont, CO: Sopris West.

Gresham, F.M. (2002). *Responsiveness to intervention: An alternative approach to the identification of learning disabilities.* In R. Bradley, L. Danielson, & D.P. Hallahan (Eds.), *Identification of learning disabilities research to practice* (pp. 467–521). Mahwah, NJ: Erlbaum.

Gross-Glenn, K., Jallad, B.J., Novoa, L., Helgreen-Lempesis, V., & Lubs, H.A. (1990). Nonsense passage reading as a diagnostic aid in the study of adult familial dyslexia. *Reading and Writing: An Interdisciplinary Journal, 2,* 161–173.

Guthrie, J.T. (2004, May). *Classroom practices promoting engagement and achievement in comprehension.* Paper presented at the Reading Research Conference of the International Reading Association, Reno, NV.

Guthrie, J.T., & Alvermann, D.E. (1999). *Engaged reading: Processes, practices, and policy implications.* New York: Teachers College Press.

Guthrie, J.T., & Wigfield, A. (1997). *Reading engagement: Motivating readers through integrated instruction.* Newark, DE: International Reading Association.

Guzzetti, B.J., Young, J.P., Gritsavage, M.M., Fyfe, L.M., & Hardenbrook, M. (2002). *Reading, writing, and talking gender in literacy learning.* Newark, DE: International Reading Association.

Hall, S.L., & Moats, L.C. (1999). *Straight talk about reading: How parents can make a difference in the early years.* Chicago: Contemporary Books.

Hardenbrook, M.D. (1997, December). *Influences on reading in the development of literacies: Examining literacy autobiographies across the sexes.* Paper presented at the annual meeting of the National Reading Conference, Scottsdale, AZ.

Harper, R., & Bean, T. (2004, May). *What's hot—and what should be hot—for the reading specialist.* Paper presented at Institute 11 of the annual convention of the International Reading Association, Reno, NV.

Hartman, D. (1997, October). *Doing things with texts: Mapping the textual practices of two African American high school students.* Paper presented at the fall meeting of the National Academy of Education Spencer Post-Doctoral Fellows' Retreat, Palo Alto, CA.

Haseltine, F., & Paulsen, C.A. (1994). *Reproductive issues and the aging male.* Washington, DC: American Association for the Advancement of Science.

Haseltine, F., & Yaw, Y. (1976). *Woman doctor.* New York: Ballantine Books.

Haugh, S.S., Hoffman, C.D., & Cowan, G. (1980). The eye of the very young beholder: Sex typing of infants by young children. *Child Development, 51,* 598–600.

Hinchman, K.A., Alvermann, D.E., Boyd, F.B., Brozo, W.G., & Vacca, R.T. (2003/2004). Supporting older students' in and out of school literacies. *Journal of Adolescent & Adult Literacy, 47*(4), 304–310.

Holland, D.C., & Eisenhart, M.A. (1990). *Educated in romance: Women, achievement, and college culture.* Chicago: University of Chicago Press.

Hudson, R.F., Lane, H.B., & Pullen, P.C. (2005). Reading fluency assessment and instruction: What, why, and how? *The Reading Teacher, 58*(8), 702–714.

International Reading Association (IRA). (2001). *Second-language literacy instruction* (Position statement). Newark, DE: Author.

International Reading Association (IRA). (2002). *Family-school partnerships: Essential elements of literacy instruction in the United States* (Position statement). Newark, DE: Author.

Ivey, G. (2004, May). *Meeting the needs of struggling readers.* Paper presented at the annual convention of the International Reading Association, Reno, NV.

Keogh, B., Torgesen, J.K., & Chapman, J.W. (2004, July). *Response-to-intervention as identification: Implications for the LD field.* Paper presented at the Annual Conference of the International Academy for Research in Learning Disabilities, Ann Arbor, MI.

Kindlon, D., & Thompson, M. (1999). *Raising Cain: Protecting the emotional life of boys.* New York: Ballantine Books.

Knight, J. (1986). The adult dyslexic in remediation: The ABCs and much more. *Churchill Forum, 8*, 1–4.

Knight, J. (2002). *Starting over: A combined teaching manual and student workbook for reading, writing, spelling, vocabulary, and handwriting.* Cambridge, MA: Educator's Publishing Service.

LaBerge, D., & Samuels, S.J. (1974). Toward a theory of automatic information processing in reading. *Cognitive Psychology, 6*, 293–323.

Ladson-Billings, G. (1994). *The dreamkeepers: Successful teachers of African American children.* San Francisco: Jossey-Bass.

Law, S.A. (1974). *Blue Cross: What went wrong?* New Haven, CT: Yale University Press.

Law, S.A. (1987). Family, gender, and sexuality: What the founding fathers had to say. *The Judges Journal, 22*.

Law, S.A. (1989). "Girls can't be plumbers"—Affirmative action for women in construction: Beyond goals and quotas. *Harvard Civil Rights–Civil Liberties Law Review, 24*(1).

Law, S.A., & Neuborne, B. (1973). *The rights of the poor.* New York: Sunrise Books.

Lees, S. (1986). *Losing out: Sexuality and adolescent girls.* London: Hutchinson.

Lefly, D.L. (1997). Risk status and phonological processing (Doctoral dissertation, University of Denver College of Education, 1997). *Dissertation Abstracts International.*

Lefly, D.L., & Pennington, B.F. (1991). Spelling errors and reading fluency in compensated adult dyslexics. *Annals of Dyslexia, 41*, 143–162.

Lefly, D.L., & Pennington, B.F. (2000). Reliability and validity of the Adult Reading History Questionnaire. *Journal of Learning Disabilities, 3*, 286–296.

Lelewer, N. (1994). *Something's not right: One family's struggle with learning disabilities.* Acton, MA: VanderWyk & Burnham.

Lesesne, T.S. (2003). *Making the match: The right book for the right reader at the right time, grades 4–12.* Portland, ME: Stenhouse.

Lesesne, T.S. (2004, May). *Matching adolescents to books*. Presentation at the annual convention of the International Reading Association, Reno, NV.

Leslie, L., & Caldwell, J. (2001). *Qualitative reading inventory, 3*. New York: Longman.

Leu, D.J., Leu, D.D., & Coiro, J. (2004). *Teaching with the Internet K–12: New literacies for new times* (4th ed.). Norwood, MA: Christopher-Gordon.

Li, X., & Zhang, M. (2004). Why Mei still cannot read and what can be done. *Journal of Adolescent & Adult Literacy, 48*(2), 92–101.

Lima, C.W., & Lima, J.A. (1993). *A to zoo: Subject access to children's picture books* (4th ed.). New Providence, NJ: Bowker.

Lorber, J. (1994). *Paradoxes of gender*. New Haven, CT: Yale University Press.

Lyon, G.R., Shaywitz, S.E., & Shaywitz, B.A. (2003). A definition of dyslexia. *Annals of Dyslexia, 53*, 1–22.

Manzo, A.V., Manzo, U.C., & McKenna, M.C. (1995). *The informal reading-thinking inventory: An informal reading inventory (IRI) with options for assessing additional elements of higher-order literacy*. Fort Worth, TX: Harcourt College.

Margalit, M. (2003). Resilience model among individuals with learning disabilities: Proximal and distal influences. *Learning Disabilities Research and Practice, 18*, 82–86.

Mascolo, M.F., Li, J., Fink, R., & Fischer, K.W. (2002). Pathways to excellence: Value presuppositions and the development of academic and affective skills in educational contexts. In M. Ferrari (Ed.), *The pursuit of excellence through education* (pp. 113–146). Mahwah, NJ: Erlbaum.

Maynard, T. (2002). *Boys and literacy: Exploring the issues*. London: RoutledgeFarmer.

McCormack, R.L., & Paratore, J.R. (Eds.). (2003). *After early intervention, then what? Teaching struggling readers in grades 3 and beyond*. Newark, DE: International Reading Association.

McKeown, M.G., & Curtis, M.E. (Eds.). (1987). *The nature of vocabulary acquisition*. Hillsdale, NJ: Erlbaum.

McLaughlin, M., & Allen, M.B. (2002). *Guided comprehension: A teaching model for grades 3–8*. Newark, DE: International Reading Association.

Meltzer, L. (2004). Resilience and learning disabilities: Research on internal and external protective dynamics. *Learning Disabilities Research and Practice, 19*, 1–2.

Meyer, A., & Rose, D.H. (1998). *Learning to read in the computer age*. Manchester, NH: Brookline Books.

Millard, E. (1997). Directly literate: Gender identity and the construction of the developing reader. *Gender and Education, 9*(1), 31–48.

Miller, M.S., & Allan, K.K. (1987). *Reading the newspaper: Middle level*. Providence, RI: Jamestown.

Miller, M.S., & Allan, K.K. (1989). *Reading the newspaper: Advanced level*. Providence, RI: Jamestown.

Moats, L.C. (2000). *Speech to print: Language essentials for teachers*. Baltimore: Paul H. Brookes.

Moffat, L. (2004, May). *Boys and girls in the reading club: Conversations about gender and reading in an urban elementary school*. Poster presentation at the 49th Annual Convention of the International Reading Association, Reno, NV.

Monsour, A.P. (1985). *The dynamics and structure of adolescent self-concept*. Unpublished doctoral dissertation, University of Denver, CO.

Moore, D.W., Alvermann, D.E., & Hinchmann, K.A. (Eds.). (2000). *Struggling adolescent readers: A collection of teaching strategies*. Newark, DE: International Reading Association.

National Council of Teachers of English (NCTE). (1998). *Guidelines for a gender-balanced curriculum in English*. Urbana, IL: Author.

National Institute of Child Health and Human Development (NICHD). (2000). *Report of the National Reading Panel. Teaching children to read: An evidence-based assessment of the scientific research literature on reading and its implications for reading instruction* (NIH Publication No. 00-4769). Washington, DC: U.S. Government Printing Office.

Odean, K. (1997). *Great books for girls: More than 600 books to inspire today's girls and tomorrow's women*. New York: Ballantine.

Odean, K. (1998). *Great books for boys: More than 600 books for boys 2 to 14*. New York: Ballantine.

Olson, S., & Loucks-Horsley, S. (2000). *Inquiry and the National Science Education Standards: A guide for teaching and learning*. Washington, DC: National Academy Press.

O'Malley, J.M., & Valdez-Pierce, L. (1996). *Authentic assessment for English language learners: Practical approaches for teachers*. Reading, MA: Addison-Wesley.

Orton Dyslexia Society Research Committee. (1994, Fall). Operational definition of dyslexia. *Perspectives, 20*(5), p. 4.

O'Shea, L.J., Sindelar, P.T., & O'Shea, D.J. (1985). The effects of repeated readings and attentional cues on reading fluency and comprehension. *Journal of Reading Behavior, 17*(2), 129–142.

Paratore, J.R. (2004, March). *Designing literacy instruction to optimize children's achievement: How should research evidence guide us?* Paper presented at the Leo F. Hanley Lecture, Massachusetts Reading Association Annual Conference, Sturbridge, MA.

Parr, J.M., & Maguiness, C. (2005). Removing the *silent* from SSR: Voluntary reading as social practice. *Journal of Adolescent & Adult Literacy, 49*(2), 98–107.

Pauk, W. (2000). *How to study in college*. Boston: Houghton Mifflin.

Piaget, J. (1952). *The origins of intelligence in children* (M. Cook, Trans.). New York: International Universities Press.

Pollack, W.S. (1998). *Real boys: Rescuing our sons from the myths of boyhood*. New York: Random House.

Pressley, M. (1998). *Reading instruction that works: The case for balanced teaching*. New York: Guilford.

Prosenjak, N. (1999, February). *Reading across the grain of gender*. Paper presented at the annual meeting of the Colorado Council of the International Reading Association, Denver, CO.

Purcell-Gates, V. (1991). On the outside looking in: A study of remedial readers' meaning-making while reading literature. *Journal of Reading Behavior, 23*, 235–253.

Radway, J. (1991). *Reading the romance: Women, patriarchy, and popular culture*. Chapel Hill: University of North Carolina Press.

Rasinski, T.V. (2003). *The fluent reader: Oral reading strategies for building word recognition, fluency, and comprehension*. New York: Scholastic.

Rawson, M.B. (1968). *Developmental language disability: Adult accomplishments of dyslexic boys*. Baltimore: Johns Hopkins University Press.

Rawson, M.B. (1995). *Dyslexia over the lifespan: A fifty-five-year longitudinal study*. Cambridge, MA: Educator's Publishing Service.

Recht, D.R., & Leslie, L. (1988). Effect of prior knowledge on good and poor readers' memory of text. *Journal of Educational Psychology, 80*(1), 16–20.

Reeves, A.R. (2004). *Adolescents talk about reading: Exploring resistance to and engagement with text*. Newark, DE: International Reading Association.

Reiff, H.B., Gerber, P.J., & Ginsberg, R. (1997). *Exceeding expectations: Highly successful adults with learning disabilities*. Austin, TX: Pro-Ed.

Renninger, K.A. (1992). Individual interest and development: Implications for theory and practice. In K.A. Renninger, S. Hidi, & A. Krapp (Eds.), *The role of interest in learning and development* (pp. 361–395). Hillsdale, NJ: Erlbaum.

Richek, M.A. (2005). Words are wonderful: Interactive, time-efficient strategies to teach meaning vocabulary. *The Reading Teacher, 58*(5), 414–423.

Ritchey, K.D. (2004). From letter names to word reading: The development of reading in kindergarten. *Reading Research Quarterly, 39*(4), 374–376.

Robinson, T.L., & Howard-Hamilton, M.F. (2000). *The convergence of race, ethnicity, and gender: Multiple identities in counseling*. Columbus, OH: Merrill.

Roller, C.M. (1996). *Variability not disability: Struggling readers in a workshop classroom*. Newark, DE: International Reading Association.

Rosenblatt, R.E., Law, S.A., & Rosenbaum, S. (1997). *Law and the American health care system*. Westbury, NY: Foundation Press.

Roswell, F.G., & Chall, J.S. (1992). *Diagnostic assessments of reading with trial teaching strategies*. Chicago: Riverside.

Rumelhart, D.E. (1980). Schemata: The building blocks of cognition. In R.J. Spiro, B.C. Bruce, & W.F. Brewer (Eds.), *Theoretical issues in reading comprehension* (pp. 33–58). Hillsdale, NJ: Erlbaum.

Ryan, R.M., & Deci, E.L. (2000). Intrinsic and extrinsic motivations: Classic definitions and new directions. *Contemporary Educational Psychology, 25*, 54–67.

Sadker, M., & Sadker, D. (1994). *Failing at fairness: How America's schools cheat girls*. New York: Scribner.

Samuels, S.J. (2002). Reading fluency: Its development and assessment. In A.E. Farstrup & S.J. Samuels (Eds.), *What research has to say about reading instruction* (3rd ed., pp. 166–183). Newark, DE: International Reading Association.

Saul, E., & Dieckman, D. (2005). Choosing and using information trade books. *Reading Research Quarterly, 40*(4), 502–513.

Schiefele, U. (1992). Topic interest and levels of text comprehension. In K.A. Renninger, S. Hidi, & A. Krapp (Eds.), *The role of interest in learning and development* (pp. 151–212). Hillsdale, NJ: Erlbaum.

Shaywitz, B.A., Fletcher, J.M., & Shaywitz, S.E. (1994). The conceptual framework for learning disabilities and attention-deficit/hyperactivity disorder. *Canadian Journal of Special Education, 9*(3–4), 1–32.

Shaywitz, S.E. (2003). *Overcoming dyslexia: A new and complete science-based program for reading problems at any level*. New York: Alfred A. Knopf.

Shaywitz, S.E., & Shaywitz, B.A. (2006). *Focus on basics: The neurobiology of reading and dyslexia*. Boston: National Center for the Study of Adult Learning and Literacy. Retrieved January 8, 2006, from http://www.ncsall.net/?id=278

Shaywitz, S.E., Towle, V., Keese, D., & Shaywitz, B.A. (1990). Prevalence of dyslexia in boys and girls in an epidemiologic sample. *Journal of the American Medical Association, 264*, 143–157.

Silvey, A. (2004). *100 best books for children*. Boston: Houghton Mifflin.

Simpson, E.B (1979). *Reversals: A personal account of victory over dyslexia*. Boston: Houghton Mifflin.

Snow, C.E., Burns, M.S., & Griffin, P. (Eds.). (1998). *Preventing reading difficulties in young children*. Washington, DC: National Academy Press.

Snow, C.E., & Strucker, J. (2000). Lessons from preventing reading difficulties in young children for adult learning and literacy. In J. Comings & B. Garner (Eds.), *Annual review of adult learning and literacy: A project of the National Center for the Study of Adult Learning and Literacy* (Vol. 1, pp. 25–73). San Francisco: Jossey-Bass.

Snowling, M.J., Stothard, S.E, & McLean, J.M. (1996). *Graded Nonword Reading Test*. Bury St. Edmunds, England: Thames Valley Test Company.

Stahl, K.D. (2005). Improving the asphalt of reading instruction: A tribute to the work of Steven A. Stahl. *The Reading Teacher, 59*(2), 184–192.

Stahl, S.A. (1999). *Vocabulary development*. Newton Upper Falls, MA: Brookline Books.

Stanovich, K.E. (1986). Matthew effects in reading: Some consequences of individual differences in the acquisition of literacy. *Reading Research Quarterly, 21*(4), 360–407.

Story-Huffman, R. (2002a). *Caldecott on the Net: Reading & Internet activities*. Fort Atkinson, WI: Upstart Books.

Story-Huffman, R. (2002b). *Newbery on the NET: Reading & Internet activities*. Fort Atkinson, WI: Upstart Books.

Tallal, P. (2000). The science of literacy: From the laboratory to the classroom. *Proceedings of the National Academy of Science, 97*(6), 2402–2404.

Thistle, L. (1995). *Dramatizing myths and tales: Creating plays for large groups*. Palo Alto, CA: Dale Seymour Publications.

Torgesen, J.K. (2004, July). *Preventative instruction for children with phonologically based reading disabilities: Results from three studies*. Presentation at the annual conference of the International Academy for Research in Learning Disabilities, Ann Arbor, MI.

Torgesen, J.K., Rashotte, C.A., Alexander, A., Alexander, J., & MacPhee, K. (2003). Progress towards understanding the instructional conditions necessary for remediating reading difficulties in older children. In B.R. Foorman (Ed.), *Preventing and remediating reading difficulties: Bringing science to scale* (pp. 275–298). Timonium, MD: York Press.

Torgesen, J.K., Wagner, R.K., & Rashotte, C.A. (1997). Prevention and remediation of severe reading disabilities: Keeping the end in mind. *Scientific Studies of Reading, 1*(3), 217–234.

Urberg, K.A. (1982). The development of concepts of masculinity and femininity in young children. *Sex Roles, 8*, 659–668.

Vail, P.L. (1991). *Common ground: Whole language and phonics working together*. Rosemont, NJ: Modern Learning Press.

Valdez-Pierce, L. (2003). *Assessing English language learners*. Washington, DC: National Education Association.

Vogel, S.A. (1990). Gender differences in intelligence, language, visual-motor abilities, and academic achievement in students with learning disabilities: A review of the literature. *Journal of Learning Disabilities, 23*(1), 44–52.

Vogel, S.A., & Reder, S. (1998). Literacy proficiency of adults with self-reported learning disabilities. In M.C. Smith (Ed.), *Literacy for the 21st century: Research, policy, practices, and the National Adult Literacy Survey* (pp. 159–171). Westport, CT: Praeger/Greenwood Press.

Vogel, S.A., Vogel, G., Sharoni, V., & Dahan, O. (Eds.). (2003). *Adults with learning disabilities in higher education and beyond: An international perspective.* Timonium, MD: York Press.

Vogel, S.A., & Walsh, P.C. (1987). Gender differences in cognitive abilities of learning-disabled females and males. *Annals of Dyslexia, 37,* 142–165.

Vygotsky, L.S. (1978). *Mind in society: The development of higher psychological processes* (M. Cole, V. John-Steiner, S. Scribner, & E. Souberman, Eds. & Trans.). Cambridge, MA: Harvard University Press. (Original work published 1934)

Watson, J.D. (1980). *The double helix: A personal account of the discovery of the structure of DNA.* New York: Atheneum. (Original work published 1968)

Weaver, C. (1998). Toward a balanced approach to reading. In C. Weaver (Ed.), *Reconsidering a balanced approach to reading* (pp. 11–65). Urbana, IL: National Council of Teachers of English.

West, T.G. (1991). *In the mind's eye: Visual thinkers, gifted people with learning difficulties, computer images, and the ironies of creativity.* Buffalo, NY: Prometheus Books.

Whitehead, F., & Maddren, W. (1974). *Children's reading interests* (Schools Council Working Paper No. 52). London: University of Sheffield Institute of Education, Schools Council Research Project into Children's Reading Habits.

Wilson, B.A. (1992). *Wilson Reading System.* Oxford, MA: Wilson Language Training.

Winner, E. (1996). *Gifted children: Myths and realities.* New York: Basic Books.

Wireless Generation. (2004). m class DIBELS software [Computer software]. New York: Author.

Wolf, M., & Katzir-Cohen, T. (2001). Reading fluency and its intervention. *Scientific Studies of Reading, 5*(3), 211–239.

Wolf, M., & Obregon, M. (1997). The "double deficit" hypothesis: Implications for diagnosis and practice in reading disabilities. In L. Putnam (Ed.), *Readings on language and literacy* (pp. 177–210). Cambridge, MA: Brookline Books.

Wood, J.M. (2004). *Literacy online: New tools for struggling readers and writers.* Portsmouth, NH: Heinemann.

Young, J.P. (2000). Boy talk: Critical literacies and masculinities. *Reading Research Quarterly, 35*(3), 312–337.

Literature Cited

Ahmedi, F., with Ansary, T. (2005). *The story of my life: An Afghan girl on the other side of the sky.* New York: Simon Spotlight Entertainment.

Aldana, P. (1996). *Jade and iron: Latin American tales from two cultures.* Toronto, ON: Groundwood Books/Douglas & McIntyre.

Balkwill, F., & Rolph, M. (2002a). *Gene machines.* New York: Cold Spring Harbor Laboratory Press.

Balkwill, F., & Rolph, M. (2002b). *Germ zappers.* New York: Cold Spring Harbor Laboratory Press.

Balkwill, F., & Rolph, M. (2002c). *Have a nice DNA.* New York: Cold Spring Harbor Laboratory Press.

Brody, L. (1989). *Cooking with memories: Recipes and recollections.* New York: Penguin.

Bett, B. (1997). *Planet ocean*. London: Portland Press.

Cook, K. (1997). *What girls learn: A novel*. New York: Pantheon.

Curie, E. (2001). *Madame Curie: A biography* (V. Sheean, Trans.). New York: DaCapo Press. (Original work published 1937)

Dahl, R. (1998). *Danny the champion of the world*. New York: Puffin.

Delacre, L. (1989). *Arroz con leche: Popular songs and rhymes from Latin America*. New York: Scholastic.

Delacre, L. (1990). *Las Navidades: Popular Christmas songs from Latin America*. New York: Scholastic.

Delacre, L. (1996). *Golden tales: Myths, legends, and folktales from Latin America*. New York: Scholastic.

Farndon, J. (2000). *The big book of the brain: All about the body's control center*. New York: Peter Bedrick Books.

Fink, J.N. (Ed.). (2000). *What's fair? What's just? What's the difference? Voices from the CityArts Kids for Justice Mural project*. New York: The Gorilla Press.

Fink, J.N. (in preparation). Danny the Champion of the World *project: Art, cars, dreams, and pheasants*. New York: The Gorilla Press.

Hintz, M. (1998). *Haiti* (Enchantment of the World). New York: Children's Press.

Keller, E.F. (1983). *A feeling for the organism: The life and work of Barbara McClintock*. San Francisco: W.H. Freeman.

Kohen, J. (1991). *Cultures of the world: Venezuela*. Freeport, NY: Marshall Cavendish.

MacLachlan, P. (1985). *Sarah, plain and tall*. New York: Harper and Row.

Myers, W.D. (1996). *Toussaint L'Ouverture: The fight for Haiti's freedom*. New York: Simon & Schuster Books for Young Readers.

Orozco, J. (1997). *Diez deditos: Ten little fingers & other play rhymes and action songs from Latin America*. New York: Dutton Children's Books.

Redmond, I. (2000). *Gorilla, monkey & ape* (Eyewitness Books). New York: Dorling Kindersley.

Rogers, L., & Rogers, B.R. (1999). *The Dominican Republic* (Enchantment of the World). New York: Children's Press.

Rose, S., & Lichtenfels, A. (1997). *Brainbox*. London: Portland Press.

Rosner, M. (2000). *Scientific American: Great science fair projects*. New York: Wiley.

Scieszka, J. (Ed.). (2005). *Guys write for guys read: Boys' favorite authors write about being BOYS!* New York: Viking.

Sharman, H. (1997). *The space place*. London: Portland Press.

Showers, P. (2004). *A drop of blood*. New York: Harper Trophy.

Torres, L. (2004). *El festival de cometas: The kite festival*. New York: Farrar Straus Giroux.

VanCleave, J. (2001). *Teaching the fun of science*. New York: Wiley.

Verheyden-Hilliard, M.E. (1985). *Scientist from Puerto Rico, Maria Cordero Hardy*. Bethesda, MD: The Equity Institute.

Walker, P.R. (1988). *Pride of Puerto Rico: The life of Roberto Clemente*. San Diego, CA: Harcourt.

Wiese, J. (2002). *Sports science: 40 goal-scoring, high-flying, medal-winning experiments for kids!* New York: John Wiley & Sons.

INDEX

Note. Page numbers followed by *f* and *t* indicate figures and tables, respectively.

DANIELS, ROY: accommodations used by, 76; alternative strategies used by, 75–76; content area–dependent fluency of, 79–80, 84, 138; current career of, 70; current reading ability of, 77; DAR interpretive profile of, 78f; disparate abilities of, 70–71; hands-on play activities of, 72, 82, 139; interest-based reading by, 71; reading development of, 79; schema familiarity of, 73; self-confidence of, 73–75; sociocultural support of, 72–73

DANNY THE CHAMPION OF THE WORLD (DAHL), 112–114

DANNY THE CHAMPION OF THE WORLD PROJECT (FINK), 114

DAR TEST, 78f

DARTTS. *See* Diagnostic Assessments of Reading With Trial Teaching Strategies

DAVIS, S., 94

DECI, E.L., 136

DECKER, S.N., 147

DEEM, GEORGE, 2

DeFRIES, J.C., 147

DEGREES OF READING POWER (DRP) SYSTEM, 20

DELACRE, L., 49, 52

DEWEY, J., 145

DIAGNOSTIC ASSESSMENTS OF READING WITH TRIAL TEACHING STRATEGIES (DARTTS), 7, 14, 15t, 77, 78f, 151t

DIAGNOSTIC READING ASSESSMENTS (DRAS), 131

DIBELS. *See* Dynamic Indicators of Basic Early Literacy Skills

DIEZ DEDITOS (OROZCO), 49, 52

DIVERSITY, 148

DOLAN DNA LEARNING CENTER (COLD SPRING HARBOR, N.Y.), 84

DOMINICAN REPUBLIC, THE (ROGERS & ROGERS), 51–52

DOUBLE HELIX, THE (WATSON), 82

DRA. *See* diagnostic reading assessments

DRAMA, 53, 140

DRAMATIZING MYTHS AND TALES (THISTLE), 53

DRAWING, 140

DROP OF BLOOD, A (SHOWERS), 81

DRP. *See* Degrees of Reading Power system

DUBLER, SUSAN, 47

DUBOIS, RENE, 46

DURING-READING ACTIVITIES, 25–26.

DYKSTRA, R., 57

DYNAMIC INDICATORS OF BASIC EARLY LITERACY SKILLS (DIBELS), 130

DYSLEXIA, 2, 6, 13f, 101, 146

DYSON, A.H., 94

E

EBERT, H. GIRARD, 8

EDWARDS, J., 94

EISENHART, M.A., 98

ELEMENTARY SCHOOL STUDENTS, RESOURCES FOR: cultural, 63–66; interest-based reading, 30–32, 36–37; magazines/newspapers, 33–35; Readers Theatre, 40–41; science-related, 86–87

EMPATHY, 96, 117

F

FAMILY: as mentors, 17–28, 44–46, 54, 56, 96–97; reading difficulties in, 129. *See also* mentoring support

FAMILY-SCHOOL PARTNERSHIPS (IRA), 56

FARNDON, J., 81

FARSTRUP, A.E., 27t

FASCINATION, 45

FEELING FOR THE ORGANISM, A (KELLER), 82

FEMININITY, GENDER ASSUMPTIONS ABOUT, 98–101, 117–118. *See also* gender and reading

FESTIVAL DE COMETAS, EL (TORRES), 49

FESTIVALS, 116

FICTION: additional resources for, 33; gender and, 108t, 109–111; writing activities, 140

FIELD TRIPS, 140

FINDERS, M.J., 94

FINK, R.P., 13t, 15t–16t, 18, 22t, 70, 75, 80, 112, 114, 128, 130, 137, 144, 145, 149t
FINUCCI, J.M., 96, 144, 147
FISCHER, K.W., 22t, 70, 97t, 137, 151
FISHCO, V.V., 7, 151t
FLETCHER, J.M., 10, 146
FLIPPO, R.F., 127, 131–132, 132t, 144
FLORIDA NONSENSE PASSAGES, 15t, 151t
FLOW EXPERIENCES, 11, 45, 95
FLUENCY DEVELOPMENT: age factors in, 10; commercial programs for, 28; content area–dependent, 79–80, 84–85, 138; definition of, 10; facilitation of, 27–28; problem identification, 130; silent reading essential for, 137–138
FLUENT READER, THE (RASINSKI), 28
FOLK DANCES, FOR BILINGUAL READERS, 53
FOLK TALES/LITERATURE, FOR BILINGUAL READERS, 48–50, 54, 59–63
FOLLOW-UP ACTIVITIES, 26
FOORMAN, B.R., 10, 127
FOUNTAS, I.C., 19–20
FRANCIS, D.J., 10
FRANCIS, DONALD, 2, 23
FREE READING, 20, 21f
FRUSTRATION LEVEL, 131
FYFE, L.M., 94

G

GADSDEN, V., 148
GARDNER, H., 18, 69–70, 73, 79–80
GASS, S.M., 57
GENDER AND READING: additional resources for, 122–123; atypical female frameworks, 103–106; career expectations, 97–98, 118; critical literacy and, 106–107, 108t; experiential differences, 94–95, 117; femininity and, 98–101, 117–118; gender balance activities, 110t–111t; mentoring differences, 96–97; mentoring support for, 106–112; myths concerning, 93–94; personality traits and, 96, 117; pleasure reading, 95–96; research study results, 97t, 99t, 117–118; sharing views on,

109–112; stereotype development, 94; "target books" for, 107–109; text choices, 95, 117; traditional female framework, 101–102; twin texts for, 107; youth-oriented topics, 112, 119–123. *See also* Brown, Susan; Haseltine, Florence; Law, Sylvia
GENDER BALANCE ACTIVITIES, 110t–111t
GENDER STEREOTYPES, 94, 98–101, 117–118
GENE MACHINES (BALKWILL & ROLPH), 81
GERBER, P.J., 75, 76, 130
GERM ZAPPERS (BALKWILL & ROLPH), 81
GILGER, J.W., 147
GILLIGAN, CAROL, 109–111, 148
GINSBERG, R., 130
GIRLS' CLUBS OF AMERICA, 56
GOLDSTEIN, SAMUEL, 139
GOOD, R.H., 130
GORILLA, MONKEY & APE (REDMOND), 81
GORILLA PRESS, 112–114, 114f
GOTTFREDSON, L., 144
GRADED NONWORD READING AND SPELLING TEST, 15t, 151t
GRAVES, D.H., 115t
GRAY, J.H., 98–99
GREAT BOOKS FOR BOYS (ODEAN), 109
GREAT BOOKS FOR GIRLS (ODEAN), 109
GREAT LEAPS READING, 28
GREENE, J.F., 143, 144
GRESHAM, F.M., 146
GRIFFIN, P., 18
GRITSAVAGE, M.M., 94
GROSS, MINNIE, 19, 23–24
GROSS-GLENN, K., 151t
GUIDED COMPREHENSION (MCLAUGHLIN & ALLEN), 20
GUIDELINES FOR A GENDER-BALANCED CURRICULUM IN ENGLISH (NATIONAL COUNCIL OF TEACHERS OF ENGLISH), 109
GUTHRIE, J.T., 18, 133, 144
GUYS WRITE FOR GUYS READ (SCIESZKA), 107–109
GUZZETTI, B.J., 94

H

HAITI (HINTZ), 51
HALL, S.L., 137, 143
HANDS-ON ACTIVITIES, 72, 82–84, 139–140
HANNA, G., 7, 151*t*
HARDENBROOK, M.D., 94
HARPER, R., 108*t*
HARTMAN, D., 114
HARVARD GRADUATE SCHOOL OF EDUCATION,
  6, 150
HASELTINE, FLORENCE, 2, 94, 97, 103–104,
  118. *See also* gender and reading
HAUGH, S.S., 94
HAVE A NICE DNA (BALKWILL & ROLPH), 81
HELGREEN-LEMPESIS, V., 151*t*
HIGH SCHOOL STUDENTS, RESOURCES FOR:
  cultural, 66–67; gender/social issues,
  119–123; interest-based reading, 32–36,
  37–39; magazines/newspapers, 33–35;
  Readers Theatre, 41; science-related,
  87–88
HINCHMAN, K.A., 144
HINTZ, M., 51
HIRSCHBERG, MARLENE, 11, 98
HOFFMAN, C.D., 94
HOLLAND, D.C., 98
HOLT, MELISSA, 100
HUDSON, R.F., 28

I

IDA. *See* International Dyslexia
  Association, Orton Dyslexia Society
  Research Committee
IMMORDINO-YANG, M.H., 22*t*
INDEPENDENT READING LEVEL, 131
INFERENCE, 132
INFORMAL READING INVENTORIES (IRIs), 131,
  132
INFORMATIONAL TEXTS, FOR BILINGUAL
  READERS, 51–52
INSTRUCTIONAL LEVEL, 131
INTEREST-BASED MODEL OF READING:
  additional resources for, 30–41;
  components of, 17, 45, 50, 135–136;

comprehension strategies in, 24–26;
  determining student interests in, 18–20;
  fluency development in, 27–28, 27*t*;
  gender and, 95, 117; mentoring support
  for, 17–18, 48, 138–139; multiple
  intelligences and, 80, 85; program
  balance in, 21–23; reading entry points
  in, 23–24; research study behind, 2–17,
  28–29; success of, 29; teaching
  implications of, 136–141
INTEREST-BASED READING: age factors in,
  9–10, 10*t*; bilingual readers and, 45–46,
  50; entry points in, 23–24; gender and,
  117; high-interest books, 36–39; as
  Interest-Based Model of Reading
  component, 17, 45, 50, 135; mentoring
  support for, 18–20; multiple intelligences
  and, 71; reader engagement and, 133;
  reading interest inventories for, 18; by
  successful striving readers, 8–9, 9*t*, 28;
  teaching implications of, 136
INTERNATIONAL DYSLEXIA ASSOCIATION
  (IDA), 6, 146. *See also* Orton Dyslexia
  Society Research Committee
INTERNATIONAL READING ASSOCIATION (IRA),
  19, 56, 57, 119
INTERNET ACTIVITIES, 20, 83*f*. *See also*
  websites
INTERVIEWS: for determining reading
  interests, 19; in research study, 148–150,
  149*t*; self-in-relationship protocol, 151
IRA. *See* International Reading Association
IRI. *See* informal reading inventories
ISAACS, S.D., 96, 147
IVEY, G., 35

J–K

JADE AND IRON (ALDANA), 48–49
JALLAD, B.J., 151*t*
JAMESTOWN TIMED READINGS PLUS, 28
KAMINSKI, R.A., 130
KATZIR-COHEN, T., 128
KEESE, D., 145
KELLER, E.F., 82

KENNEDY, B., 151
KEOGH, B., 146
KNAPP, ROBERT, 2, 95
KNIGHT, C.C., 70, 137
KNIGHT, J., 143, 144
KOHEN, J., 51

L

LADSON-BILLINGS, G., 148
LANE, H.B., 28
LAW, SYLVIA, 2, 94, 105–106, 118. *See also* gender and reading
LEES, S., 98
LEFLY, D.L., 12, 144, 147, 150–151, 151*t*
LELEWER, NANCY, 2
LESESNE, T.S., 119
LESLIE, L., 12, 131
LETTER IDENTIFICATION, 12, 71, 128, 129
LEU, D.D., 82
LEU, D.J., 82
LEVY, G.D., 94
LI, J., 70
LI, X., 43
LICHTENFELS, A., 81
LIMA, C.W., 19
LIMA, J.A., 19
LINCOLN SCHOOL (BROOKLINE, MA), 20, 21*f*, 52, 55, 112, 113*f*, 114*f*
LITERACY ONLINE (WOOD), 82
LITERACY SKILLS, academic, 58, 139; critical, 106–107, 108*t*; diagnostic assessment of, 130; early, reading difficulties and, 128
LITERACY VOLUNTEERS OF AMERICA, 56
LORBER, J., 98
LOUCKS-HORSLEY, S., 83–84
LUBS, H.A., 151*t*
LYCEE FRANÇAIS (PARIS), 46
LYON, G.R., 146

M

MACLACHLAN, P., 110*t*
MACPHEE, K., 128
MADAME CURIE (CURIE), 81
MADDREN, W., 96

MAGAZINES: for interest-based reading, 20, 33–35; reading habits and, 16*t*
MAGUINESS, C., 20
MANZO, A.V., 131
MANZO, U.C., 131
MARGALIT, M., 75
MASCOLO, M.F., 70, 137
MATCHING BOOKS TO READERS (FOUNTAS & PINNELL), 19–20
MATTHEW EFFECTS, 79, 138
MAYNARD, T., 94
MCCLINTOCK, BARBARA, 82
MCCORMACK, R.L., 144
MCKENNA, M.C., 131
MCKEOWN, M.G., 23
MCLAUGHLIN, M., 20
MCLEAN, J.M., 7
MEANING CONSTRUCTION, 28–29; contextual reading strategies for, 12–13
MELTZER, L., 75
MENTORING SUPPORT: additional resources for, 67–68; for bilingual readers, 47–56; by community, 56; expectations and, 140; by family, 44–46, 54, 56; gender differences in, 96–97, 117; for gender issues, 106–112, 108*t*, 110*t*–111*t*; importance of, 47–48, 138–139; as Interest-Based Model of Reading component, 17–28, 48, 135; for multiple intelligences, 80–85; by reading buddies, 54–55, 55*f*; by teachers, 47, 54; teaching implications of, 138–139, 140–141; for teaching writing, 112–116, 114*f*, 115*t*, 116*f*
METACOGNITION, 132
MEYER, A., 144
MIDDLE SCHOOL STUDENTS, RESOURCES FOR: cultural, 63–66; gender/social issues, 119–123; interest-based reading, 32–36, 37–39; magazines/newspapers, 33–35; Readers Theatre, 41; science-related, 87
MILLARD, E., 94
MILLER, M.S., 25
MOATS, L.C., 137, 143

MONSOUR, A.P., 151
MOORE, D.W., 144
MORSE, F., 72, 139
MOTIVATION, INTRINSIC, 136
MULTIPLE INTELLIGENCES: content area–dependent fluency and, 79–80, 84–85, 138; content area resources for, 81–82, 83*f*; Daniels, Roy, as example of, 70–77, 85; hands-on activities for, 82–84; Interest-Based Model of Reading and, 80, 85; looking for, 80–81; mentoring support for, 80–85; teaching implications of, 138; theory of, 69–70. *See also* Daniels, Roy
MULTISENSORY METHODS, 144
MUSEUMS, 84, 91–92
MUSIC, FOR BILINGUAL READERS, 52
MYERS, W.D., 51
MYSTERIES OF INTERNET RESEARCH, THE (COHEN), 20

N

NATIONAL ACADEMY OF EDUCATION, 6
NATIONAL COUNCIL OF TEACHERS OF ENGLISH, 109
NATIONAL RESEARCH COUNCIL, 20
NATIONAL SCIENCE EDUCATION STANDARDS, 83–84
NATURE, ADDITIONAL RESOURCES FOR, 34–35
NAVIDADES, LAS (DELACRE), 49, 52
NELSON-DENNY READING TEST, 7, 14, 15*t*, 77, 151*t*
NEWBERY ON THE NET (STORY-HUFFMAN), 20
NEWSPAPERS: comprehension strategies for, 25; for interest-based reading, 33–35; reading habits and, 16*t*, student, 20
NONFICTION: for bilingual readers, 50–52, 64–67, 82; gender and, 111–112
NONLINEAR DEVELOPMENTAL PATHWAYS, 78, 85, 137

O

OBREGON, M., 128
ODEAN, K., 109
OLSON, S., 83–84

O'MALLEY, J.M., 57, 58
100 BEST BOOKS FOR CHILDREN (SILVEY), 19
ORAL READING, 14, 28, 131, 137
OROZCO, J., 49, 52
ORTON DYSLEXIA SOCIETY RESEARCH COMMITTEE, 144, 146
ORTON-GILLINGHAM APPROACH, 144
O'SHEA, D.J., 27*t*
O'SHEA, L.J., 27*t*

P

PAINTING, 140
PARAGRAPH-BY-PARAGRAPH COMPREHENSION STRATEGY, 25–26
PARATORE, J.R., 57, 144
PARR, J.M., 20
PAUK, W., 25–26
PENNINGTON, B.F., 12, 144, 147, 150–151
PERSISTENCE, 96, 117
PHONICS: balance needed with, 21; ineffective application of, 11, 12, 28; systematic teaching of, 137, 143
PHONOLOGICAL SKILLS: decoding, 14, 21–22, 22*t*, 28, 137; diagnostic assessment of, 132; ongoing problems with, 11, 12, 14, 28, 137; problem identification, 129; SDS strategy for, 21–22, 22*t*; teaching approaches for, 143
PHRASES, SPEAKING IN, 129
PIAGET, J., 18
PIG LATIN TEST, 15*t*, 151*t*
PINNELL, G.S., 19–20
PLACKER, T., 94
PLANET OCEAN (BETT), 81
PLAY, HANDS-ON, 72, 139–140
PLEASURE READING: gender and, 95–96; reading habits and, 16*t*
POETRY: additional resources for, 124–125; festivals, 116; play activities involving, 140; writing, 114–115, 116*f*
PRESSLEY, M., 137
PRIDE OF PUERTO RICO: THE LIFE OF ROBERTO CLEMENTE (WALKER), 50–51
PRONUNCIATION PROBLEMS, 129

ROSWELL, F.G., 7, 151*t*
ROTENBERG, E.J., 70
RTI. *See* Responsiveness to Intervention
RUMELHART, D.E., 12
RYAN, R.M., 136

S

SADKER, D., 94
SADKER, M., 94
SAMUELS, S.J., 12, 27, 27*t*
SANABRIA, CRUZ, 46–48, 52, 54. *See also* bilingual readers, successful
SANVILLE, PRISCILLA, 96, 100
SARAH, PLAIN AND TALL (MACLACHLAN), 110*t*
SCHEMA FAMILIARITY: context-reliant reading and, 12; Daniels, Roy, and, 73; fluency development through, 28; as Interest-Based Model of Reading component, 17, 135; by successful striving readers, 12, 28; teaching implications of, 136
SCHIEFELE, U., 136
SCHOLASTIC MAGAZINE, 2
SCIENCE: additional resources for, 34–35, 86–92; gender stereotypes and, 100–104; hands-on activities involving, 82–84, 140; teaching approaches for, 81–84. *See also* Daniels, Roy; multiple intelligences
SCIENTIFIC AMERICAN: GREAT SCIENCE FAIR PROJECTS (ROSNER), 81
SCIENTIST FROM PUERTO RICO, MARIA CORDERO HARDY (VERHEYDEN-HILLIARD), 50
SCIESZKA, J., 107–109
SDS. *See* Syllabification for Decoding Strategy
SELF-IN-RELATIONSHIP INTERVIEW PROTOCOL, 151
SELIG, MAUREEN, 100–101, 117
SELINKER, L., 57
SEMANTIC IMPRESSIONS VOCABULARY METHOD, 22
SHARED WRITING, 115, 115*t*
SHARMAN, H., 81
SHARONI, V., 144
SHAYWITZ, B.A., 94, 145, 146

SHAYWITZ, S.E., 94, 128, 129, 145, 146
SHOWERS, P., 81
SILENT READING, 20, 21*f*, 137–138
SILVEY, A., 19
SIMPLIFIED REPEATED READING METHOD, 27–28, 27*t*
SIMPSON, EILEEN, 2
SINDELAR, P.T., 27*t*
SKILL THEORY, 70
SNOW, C.E., 18, 20, 129, 137, 144
SNOWLING, M.J., 7, 151*t*
SOCIAL STUDIES, ADDITIONAL RESOURCES FOR, 34, 119–123
SOLOMON SCHECHTER SCHOOL (NEWTON, MA), 116
SONG, 140
SOUND ANALYSIS, ONGOING PROBLEMS WITH, 11, 71
SPACE PLACE, THE (SHARMAN), 81
SPELLING, ONGOING PROBLEMS WITH, 14, 137
SPORTS, ADDITIONAL RESOURCES FOR, 34
SPORTS SCIENCE (WIESE), 83
SSR. *See* Sustained Silent Reading
STAHL, K.D., 23
STAHL, S.A., 23
STANOVICH, K.E., 9, 73, 79, 138
STARARTE GALLERY (NEW YORK, NY), 113–114, 114*f*
STORY-HUFFMAN, R., 20
STORY OF MY LIFE, THE (AHMEDI), 111*t*
STORY WRITING/TELLING, 140
STOTHARD, S.E., 7
STRIVING READERS: compensated/partially compensated, 13–14, 13*t*; definition of, 146; teaching approaches, 143–144; underestimating abilities of, 80–81
STRIVING READERS, IDENTIFICATION OF: diagnostic assessment instruments for, 130–132, 132*t*; early, importance of, 127–128; early reading difficulties, 128–129; later reading difficulties, 129–130; reader engagement and, 133; test scores and, 133